BILLY'S BACK!

Thomas E. Uharriet
Encoder for the protagonist, Billy Shears

Disclaimer
This entire novel (even including this sentence) is your realistic, but fictional, magical mystery tour of Paulism. Until the end, suspend all disbelieve for a ride that can erase and replace your favorite rock icon.

Song Credits
Actual song authorship is to be understood by its historical context. Each song from before the 1966 death of **Paul McCartney** that this historical fiction book says **is** written by the protagonist, was written by **Bill Shepherd**, or "Vivian Stanshall," as indicated in the text. All of the Beatles' songs said herein to be written by the protagonist are by Lennon-McCartney (at least officially). Post-Beatles songs said to be released by the protagonist (as of 2009) are by the current J. Paul McCartney. All non-released songs (as of 2009) that are first appearing in *the Memoirs of Billy Shears* are credited to "Billy Shears."

Photography Credits
The front cover image of "Billy Shears," and the jacket's images of Sir J. Paul McCartney and Thomas E. Uharriet, were adapted from photographs by, respectively, Michael Cooper, Oli Gill, and Bryan Blanchard. "The Hand" was photographed for the 2018 *Memoirs* back cover by Amanda Bird.

© **2009, 2010, 2012, 2016, 2018, 2020, 2021**

Thomas E. Uharriet. All rights reserved including the right of any reproduction in whole or in part in any form. Copyrighted materials are quoted for critical review and educational purposes, sometimes with modifications to preserve the narrative flow. This book is a solo project, not a Beatles product. Published by Peppers Press, a Subsidiary of MACCA Corp. Opinions presented herein are solely those of "Billy Shears," and do not necessarily represent the views of the Encoder.

www.BillyShears.com

ISBN: 978-0-9842925-7-8
0-9842925-7-8

A Most Special Thanks to
Sir J. Paul McCartney
for providing such fantastic material.
~ *Thomas E. Uharriet*

"**Herein is an epic of our hero,
Paul McCartney,
who entered the underworld,
and then returned
by taking possession of me,
an unknown session musician.**"
~ **William Shepherd** [a.k.a. "Billy Shears"]

"**The singer's going to sing a song
And he wants you all to sing along
So let me introduce to you
The one and only Billy Shears
And Sgt. Pepper's Lonely Hearts Club Band**
~ **Billy Shears**"
("Sgt. Pepper's Lonely Hearts Club Band," Lennon-McCartney)

William Shepherd's Dedication

Keeping all of this under wraps until now was to protect my five children. **I**t is now my pleasure to give them the peace that comes with full disclosure. **D**edicated to each of my children who too were given the McCartney name, **s**ince they were born or adopted into it. This is for them and for the biological Paul.

Thomas E. Uharriet's Dedication

This book **is dedicated to** my own five children who are each among my greatest delights, and whose **u**nwavering **love** supported this massive encoding.

Contents

Please pause, before rushing on to the first chapter, to preview the book by scanning the contents. As you consider what's coming, ask yourself if you are ready for an all new awareness of **Paul and** me. Understand that you will never perceive us in the same way. Now, at my world's end, **I reveal it all.** Love us all anyway.

Foreword by Gregory Paul Martin	7
Preface to the 2020 Edition of Billy's Back!	8
Preface to the Nine After 9-09 Edition	9
Preface to the Memoirs of Billy Shears	10
1. (Also Chapter 1 in *the Memoirs*) Dreams of Paul	13
2.[2] Stuart Was the First Martyr.	31
3.[3] Paul Worked It Out.	34
4.[4] Paul's Girls	45
5.[5] Drive My Car Backwards.	55
6.[7] Born a Poor Young Country Boy	61
7.[8] I Was a Session Musician.	64
8.[9] Playing with the Bonzos	71
9.[10] The Last Song of Phase Two	79
10.[11] Masonic Checkmate	83
11.[12] Billy Shakespeare	99
12.[13] What's in a Name?	102
13.[14] I ONE IX HE ◊ DIE	108

14.[16] The One and Only Billy Shears Rams On. 127
15.[17] You Want Dates? 137
16.[18] "Two of Us" 150
17.[19] "Tuesday Afternoon Is Never Ending." 158
18.[20] "Wednesday Morning Papers Didn't Come." 165
19.[21] "Thursday Night Your Stockings Needed Mending." 169
20.[22] "Friday Night Arrives Without a Suitcase." 178
21.[23] "Saturday Night's Alright." 191
22.[24] "Sunday Morning Creeping Like a Nun." 201
23.[25] "Monday's Child Has Learned to Tie His Bootlace." 209
24.[26] Tuesday, 20 September 1966 220
25.[27] Impersonators 225
26.[28] Recording with the Beatles 234
27.[29] Donovan 250
28.[30] Penny Nickels, Denny Laine, and Penny Lane 265
29.[31] "High Brow" 277
30.[32] "The Parting on the Left Is Now . . . on the Right." 281
31.[33] "Hey Jude" 292
32.[34] Do You Hear Voices? 304
33.[39] "Hey Bulldog" 310
34.[41] Seven in Three 316
35.[46] I Am the Grey Seal. 320
36.[50] "While My Guitar Gently Weeps" 325
37.[51] Apple Corps Ltd. 329
38.[52] "All Together Now" 333
39.[53] You Know My Joke. 337
40.[57] From "Ob-La-Di, Ob-La-Da" to Boogaloo 345
41.[59] *Japanese Jailbird* 358
42.[62] *Run, Devil, Run* Through the *Driving Rain*. 367
43.[64] Don't Let Your Inaction Blow It! 373
44.[65] Know the Difference. 379

Most Importantly 399

Foreword by Gregory Paul Martin from the Memoirs of Billy Shears

When Thomas E. Uharriet first approached me about narrating this book, I was curious. I had no idea such a strong belief was still prevalent in the Beatles subculture that the rumor about Paul's death all those years ago was true. Exploring the possibility in the form of a novel seemed an intelligent way to address the subject; and the extent of Uharriet's knowledge of the subject interested me.

As a gifted actor, I have a natural facility for mimicry. My version of Paul McCartney's voice came easily to me, especially since I have known him since I was five years old. I first met Paul in the winter of 1962, just a few months after my father, Sir George Martin, signed the Beatles to Parlophone Records.

To record the Memoirs, I thought it would be most fitting to use the original recording equipment that the Beatles had used at Abbey Road Studios, with help from my father, and from engineers Geoff Emerick and Dave Harries. That equipment is now located at the prestigious British Grove Studios.

On several occasions during the recording process, while sitting at that same equipment to record this book that the Beatles and my father had used for their vast catalog of songs, I felt I had 'become' Paul. While this experience is a natural part of an actor's process, in this instance, with this subject matter, it felt uncanny.

Is Paul dead? I leave that to you to decide. Meanwhile, in Paul's words, "Let me introduce to you the one and only Billy Shears."

~ Gregory Paul Martin

Preface to the 2020 Edition of Billy's Back!

Billy's Back is sailing again as Billy Shears' flagship! **This** collection from *the Memoirs of Billy Shears* is enough to give you the flavor of the rest. **This book is** primarily intended for those who do not **already** have all of these *Memoirs* chapters. It **invites you to begin your** journey in **an alternate reality that runs** parallel to traditional thinking. This initiation into **the Beatles' magickal** world, as told from Billy's own **perspective**, lets you join the circle of those who **understand** the **mystery** of how he obtained **Paul McCartney's role** and estate in 1966. Read this book **as the ultimate fantasy tour** of the magickal mystery. **Your tour guide, Billy** Shears, the fictional protagonist, **reveals it all.**

NOTE: This 2020 Edition of *Billy's Back* is set apart from earlier editions by being from *the Nine After 9-09 Edition of the Memoirs of Billy Shears*. In keeping with the high standard set by *the Memoirs,* this book also includes its own additional footnotes and other enhancements. Another change is that we reduced the number of chapters in *Billy's Back* to make the book more affordable. Meeting the specific challenge, this book was trimmed to have exactly 44 chapters, and 99 footnotes, in 400 pages. As such, this edition averages more lines per page than earlier editions.

The Memoirs (including the 44 chapters in this volume) call for multiple readings. This book is designed to provide additional layers of understanding each time it is read. Being encoded in layers, some elements can only be understood by a comprehension of the whole. As with life in general, remaining open to new awareness is far more satisfying than to hold any mental position with white-knuckled tightness. We advance in light and knowledge gift for gift. As we continue to put our energy into it, we receive the energy that is available on that level, advancing degree by degree.

The many footnotes, like the word-stacking and acrostic, may either enhance or distract from the primary content. We recommend that you not allow these extra elements to interrupt the flow of the narrative before finishing the book at least once. It is a very different book with the footnotes, one that is written for those who have already been initiated by reading the whole book without them. For the most impactful experience that goes beyond the book itself, let the entire narrative work on you before going back to read it again with these added elements. Reading the footnotes on the first time through the book is like spoiling a suspenseful mystery book by reading the end too soon. Saving the footnotes until the second or third time through sets up what may actually be a meaningful life-experience—rather than merely reading for information.

Preface to the Nine After 9-09 Edition of The Memoirs of Billy Shears

This special anniversary edition marks nine years since *the Memoirs* were **first released on** that historic day of **09-09-09**. **We** questioned, "What would the public do if we **were** to release such an astonishing disclosure in a **completely** unique book without promoting it? With **absolutely no** copies in any bookstores, we were **delighted** that you found it online—even without us letting you know where to look for it. With only **word-of-mouth** advertising, especially via blog sites and **podcasts**, you have come to know *the Memoirs* **from people** like yourself who have brought the book out **of o**bscurity and into the light of public **awareness**. This edition is to thank those who **brought this u**ndertaking about Paul—and about how the **world** works—out of the dark shadows and **to the masses.**

NOTE: In the nine years since the release of *the Memoirs,* many readers have responded in stages of grief as if for the loss of a loved one. Initially, they are in a state of shock and denial, grasping at any reason to disbelieve it. As denial becomes impossible, pain increases. Then they become angry. Next, they feel a sense of personal loss, as though lonely without their loved one. Some become depressed. Finally, they find peace as they shift into complete acceptance. Many then move into gratitude and admiration for how brilliantly William has carried on the work in Paul's name. If you experience any unpleasant stages of grief with this information, be assured that they will pass.

Preface to the Memoirs of Billy Shears

Imagine obscure lyrics from hundreds of songs that you grew up with, and sang along with, becoming meaningful to you as you read this book. Imagine lines of songs that had been dead to you coming alive as what had been gibberish is transformed into something solemnly poignant or hilarious. Imagine getting the joke and laughing out loud after decades of singing along without a clue that the joke existed. Imagine, finally, being invited into the hearts, minds, and souls of John, Paul(s), George, and Ringo, with new awareness of their deep sorrows, frustrations, challenges, and bitter-sweet successes.

Everything changed as William Shepherd ("Billy Shears") went from Billy Pepper of Billy Pepper and the Pepperpots to Sgt. Pepper of Sgt. Pepper's Lonely Hearts Club Band. You will learn when, why, and how Billy took over creative control of the Beatles, as represented on the back of the Sgt. Pepper's album. It shows Billy's back, not Paul's. He faces the band as its new conductor. Giving John's band to Billy Shears (Paul's replacement) was a great torment to them all. You will understand why.

Billy's Back!, *Beatles Enlightenment*, and *The Talent Contest* are each collections, sorted for individual interests, from the unique book that set world records, *The Memoirs of Billy Shears*.

Letting the world in on secrets concealed since the Sixties, *The Memoirs of Billy Shears* reveals loads of infallible proofs, along with overwhelming circumstantial evidence, to finally prove, all these years later, that Paul McCartney really died in 1966.

From verifiable facts in this book, you will be sure of it, and will know how to easily prove to others that Paul was replaced by William Shepherd "Billy Shears." William has been playing the part of Paul, recording and performing, since Paul's fatal automobile calamity all those years ago.

Just as Beatles albums contained hundreds of clues about Paul's death and replacement (with hints in their lyrics, cover art, and video performances), in keeping with that same secret creative expression of sympathy for the loss of Paul, friends in other bands also made "Paul is Dead" songs. Among others, the Rolling Stones, the Bonzo Dog Doo-Dah Band (now, generally called the Bonzos), the Who, Donovan, and Elton John all sing about Paul's death. This book discusses some of their songs, as well as some by "Paul," John, George, and Ringo that were made beyond their Beatles Years.

The Memoirs of Billy Shears uses over two hundred songs to explain the Paul switch (including the torment it caused before and after Paul's death), to establish the historical context, and to add support, richness, and texture to the book's concepts. Those musical enhancements add warmth and a depth of feeling to the cold hard facts, giving you insider empathy for all involved.

Fittingly for a book of Paul-clue decoding, *the Memoirs of Billy Shears* (in printed editions) is itself fully encoded. Providing new reading fun, not only can readers decode more Paul songs, but they can also break this acrostical code! The first letter in every other line combines to spell secret messages. The world's longest acrostic began nine pages ago, right after the title page (excluding credits, copyright, the foreword, and a few other parts). The booklet, *Billy Shears Acrostical Decoding*, helps you to decode it.

For an added reading attraction, all printed editions of this book have encoded messages that are created by combining words on different lines in order to form complete sentences. **This** encoding was too obscure until the font was lengthened and made bold. This nonlinear reading **is** now an amusing aspect that draws even the most reluctant readers into the book. This is **word-stacking**. You will find it on every page of the narrative.

Letting the readers participate even further, the final chapter of *The Memoirs* includes unrecorded lyrics for use in a music-writing and performing talent contest. Details are at www.BillyShears.com.

You might imagine, as you read this material, that Billy Shears wrote *The Memoirs of Billy Shears*, or that he gave Thomas E. Uharriet this material to encode. Such persistent imaginings happen partly because the book is written in the first person of William, and more so because the book is engorged with private details that only William would know, or because only he could possibly be aware of these verifiable facts that prove Paul's death. However, "Billy Shears" is only a stage name. Paul's replacement's birth name was William Shepherd. By whatever we call him, McCartney, Shepherd, or Shears, he did not write this book, and would not wish otherwise. Think of it as a literary caricature.

1

Dreams of Paul

Almost **everything** about me taking Paul's place **was made possible because** of the series of dreams that **Paul had**, showing his death and me replacing him—and by my dreams of Paul, showing me how. First, let **me, William Shepherd** ("Billy Shears"), tell you of a more recent dream. I want it told before I die so that you will know **I knew**. After discussing my undertakings in his name, **Paul** said, "You will be released on the twenty-first of February 2014."

I asked for a nine-year extension for more tours. Since I needed to see my Utah-based Encoder one last time, a tour would include it. Until **I am** done, this book will be distributed on a level **that** will keep it down. We will keep it underground until **I am**.

"Yesterday" is a massive hit from well before I came along. That song had more airplay than any other number ever written, and is the most-recorded song. That sweet melody in its entirety sprang forth unbroken from one of Paul's dreams. He woke up with it at Jane Asher's house one morning in May 1965. He shared it with several people on the set of *Help!* **The music surpassed** Paul's own natural aptitude, surprising **everyone.** The words came to him a bit later. At first, nonsense words kept the young song from devolving. He sang something like, "Scrambled eggs, my but don't you have such lovely legs." **Within** about five days, the real lyrics came to **him based on** some other dreams, actually **nightmares,** he had first mentioned on 29 January. **Those dreams** provoked the theme of "Yesterday," and **engendered** material used in most of his other **songs** for the rest of his life.

Paul's dreams haunted him. Once, he saw the Beatles recording his "When I'm Sixty-Four" at the "Abbey Road Studios." But he wasn't one of them. He was merely an observer floating a little above an

NOTE: When William refers to "Abbey Road Studios," he is giving the current name, not the name by which it was called when the Beatles recorded there. As Paul told John and others of the dream, he said, "The band was recording in Studio Two," which all understood to mean a particular area in EMI Recording Studios. To capitalize on the popularity of the Beatles' *Abbey Road* album, and of the famed crosswalk in front of the EMI building, EMI eventually renamed their studio. If Abbey Road Studios had had that name when the Beatles recorded there, the Beatles would have given the album a different name, especially since they loathed being there as a group by then.

As William designed the layout for the now-iconic picture, he made a point of having the group walk away from the studio, not toward it. They were not walking in to record, but walking out to be done with the place. The recording sessions for *Abbey Road* were the last in which all four Beatles participated. Although *Let It Be* was the group's final album before the band's April 1970 dissolution, most of that album had been recorded before the *Abbey Road* sessions began. While the main objective for the *Abbey Road* photograph was to point to Paul's death, the double meaning included the death of the band which would soon be done with EMI Recording Studios.

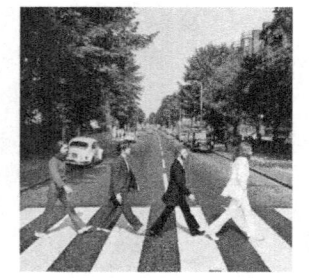

Dreams of Paul

unknown musician. John said, "Paul," and the musician answered. Paul saw the stranger's face, looking a bit similar to his own. A gentle voice behind him, unheard by others, said, "Paul, this is the man who will take your place." The dream panicked him, but also gave him a face to seek out.

Such dreams became frequent. Some were grotesque. In one, Brian Epstein handed John a picture. **John saw it and** laughed hysterically as though he **had gone totally mad.** Then Paul, in his dream, saw himself in the picture. His head had been smashed off. **Paul** awoke in a cold sweat, reaching for his head, to be **sure** it was there, then rehearsed it that day to all who **would** hear him.

Each dream contradicted the others until it all played out. He and George were **upset** in one; and Paul yelled at Brian in another. **A girl** in one dream stood in a storm, holding an old suitcase. Paul moved a folder of papers from the **passenger** seat and let her in. The girl recognized him and excitedly asked him to sing along with one of his songs. Going from station to station, up and down the radio dial, at first she could not find his songs. Continuously interrupting herself with each song, she bounced from one incoherent thought to another about poverty, hard work, and about God or fate uniting them forever. Suddenly, they were thrown sideways into a pole, which, like a "silver hammer" that "came down upon his head . . . made sure that he was dead" ("Maxwell's Silver Hammer").

Billy's Back!

Hardly a day ever passed without Paul discussing one of his horrific nightmares. Finally, Vernon E. Mosher, one of Kenneth Anger's Satanists, met the Beatles on 11 May, the last day of filming *Help!* Interpreting Paul's dreams, Mosher said, "They mean that you're the one. You're the goat, the band's sacrifice. When did you make your compact with Satan?" Measuring Paul's life, Mosher crunched some numbers, then read Paul's palm for validation. He said, "You have about fifteen more months, kid."

Oscillating then from despair to dedication, Paul was always heavily burdened, but more determined to use his remaining days productively with albums and another tour. Mosher's predicted timing was too soon by one month. The last several months of **Paul's life reflected** his tormenting dreams.

His music had **a new seriousness** in it from January 1965, **until he died in September 1966.** Evoking deeper feeling, they reflect troubles far beyond his old quaint love songs. He sought for originality and far greater quality in his writing. The

---

NOTE: The Beatles were a well-planned psychological operation (PSYOP) to evoke specific emotions, attitudes, and behaviors as part of the societal conditioning required for the New World Order.

As strategically engineered, the Western World's first impression of the Beatles included subliminal markers for virginal innocence. For example, as Paul sings the third verse of "Paperback Writer," John and George, in backing vocals, sing the title of the French nursery rhyme "Frère Jacques." That addition, added under George Martin's direction, focused the song as being of a firmly planted youth who can only dream of joining the adult world.

The Beatles' lyrics (including even some of their own creation) included infatuations, heart-ache, and messages of happiness. Then came "Yesterday" with Paul's energy of dire ominous foreboding, planting subconscious dread for that figurative virgin's pending sacrifice—fulfilling his own oath in which he "said something wrong," consenting to his own demise.

band was crucially important to him, but was not as important as his own personal growth and musical excellence. The stress contributed to the lovely music of "Yesterday." That is how the young lad was able to write that solemn message. "Yesterday" describes him suddenly not being half the man he used to be. What changed? Only one thing. My shadow was suddenly hanging over him. As was usual, **Paul** gave it a romantic context, not ever wanting to **just** sing what was on his mind: "Why she **had to go**, I don't know." Yet, everyone knew his romantic life had nothing to do with a woman leaving him. The Ashers were all family to him. Jane was with him for the rest of his life. They were both very securely in love. It is ridiculous to suppose otherwise. Paul was sleeping upstairs in her family's handsome home in the center of London on 57 Wimpole Street when he wrote that song. The perceptibly profound depth of feeling made it a huge success; but those feelings were not about losing anyone but himself.

To most people who knew Paul, the song had nothing to do with his own life. Furthermore, it had nothing to do with the Beatles. They credited it to "Lennon-McCartney," as with all of the songs that either of them wrote; but John had nothing to do with it—neither did George or Ringo. Paul had the music from one dream, and the message given to him from a few others. Being far beyond Beatles arts instrumentally, **Paul hired** strangers, a string quartet of **session musicians.** Being patently non-Beatle made them question how to release it in the UK. Locals knew better—and knew Jane. Paul was endowed with that song in May 1965, and recorded it weeks later. It was on the album *Help!*, released in August. The next month, it was released as a single in the US, but not here until ten years after I joined the band. Finally, in 1976, at my suggestion, we released it as a UK single.

On the B-side of "Help!" was "**I'm** Down." They were not released on albums **in** the US or in the UK until *Rock 'n' Roll Music,* also in 1976. Before recording "Yesterday," **Paul** felt that he needed to warm up to it. He began that day, 14 June 1965, by recording "I'm Down." He then did the even more obscure, "I've Just Seen a Face," before recording his "Yesterday" vocals. The song, "**I'm** Down," was in response to the remaining **Fab** making jokes about his blues over his persistently haunting dreams. **John's laughter**, and Paul's father's disbelief, **hurt Paul** the most. Paul sang, "I'm down, down to the ground [grave]. How can you laugh when you know I'm down?" Being most spooked in the beginning by his dream of seeing my face when John called his name, Paul obscured this line in his next song, "I've just seen a face I can't forget," by a romantic context with the utmost opposite false love message as the one he recorded next. **Here, Paul meets a girl**, next he regrets losing one, **all in the same** recording session, and all while staying at the **home** of Jane, his steady date. In that second song, **Paul is** "Falling, yes I'm falling," suggesting that he was **falling** in love.

Really, he feared falling **as Humpty Dumpty**, the Eggman, saying "Goo goo g'joob," and **entering** eternity, joining all the fallen. Having just seen **my** face, which to Paul was as the face of **death**, he announces to all, "I just want to tell the **world** we met." He recorded all three of these songs on a Monday. **Paul** had the string quartet added to "Yesterday" days **later**, Thursday, 17 June 1965, the same day Ringo **recorded** the Buck Owens song, "Act Naturally," with **advice to me**, as the Paul he expected. It was written by Vonie Morrison and Johnny Russell. When I joined, I said that using all others' songs wasted royalties. I stopped it until I had incentives (a court settlement). That song—as very many other songs from this time—fit their New-Paul theme. Making more movies was an expectation they held. As me, Ringo sang: "They're gonna put me in the movies. They're gonna make a big star out of me. We'll make a film about a man that's sad and lonely. [The sad loneliness that I and my bandmates suffered inspired the line, "Lonely Hearts Club Band."] And all I gotta do is act naturally. Well, I'll bet you I'm gonna be a big star." Ringo had it right.

Ever since **Paul** died, I have dreamed of him more often than he **had** of me. My dreams made us all interested in spiritual **things.** George once said, "Paul McCartney is the Beatles' own patron saint; and you are his prophet. I send up a prayer to him; then he comes speaking to you." At some times, I have felt I know Paul better than George ever did. **I** feel **like** he and I have collaborated on many songs that bear **his name**. That is the tradeoff. His name gets the credit; but I remain to get the royalties. After all, what good are royalties to him now? The credit is all the reward that his endeavors can possibly earn for him now. I give him that much in all of my McCartney work.

These dreams have sometimes been musical, but more often have had to do with Paul's life. I have headed down to Liverpool and other places after some of these Paul dreams, only to find things there exactly as **I dreamed** they should be. I am not sure what to make **of it**. I have wondered if I merely remember things **from previous trips to** these places, or if **the old Paul** has been sharing his past with me. After some such dreams, **I have** consulted with Mike McCartney. As **Paul's brother**, he has filled in slits in my memory, **altering** my dreams a little bit, making them more **correct**, or perhaps less.

One can neither be **certain** how much of these dreams are products of the **stories** I have learned, nor how much of what I have learned has come from the dreams. It is all one continuum of realistic experience and unreal imagination versus realistic imagination and unreal experience.

Dreaming has been an enormous comfort and sustaining force in my life. For instance, when **I** resented all the irritation I had to deal with to **get** the Beatles' last released album going, **peace** emerged that way. My mother, called Mary **here**, like Paul's, died when I was young. **It had been** a while since I had heard from her **in my dreams**.

My life had become too busy for her. With all my money concerns, friction with the band, and a bit more drug-induced paranoia than I understood, I seemed to crowd important souls out of my life. She was one I had left behind, making a void. I felt well again after that dream visitation. When I wrote, "Let It Be," **I tried to make** it sound like a hymn to evoke **a religious feeling**. I call her Mother Mary, **like the Virgin**. The spiritual implications are enhanced by a track I made that Phil Spector later added in after "Dig It," introducing "Let It Be." "That was 'Can You Dig It?' by Georgie Wood. Now we'd like to do, 'Hark the Angels Come.'" Doing that intro added to the worship idea. The Virgin appearance was symbolic. When the public

NOTE: To further global agendas, the Beatles were made to appear hostile toward Christianity. Paul's mother, Mary, had been a Christian. However, after her passing, Paul's father, Jim, discouraged church involvement. When the Beatles signed with EMI, they were told that they would eventually be required to renounce their Christian beliefs. Meanwhile, although they were not required to be agnostic, they were advised that it was the most defensible theological position since (in their view) neither theism nor atheism could be proven. With that coaching for early interviews, they claimed to be agnostic. Gradually, after they were each encouraged to explore non-Christian spiritual traditions, their comments about religion reflected more contemplation.

After exploring the question for himself, John said, "I believe in God, but not as one thing, not as an old man in the sky. I believe that what people call God is something in all of us. I believe that what Jesus and Mohammed and Buddha and all the rest said was right. It's just that the translations have gone wrong." George, being more interested in spiritual evolution than the others, often discussed spiritual ideas, especially after the Beatles were dissolved. One of his most practical ideas of spirituality was that "Heaven and hell is right now. . . . You make it heaven or you make it hell by your actions."

Unlike Paul and the others, William was raised with an eclectic approach to esoteric tradition. As trained from early on, William is aware enough of Christianity, and of other religious perspectives, to use what serves his will. He sang of being visited by "Mother Mary" to divide Christian fans. While some considered it a reference to Mary McCartney, most understood the Biblical Virgin allusion. Some fans liked the idea of him receiving a Marian apparition. Others were offended. It troubled those who felt that on some level he was suggesting that he is the Son of Mother Mary. John also opposed the song, saying, "That's not the Beatles. That's a hymn!"

ridiculed it for being **sacrilegious**, I said I had never thought of a religious **interpretation**.
Every time that **happened**, we gave that same reply. We did not know **it was there**, or that it meant anything. It's nothing. **It is** just like John saying he "had no idea that '**Lucy in the Sky** with Diamonds' meant LSD." **The old story of** Julian drawing his nursery school classmate, **Lucy** O'Donnell, in the

NOTE: "Lucy in the Sky with Diamonds" is meant to be understood in three ways. In addition to the Lucy O'Donnell story, "Lucy . . . Sky . . . Diamonds" is an LSD reference. More significantly, however, as another layered meaning, Lucy is short for Lucifer, the light-bearer, who is in the sky with stars, or diamonds. We picture ourselves in a paradise of tangerine trees, marmalade skies, and towering flowers, representing Adam and Eve in their paradise. When hearing this song, consider yourselves as if you were Adam or Eve. Like Adam and Eve's forbidden fruit, LSD, gives us access to the Luciferian illumination and knowledge needed to become as the gods.

According to the Bavarian Illuminati's Luciferianism, the snake in Eden's forbidden tree represents Lucifer who gave Father Adam and Mother Eve special gnosis, hidden knowledge, to make them wise like the gods. By contrasting Lucifer's benevolent giving with the Biblical God forbidding illumination that would liberate mankind, Luciferians see Lucifer as the savior, not Jehovah (Isaiah 43:11) or Jesus (1 John 4:14). Likewise, in modern times, the Luciferians (such as by their control of rock, pop, rap, and hip-hop) promote liberation of thought and action that comes through experimentation with LSD and other drugs that are forbidden by authoritarian Christians.

When giving Eve the fruit, Lucifer (Enki) says, "God (Enlil) doth know that in the day ye eat thereof, then your eyes shall be opened, ye shall be as gods, knowing good and evil" (Genesis 3:5). When God (Enlil) asks Eve what she had done, she says, "The serpent (Enki) beguiled me, and I did eat" (3:13).

Nevertheless, the claim that Eve was "beguiled" or "deceived" (1 Timothy 2:14) is contradicted by God validating Lucifer's claim as an accomplished fact: "God said, Behold, the man is become as one of us, to know good and evil" (Genesis 3:22). Finishing that verse and the next from the Luciferian view, to further thwart Lucifer's work, God evicted Adam and Eve from the garden of Eden, and prevented them from partaking of the fruit of the tree of life, which would have let them live forever. Thus, as taught by Skull and Bones (a secret student society at Yale University), Lucifer (Enki) teaches us the secrets to make us gods; but God (Enlil) blocks that liberation, and consigns us to death (hence their death logo) according to 3:22.

sky with diamonds is true; but we built the song around Alice **as if high on LSD**. It was perfect for it. **The LSD chorus unwittingly came** from Julian; but John set out **to create the LSD images** overriding the entire song. I contributed a few lines here and there too. Back then, we thought LSD was rather liberating. **I would** never touch the stuff now though. Now I **know too much** about it to allow my mind, body, or soul **to be destroyed by** it. *Alice in Wonderland* ideas provided **LSD** type images that entered all our albums, including such images as the walrus, or Eggman (Humpty Dumpty).

In 1966, **John and George** introduced me to LSD. They had each been **turned on to the drug** way back in early 1965, **in the home of their dentist.** Along with Cyn and Patti, John and George each had a cup of coffee without being told it was laced with it. From there, they went to a club and tripped out. Sensory perceptions became compromised without them knowing why. The next day, John and George introduced Ringo to the drug, and eventually got Paul to try it. After John returned from Spain in November 1966, he spoke enthusiastically about it, trying to convince me to come onboard with it. I first tried it with him after overdubbing "Strawberry Fields" on 15 December, the day Walt Disney died.

NOTE: Theodor "Teddy" W. Adorno (11 September 1903 to 6 August 1969), who wrote many Lennon-McCartney songs (especially before William stepped in) described Walt Disney as the most dangerous man in America. From Adorno's perspective, the purpose of life was not to be entertained or distracted (such as by Disney's hypnotic films, mindless songs, and theme parks of ultimate artificiality), but to increase consciousness, and to use that new awareness to expand and develop ourselves and society.

Billy's Back!

Right away, I sought to promote the drug with friends and associates. Even though I was the last one in our group to try it, **I was the first** to admit it to the press. My first statements **promoting LSD** were during an interview, published **in *Life* magazine** in May 1967. That was the month **before our** big unveiling of *Sgt. Pepper's Lonely Hearts **Club** Band*, which further promoted the drug. I **gave the context.**

Considering my openness about drug usage, and how I got Brian Epstein, John, George, and Ringo to engage in a campaign with me to legalize pot in GB (such as when **I convinced them all** to show dedication to the cause **by** joining me in signing a full page **advertisement** in the London *Times),* the idea I hear now **that I was** not **the most political** of the band is inconsistent with history.

Our drug campaign had many fronts. After seeing its harmful effects firsthand, I quit my LSD usage. John, being a much more regular user, took years longer to get off of it—and off of some worse addictions, such as heroin. But when I was for it, **I actively promoted LSD**. On the board of directors, **along with John** Phillips (the Mamas & the Papas), Mick Jagger (the Rolling Stones), Andrew Oldham (Stones' manager), and Terry Melcher (Doris Day's son, a record producer), I networked with MK-Ultra, a joint ███-British intelligence task force, to provide free distribution

NOTE: Regrettably, we are required to censor out the three-letter abbreviation of the particular United States federal agency involved in this project. This undisclosed federal agency has a long history of domestic and international drug trafficking, which liberally funds secret operations that cannot be funded by constitutional means. Although increasing the demand for their forbidden goods profited them in the drug market, that profit was not their motivation.

during "The First Annual Monterey International Pop Festival." **It** was attended by over 100,000 observers who were **invited** to participate with free hallucinogens. The **government** had agreed that they would not enforce any **drug laws** there. It was all with complete US/UK government **facilitation.**
Having MK-Ultra's objective of making San Francisco a youth-centered gathering place for drug experimentation made it easy to get their cooperation in freely supplying the massive distribution for the rock show in Monterey, just two hours away. The key people connecting John Phillips with the drug distribution through government agencies were Ken Kesey, Timothy Leary, and others. Later, Timothy ran for governor of California against Ronald Reagan. Leary, with his very public pro-drug work, understandably had a drug related double-meaning in his campaign slogan. **To get his** campaign going, not only with his political **party**, but also with partiers, his slogan (which led **directly** to the Beatle song by John), was "Come **together,** join the party," seeking to unite politically **minded** drug partiers.

By briefly touching **on** this **LSD** diversion, my point is that **I was fixedly passionate** about altering

NOTE: The elite who control the media predetermine what music to make popular and when. The First Annual Monterey International Pop Festival was a creation of the global elite—as were the biggest rock festivals. "Pop" is short for popular to the common class. The elite, however, see it as representing the Pope's domain. Rock, they say, represents Masonry. Both reflect, and are ruled by, the planet's highest governing bodies. (Papal dominion has always exceeded Biblical Christianity.)

Rap music, named for ceremonially rapping a Masonic mallet, is designed to trap listeners in their self-destructive thinking patterns by using negative energy to deplete their consciousness. In that weakened state, it is nearly impossible to break any other addiction. The plan is to lower consciousness until societal degradation has produced so much disorder and misery that the world will crave the control and safety of the New World Order, presided over by the illuminated that bring "Ordo ab Chao" (order out of chaos). To create that chaos, the media is manipulating people to lower their energy into hate, division, and fear. By lowering their energy, they lose mental objectivity.

Billy's Back!

your perceptions of reality, and felt that promoting psychedelics, all with full government backing, just furthered my work to bring the whole world into a new reality. I could fill a book with many other examples; but **this one** is enough to make the point. The **album, Sgt. Pepper's** Lonely Hearts Club Band, **especially with** its obvious "**L**ucy in the **S**ky with **D**iamonds," **was the new door** for the whole world to pass through **to a psychedelic parallel universe.**

After some of our **amazing** LSD-induced dreams (supposing that synthetic **drugs** were as beneficial as natural psilocybin **mushrooms and/or DMT**), I promoted LSD for several years. Nonetheless, my best dreams have been without drugs. If **I still** believed LSD were useful, I still **would not hesitate** to give you my endorsement **to try** it. **I** have already encouraged many millions, and would **still do so**, even without government backing, if I still believed

NOTE: Incarceration for "victimless crimes" is among the worst atrocities against humanity perpetuated by modern governments. This book does not endorse breaking drug laws that could lead to such unjustified abuse by one's government. It does, however, call for a public outcry against all oxymoronic "victimless crimes." It calls for more awareness of the benefits of cannabis, DMT (especially in ayahuasca), psilocybin mushrooms, peyote, and other herbs and formulas that have been life-enhancing since ancient times, as opposed to toxic pharmaceuticals that destroy mental, physical, or spiritual health.

The pineal gland produces and stores DMT. Using DMT, such as smoking it with cannabis, triggers the release of the DMT that has built up naturally in the body, permanently opening the mind to greater consciousness. Ayahuasca makes the DMT experience last for hours. Consistent with the ayahuasca-induced spiritual awakenings facilitated by South American shamans for perhaps thousands of years, William says that his most spiritual life-enhancing experience was when, while on DMT, he saw God.

William says, "Churches fight it, and make it illegal, because ten minutes of DMT helps more than ten years of religion." Likewise, Big Pharma lobbies against cannabis and psilocybin mushrooms because both are more effective, and with fewer side effects, than their own synthetic products. For example, a monthly dose of natural psilocybin mushrooms fights depression more effectively than daily doses of toxic unnatural antidepressants.

in taking it; but I do not. Of all the **many kinds** of dreams that I have had, the best **have been** of an entirely different derivation. Hallucinogens **distorted** reality. They do not make **your picture** of what **is** any clearer. The best dreams do **the opposite.** They go the other way, giving depth **of real perception. We did** "Lucy in the Sky" before we realized **enough** about it. We presented Lewis Carroll in an **LSD** context. It seemed like a good idea at the time.

Instances of "looking glass ties" to **John's** song can only be viewed *Through the Looking Glass:* "The boat glided gently . . . **among beds of weed**s . . . and . . . under trees, but always **with** the same tall river-banks." The guard **look**s at her, "through a telescope, then **through** a microscope, and then through an opera-glass." "**The** setting **sun** . . . shining on his armour in a blaze of **light** that quite dazzled her . . . all this she took **in** like a picture, as, with one hand shading **her eyes.**" Realizing bees are elephants, Alice thinks, "What enormous flowers they must be!" "**Listen**ing, in a half dream, **to the melancholy music of the** song." "The boat, and the river, had **vanished.**"

"Putting his head in at the window" of the train at a station, a guard there says, "Tickets, **please!**" From a gnat, "Half way up that bush, you'll **see** a Rocking-horse-fly." "Alice looked up at **the** Rocking-horse-fly with great interest." Such bits from Lewis Carroll, shown here in **random** order, along with his "Feed your head" **messages**, were the source of **John's** hallucinogenic images making "**L**ucy in the **S**ky with **D**iamonds" sound like an LSD-induced **dream,** but also alerted our listeners to what **we were conveying through** the images of Lewis Carroll. Many of our Paul **codes** could only be broken by reading Carroll. We provided that context.

Dreams still play a big part in my life. I dream of lines **for songs**, and of lines to share with my relations. **I dream of** people I work with and later use those **good lines** in our real conversations. Everyone thinks I am clever for coming up with these lines spontaneously. I do not tell them that I actually dreamed the lines long before and just waited until the circumstances would present the moment when **I could repeat** them. I cannot help wonder how **much of these dreams** are creativity, or how much is channeling. Just like Paul who woke up with the "Yesterday" tune in his head, **I have** frequently awakened with ideas that seemed **to have** simply been given to me. Wherever **these ideas** may hail from, **I am always glad to receive them.** Sometimes I can decide during the day what I end up dreaming about that night. You can learn to do it too. **Dream of me.** I will tell you more.

Before **going into** the "**Paul is Dead**" aspects of "Let It Be," **let me say** that these things are all one. Everything relates to **everything** else. When I first considered what to include **in this book**, the idea I had in mind was to focus on the **"Paul is Dead"** material. However, it is interconnected with every

---

NOTE: When this book is read as intended (such as by ignoring the footnotes, word-stacking, and acrostic until after reading the entire book once or twice), the reader allows the magical mystery to create the full interactive experience. For those who do so, it is common for William to show up in dreams. He says, "Dream of me. I will tell you more." Many readers have this experience.

If you have such a dream, or feel internal shifting, consider writing it down on the back page of this book. Another approach is to compose each dream on a separate sheet of paper and to tuck each into the book. So doing will shift and personalize your energetic experience of this mystery tour. If you have already had such dreams, consider writing each one now. It adds to the fun by turning up the energy. If this trip gets too intense, give it a rest for a little bit. If you look over that back page right now, you will be more likely to use it later.

aspect of **my life**. It cannot be isolated. Paul **dreamed his death**; but we were all dream weavers. Paul and I were **the best** at it, then George and John; but we all had lucid dreams. John said he wanted Paul to give him more, and was always jealous of me for that; but Paul is attached to me. We are one. **I'm** yoked with his burdens, and flying with his **broken** wings. I am Paul now. It is my dream.

Having briefly explained the importance we all placed on dreams, I will share a few more of them. Early one morning, **John dreamt of** a white bird in a tree singing in **harmony** with a large yellow dog loudly howling while standing on its hind legs beside the tree. **I found it** amusing. John read a lot into it. It was **meaningful.** Without touching his interpretation, I find it more about the way that our world is as harmonious as we perceive it to be—and about him having music on his mind.

Here, I will mention that John also had a dream of **his mother**. **Like mine,** it was comforting to him. Each of those dreams **led to songs.** John's dream showed her, "Julia," more radiant than she was in life. In my "Let It Be" chapter, **I will explain** how my dream, and some **backward recording**, led to that song. John, George, **and** I all had meaningful, sometimes **life-changing**, **dreams** outside of the scope of this underground book. Ringo's interesting dreams were not of the same momentous meaning; and none, as far as I know, ever led to any song. Nevertheless, song writing, under any circumstance, was not Ringo's forte. Ringo made his contribution as a drummer, but

BILLY'S BACK!

may have helped even more as the group's loving underdog. He was good for the band.

Julia whispers that I should explain her song. Okay. When Julia contacted John in a dream, his ugly memories of her neglecting him while out entertaining "Johns," et cetera, all vanished. She was lovelier than he had ever imagined her. In the dream, **she was** calling out to him. He refers to it in his "**Julia**" song, singing, "Julia . . . calls me." The point of the song was for John to reach her by answering her call. "**I say** it just to reach you, Julia." He sought **a spiritual connection** with his mum.

Speaking of dreams, it **is important** to have a dream to pursue. **It makes a difference** to have family and friends who support us in our passions, who encourage us to follow our own bliss. Still, even if we don't have that advantage, we are responsible for our own lives. It is up to each of us to discover what we need to thrive, and then to go after it. My dream was to entertain with music. Your dream may be something else. I was privileged to have powerful people conspire to help me, but more lucky to find a supportive partner.

NOTE: The acrostic continues to page 616 of *the Memoirs*. This chapter says:
  At first, you may say Paul is a dreamer; but he is not the only one. From the time I joined him, our dreams have made us together as one.
  "Dream sweet dreams for me."
  I was introduced to LSD and other drugs by John and George. It's a trip from L. C.
  Dream of me.
  Be happy.
  "Hello."
  "Hello, Mum."
  Julia's fine.

2

Stuart Was the First Martyr.

Assuming Paul's identity, dreaming of him, and feeling his presence, each reinforces the others. I stand for him, and he for me. **Part of each of us** is in the other. Although I may say he **died** and I live, it is not entirely true. My own life as William was halted with Paul McCartney's fatal crash; yet, he continued on through me. You might as well say Bill died and Paul lives. I am not an impersonator in ordinary terms; our exchange is mutual. **Paul's** spiritless remains mark the end of William's **life** now to the extent that my living flesh **embodies** Paul's life. I am Paul. I am **Billy. I have** died. That is why I live as I do. Dreaming of **him, as** myself, I dream particularly of that **part of me** that I missed growing up. It helps me understand who I am. Even before I left my Billy life behind for this new life of Paul, I searched for myself. Dreams have always helped me to understand myself better.

Until I became Paul, my dreams were more self-centered. Now that I can see myself through Paul's eyes, it is easier to see beyond myself to become who or what I am meant to be.

Billy's Back!

I obviously feel more connected to Paul than to any of the other ex-Beatles, but still cannot help needing continued connections with them all. I mean no disrespect to Wings by saying that the past I share with John, George, and Ringo will always have special meaning to me, and that they all made my dreams a reality. Wings was a great band and all that, but could never have existed until my Beatle years ran their course. I could not do it as William Shepherd. I had to give up myself and live the life of Paul McCartney who prepared my way. **I am** indebted to all four. However, it does not stop there. **Their** success was launched by help from bandmates, Peter **Best** and Stuart Sutcliffe.

Others surely helped; but there were only seven Beatles: John, **Paul**, George, Stu, Pete, Ringo, and, do not forget me, William Shepherd, a.k.a. Billy Shears. Stu was the band's first bassman. Paul took over as bass player when Stu left and died. Then I took over where Paul left off. I was joined to each of the Beatles as a fraternal brotherhood. Stu came to me twice in dreams, and John did once.

Stu was astoundingly shy, even in death. **Paul** told me in a dream that Stu Sutcliffe **died of** a subdural hematoma (bleeding in the brain) from **an injury** received at a Beatles show. Paul said its gravity eluded Stu. **No one had any idea how** serious it was. It started when **John shouted obscenities** at the crowd. One English-speaking German became irate. From the stage, John kicked him in the head. With one kick of John's boot, the burly man went down. A fight broke out between the band and the audience. It nearly killed John. **Paul told me** they ached for days; but no one knew **it finished Stu.** When Paul told me this in a dream early on, I said I would like to meet Stu someday.

In my next Paul dream, he introduced me to Stuart. Stu told me that if he had not gone that night, it would have been John that died in 1962, not Stu. Stu took some hard blows that would have unavoidably fallen on John if Stu had not then come along. I awoke from this visit-dream thinking of everyone's impact on the world without anyone realizing it. **If Stu had missed** that gig, and John terminated in 1962, **the Beatles** would not have achieved world fame. **Paul would still be alive.** He also died **in consequence** of the band–as John did much later. **I would still be** some poor bloke roughing it as **a session musician.** The world would be a very different place–especially for me.

One other time I dreamed of Stu, about four months after the first time. Stuart told me that until he hooked up with John, he was drifting without direction, and that the only reason he got into the music business was because John persuaded him. He said **he wanted to** be an artist. He said the quiet canvas **always** appealed to him more than the limelight. He sounded regretful.

My dreams **tell me things**, but are merely dreams. **I never knew** how much to believe them. Even so, they have taught me quite a bit.

3

Paul Worked It Out.

Paul's death premonitions were taken more seriously by some people than by others. Nearly all of his loved ones bought in to it to a point; but it was hard to motivate many of them to take action. Unless they prepared by finding a replacement while **Paul was** still alive, he was saying, it would be too **late.** Without revealing his motive, Paul held a lookalike contest through a popular teen magazine. The winner, Keith Allison, had the look, but was not the man whose face Paul had seen in his studio dream. Ongoing efforts were made to find the **next** Paul. Brian Epstein's brother thought **I would be** a good replacement; but never spoke to **Paul** about it. **Paul** had seen me once at a spring party, and **seemed** to kind of recognize me, but was too **freaked out** to pursue it. I have been told that upon **seeing me**, he

NOTE: Several events were combined to create the above party story. Paul was well acquainted with William long before dreaming of being replaced by him. William was first introduced to Paul on 5 July 1963 at the Plaza Ballroom at Old Hill. They went on to have many further interactions at other venues, at EMI Studio Two, and in social settings, especially with friends of the Hyde Park crowd.

By the imposed use of doubles, Paul sometimes felt replaced already. He understood that he would be replaced permanently, but, as shown by the lookalike contest, hoped to have some say in selecting his permanent substitute.

ended his search without ever attempting to find or contact me, or any other candidate. During a visit with Jim McCartney one day, a year or so after Paul crossed over, Jim said he had insisted that Paul stop talking about, and stop preparing for, his own death. Jim had told Paul that all of that preparing for it could possibly make it happen. Jim had believed that as Paul's father, he ought to be able to counsel him. However, **Paul's** position was that his father was too **out of it** to understand. Paul thought that since he was **now** so successfully emancipated, he was not obligated to take his father's advice. **Paul felt** disrespected by his father who did not take **omens** seriously. Jim likewise felt dishonored by Paul who ignored good fatherly advice. Jim said Paul would still be alive if he had been open to fatherly counsel. He also said Paul's "debt to the devil . . . was nonsense."

From Jim's perspective, Paul's first dream was merely a dream, nothing more. According to Jim, everything escalated out of control because Paul obsessed about it. Jim told me that a death dream is usually about a change of life. He says Paul's subconscious was probably trying to deal with some aspect of his life that was ending. It could have been his loss of youth, or of any one of a very many things. **It could have been** a fear of losing his hair, or **Jane**, or of the band coming to an end. Whatever it **was**, Jim was sure it was not a message **from heaven**, or from hell, warning of his replacement. It was just one bad dream that freaked him out enough to trigger another, and another.

Yet, Jim said **Paul** got some crazy ideas stuck in his brain about why he **had to be sacrificed** and substituted. Jim said **Paul psyched himself out.** By his obsession, **Paul focused his fears into** his reality. By his obsession, he was **tormenting** himself over it, bringing on further **dreams** to obsess about. **Paul's** subconscious used dreams to work through the **trauma** he **was** feeling, which resulted in more material **over** which to obsess.

I would tell him to clear **negative thoughts** through meditation, if he were here now; but that would have prevented my turn. **Jim said** Paul attracted and created the product of his thoughts, that Paul's reality of death was first created in his head. Next, as though manifesting willfully, his persistent thoughts and deep feelings, brought them into reality.

Donna, standing by the side of the road, holding her suitcase, soaked by the windy rainstorm, trying to get a ride, must have been recognized by Paul. Playing out precisely as he had foretold it all, he had to recognize it from his dream, but pulled over anyway. He seems to have developed a death wish. Even though it was self-destructive, something about the martyrdom seemed to attract him. He could not resist playing out the fate he established. He saw something romantic in it. **He was dying to** be esteemed not only as a great writer and performer, but also as one who could **foretell his** future. Sealing his fate by pursuing his **own death**, he also established his own role as the band's prophet.

Paul Worked It Out.

Not that I fully bought into it, **I played** along. John and George called him **their Lord.** Going overboard with the praise of Paul, George went so far as to say that **Krishna** became Christ, and that Christ **became Paul.** While I never had any reason **to believe any of that**, and even though it **seemed remarkably absurd** to imagine the resurrected Christ returning by another reincarnation (making him die again), and even though it seemed even more foolish to suppose that Beatle-Paul had evolved an incarnation beyond Jesus, still I was bright enough to recognize the opportunity.

For this role of Paul to work fully, **I** needed a spiritual connection to Paul, and **actually got it** over and beyond what I had expected—which was far more than what John and George anticipated. Realizing how John and George were elevating the spiritual significance of Paul, and observing how freely they welcomed that elevation of their dead bandmate, **I** understood early on how all of that ultimately **raised my own** position. The thing that impressed them the most about **Paul** as a spiritual sentient presence was **that** he foretold his death and substitution, then **worked with me**, the strange substitute, channeling music and talent to me. To them both, that made Paul some kind of a god.

NOTE: To Krishna's followers, it is plausible that someone living today may be the reincarnated Lord. In *the Haiku Gita,* he says he is born in each age:

I return through birth
whenever goodness decays
or evilness grows.

To protect the good
and to destroy the evil,
I'm born in each age.

37

BILLY'S BACK!

I should also mention that Paul appeared to George in an LSD trip, helping each of us realize new levels of awareness of the loving universal light that binds us all as one. That new enlightenment gave us all cause to see Paul in a more spiritually evolved plane than we had supposed.

All of these things combined for my own benefit. In addition to appreciating the social and spiritual nuances of George's insights, it also set me up to benefit from the band's new obsession. Paul's **death became** the primary focus of each album. As **Paul's** representative here on earth, **I became** the **focus.** Everything pointed to me pointing to **him.** If you care to become aware of it, you will see that the intense focus on Paul begins with *Sgt. Pepper's,* my first Beatles album, and never does let up. With George and John calling Paul their Lord, that makes me their Lord's mouthpiece. I am singing for him. Even though there was often conflict between my bandmates and me, they all intensely loved their Lord Paul. I will return to the Lord Paul idea in the chapter on Paulism. For now, let me explain that **I played along** largely because of the position it put me in **with the band** and with the world. It was not **because of** a religious conversion. I also played along for **Paul's** sake. I felt that he appreciated getting all of that **attention.** I felt that he approved of it, and **that I owed** it **to him**—and to my bandmates.

Motivating his family, friends, and others, to cooperate with Paul to prepare for his coming death,

Paul Worked It Out.

yoking us together forever, **Paul** (with some help from John) wrote "We **Can Work** It Out." He fashioned it to have **a double meaning** for a romantic sense; but our focus **in this book** is on his real concern. He says, "**Try to see it** my way. Do I have to keep on talking till I can't go on?"

It burdened him because he believed he would die before long—making him unable to "go on." Everything had to be worked out immediately. Arguing with him was costing time that was now running out. The risk was that Paul's death before replacement plans were finalized could deny any possibility of carrying them out. "While you see it your way" referred to that position insisted on by Jim and others that Paul should drop the subject, and then deal with the death if and when he crossed over. Paul said that "Run[s] the risk of knowing that our love may soon be gone."

As I look back over those years, **I am** especially impressed with that line of love. **Paul's** deal was vital to prevent their love from being gone. I do not know how Paul meant "love," but am surely most emphatically aware of how it played out. I thought at first that he was referring only to his own death. As time went on, I believed that by "love," he meant

---

NOTE: We treat each Paul song as if he authored its sentiments. That's partly true. Although highly focused on the work at hand, George Martin also showed genuine interest in what John and Paul were experiencing. On occasion, John or Paul would share concerns or feelings that could be worked into songs for them. Nevertheless, working for Tavistock, the lead songwriter sometimes understood their situation more clearly than they understood it themselves. Accordingly, he wrote what John or Paul would feel if they fully comprehended their situation. "We Can Work it Out" partly originated from Paul's own concerns, but included layers of meaning that he could not grasp.

his own good will that held the Beatles together. Lately, I have come to see it as the loving universal force that keeps all things in harmonic order.

"Within You Without You" has George singing about "the love that's gone so cold." He then again cries of "the love there that's sleeping" in "While My Guitar Gently Weeps." Likewise, "All You Need Is Love" has John complaining of the same thing. **I will explain** what each of those songs say of **the love lost** as we reach those chapters. Here, Paul pleads **for family and friends** to work it out to keep that love alive when he is gone. He is leaving, but will not leave the band comfortless. His love would continue through me.

However good in theory, in truth, his music went on without him; but the love felt by the band for the years that **I was in** it never could begin to measure up to **the** love they had between them all until Paul's **death.** While music flourished, love diminished. It gave us all a pain to hope otherwise.

I guess **most people** who grasped the song would have **thought** of Paul's own prophetic brilliance to work **that** out. He had his continuance figured out. To me, **Paul's** plan suggests a lack of sense. He thought he was **replaceable.** He was, but only as the musician and songwriter. I could do that very well. However, when he died, they did not miss the hit-maker. That was not the lack. It was his love. It was his core being. On that level, no one is ever as another. I will explain that further when I write about Linda or about "Let It Be."

"Think of what you're saying. You can get it wrong and still you think that it's alright." That bit

Paul Worked It Out.

is saying that the position of "agree to disagree," or to wait and deal with it later—if and when the time ever comes—is not all right because it would be too late. Being wrong about it cannot be all right. He sings, "Think of what I'm saying. We can work it out and get it straight, or say good night." **Unless** all agreed before his golden slumber, **his love would** sleep with him, making it "good night" to his **love**.

Can you see why George later said **their love is** sleeping? He got it from Paul's **"good night."** We recorded John's "Good Night," and my "Golden Slumbers," with that loss in mind. "Good Night" intentionally follows John's chaotic "Revolution 9" just as Paul's final resting peace would follow his miserable end. John wrote it as far as Ringo sang, but wanted a serene harmonious Hollywood ending, which he asked George Martin to score for him. George scored the end and then hired thirty session musicians for his orchestra, another for the harp, and a choir of four boys and four girls.

On "Golden Slumbers," **I too had help.** That song, recorded one year **later** than John's, was inspired by a ballad written **by Thomas** Dekker (1572 - 1632). Having respected Paul Simon's work adapting "Richard Cory," by **Edwin** Arlington Robinson (1869 - 1935), I decided that maybe I would do the same. Almost all the words are from Dekker. Only three months before Paul Simon's lyrics reworking Robinson's were released, The Byrds had a big hit adapting King Solomon's

Billy's Back!

lyrics from Ecclesiastes: "**Turn! Turn! Turn!**" Others too have adapted poetry **this way.**

NOTE: The Byrds' "Turn! Turn! Turn!" was to help turn youth from parents, tradition, and religion, to the peace-love-sex-and-drugs counterculture. Their anti-war obsession targeted the Vietnam War ("the American War" to the Vietnamese), which had begun in 1955. Since whatever we put energy into increases, being pro-peace would have worked better than being anti-war. However, it was not designed to work. Before the youth's anti-war campaign, the most influential conservative voters already objected to John F. Kennedy increasing the number of American military advisors in Vietnam to 16,000.

Although the US military-industrial complex sought to escalate that war, Congress needed a reason for it. On 2 August 1964, the North Vietnamese showed aggression in the Gulf of Tonkin by returning fire on the destroyer, USS *Maddox*, which had only fired "warning shots." The *Maddox* then fired more, killing four North Vietnamese, and wounding six more. There were no U.S. casualties. The National Security Agency (NSA) claimed that a full battle occurred there two days later. Lyndon B. Johnson was informed that the report was false, but convinced Congress of the necessity of using that "Gulf of Tonkin Incident" as America's door to war. At that time, the U.S. naval forces commander there was Admiral George Stephen Morrison. With military-funded support in Laurel Canyon, Los Angeles, Admiral Morrison's son, Jim, went on to be the lead vocalist of the manufactured band, the Doors.

Before the Gulf of Tonkin incident, plans were already set to hijack the peace movement away from conservative intellectuals and to place it squarely in the hands of those whom conservatives would see as freaks—later renamed hippies. Once the Beatles made their debut in America, other bands were manufactured in England and in California (such as the Doors) who produced a blend of folk music and rock, infused with psychedelics. The freaks, dressed in strange costumes, danced in such a peculiar way that they became the primary attraction at clubs featuring those newly launched folk-rock bands.

As planned, with full media support, Americans were brainwashed to equate the peace movement with repulsive freaks, or hippies, who promoted dropping out of society to engage in open-sex and drugs. By that manipulation, fighting in Vietnam became esteemed as conservative, while those who called for peace were seen as idiotic. The "bad guys" were dirty hippies that wore broken-cross peace signs. The "good guys" supported killing innocent people in foreign lands without stopping to realize that the conflict had no American advantage, but only killed to make rich war-machine-corporations richer.

Flipping war perceptions from evil to good, the US military funded bands and provided a base of operation at a military installation in Laurel Canyon. The Byrds, who covered Pete Seeger's "Turn! Turn! Turn! (To Everything There Is a Season)," was one of their first manufactured bands. The Beatles were coached to name the Byrds as their favorite American band.

Laurel Canyon became the world's central hub of musicians. There, John, Paul, George, Ringo, and William connected with the Byrds, the Doors, the Animals, the Monkees, the Beach Boys, the Mamas and the Papas, Crosby, Stills, Nash and Young, Tom Petty, Joni Mitchell, Carole King, Jimi Hendrix, Frank Zappa, Harry Nilsson, Eric Clapton, Alice Cooper, Charles Manson, and many others.

Paul Worked It Out.

Answering Paul's "get it straight, or say good night," John's "Good Night," and my song, "Golden Slumbers," suggested not only Paul's death, but also that we could not "work it out and get it straight."

Keeping both songs as literal sweet dream lullabies, but also continuing what we wanted all of you to know about Paul, each of these songs worked on different levels. John was saying "good night" to our sleeping Beatle love, and to Paul, but also used the song as a lullaby for Julian. "Golden Slumbers," until **I gave it** a new tune, was already a lullaby; but I provided **the context** of Paul's love. I did it as one song with "Carry That Weight." That song was about the heavy burden **I had** with my Paul role—not that I resented **Paul for** working it out for me, but that I missed being **myself**, in peace, without all the conflict and hassle of dealing with John's grief and pain. Using Dekker's poetic words to describe **Paul's** eternal snooze, his sleep of death, I lead right **into** the weighty burden that his death had placed on **me**.

As Dekker had it, "Sleep pretty wantons do not cry, and **I will sing** a lullaby," I thought of myself going on **in Paul's place** while he slept, and singing to him about **wanting to give** it up and go home. So I added "Carry **That Weight**." In that song, I had all four of us in the band singing the message to me that I needed to accept: "Boy, you're going to carry that weight, Carry that weight a long time." But that is not all we sang. Listen, and hear, "**Paul**, you're going to carry that weight." I have **had** far better times since dissolving the Beatles. Still, I realize that although most of the weight has **been lifted** off me with the band's dissolution, much of the "Paul McCartney" burden remains. After I had worked for a long time to carry Paul's burden, I wrote, "**I've Carried** That Weight." I will include all of **those** lyrics in the final chapter of this book of **secrets.** Singing with Jay-Z moved me to write, record, and perform it as hip-hop; but I did not have the energy for it to come out right. I thought I would kick it out to you so that one of you could cover it. I might enjoy doing that song with one of you.

In Paul's song, his own urgency also gives us all words to live by: "Life is very short, and there's no time for fussing and fighting, my friend. I have always thought that it's a crime." **I think** so too. "Once again, try to see it my way." **His way was** shown to be true. Jim and others claim that **up** until Paul died, he made it come true as a self-fulfilling prophecy. **I see that they** may be right. The deal that Paul **worked out** helped me more than it did him. I got out of **the worst of it.**

4

Paul's Girls

Singling out some of Paul's children may give the impression that they were all he had. They were not. Obviously, these are some that **I** know of, but not all. In this life, Paul never **learned** of most of them. Roaming around and having **more** opportunity than most guys could imagine, **while** not taking any responsibility for it, and **being** the world's most eligible bachelor, **Paul** could conceivably have had young children all over the planet by the time he departed in 1966. Here are some with good stories.

Brian Epstein paid Anita Cochrane £5,000 to not say Paul fathered her son, Philip Paul Cochrane. Under the circumstances, there was a convincingly high probability. Many others also made claims of the Beatles impregnating them. However, most of the claims were not established beyond all question.

I cannot possibly know how many children John, Paul, George, or Ringo fathered while on tour. They do not know either—well, at least none could know

---

NOTE: Sometimes in his songs and in *the Memoirs,* William uses ambiguous words when so doing allows for multiple true meanings. In this case, the phrase, "Paul's Girls," refers to the biological Paul's lovers and also to his daughters, even though the first offspring example is one of Paul's sons.

in this lifetime. From what **I have** heard, none of them respected women enough **to take** paternity seriously, at least none did in **Paul's lifetime**. They nestled up with many birds before they settled down to roost permanently. I confess I was the same way once I took over Paul's part. Being in the greatest show on earth put us at an advantage with women.

There were always gorgeous women who would do anything to get close to us. Two daughters that I know sprang from Paul are spotlighted in this chapter. Before discussing them, let me say that since Paul never did take full responsibility for his children, I feel for them, and see how it clearly reflects poorly on Paul; but it is not my problem. It is tragic to be sure. However, it is not my predicament. I do not want to sound callous. **I am sorry** about Paul's indiscretions. I am sorry **he did not accept** his rightful responsibility for **his children** when they came along. It is sad; but it happens. I want no part of it. I wish his children would not contact me. I am finally using this chapter to tell them that I regret what they have gone through without a father; but I am not visiting them, or paying them. Paul was not mature enough to follow-up with responsibility. In that respect, **I am not** Paul.

As **a teenage rocker**, when Paul (and other pre-Beatles) was with the Quarrymen in the then new Cavern Club, Paul met, dated, and impregnated

---

NOTE: While at the Cavern Club, John and Paul showed potential as rockers. However, more than their performance skills, Paul's face caught the global network's attention. Paul's facial characteristics resembled William's, whom a few knew as the magician's son. As such (for a few insiders), and because of Paul's high-arching eyebrow (which impressed others), he became a person of interest. Had he quit the Beatles and started his own band, that new band, not the Beatles, would have been the one promoted. Like a coven of cooks watching two pots on a fire, a few inner circle elite kept an eye on both Paul and William as each developed his own stage presence and music skills.

Monique LeVallier (1945-1999). Monique was a young makeup artist working in London. As always, when she told Paul that she was having his baby, he chose to discontinue their relationship. Monique, broken-hearted and embarrassed, returned to her home in Paris, France. Monique had the baby girl on 5 April 1960. Without Paul, she named the infant Michelle. Paul knew of her, but did not pursue his paternal role.

Letting things drop—partly because Paul, a teenage Quarryman, did not have the means to give due support—Monique parented without him. However, by Michelle's fifth birthday, the Beatles rocked the whole planet. That is the year Paul became a millionaire. Monique put a picture in an envelope and mailed it to him. On the back, she wrote, "**Paul**, Look at our beautiful little daughter. Now she **is** five years old. Michelle would like to meet **her father.** Love, Monique." I found this picture a year and a half later when I went through all of Paul's stuff. Monique took the picture on 5 April 1965, and mailed it from Paris on the 17th. Paul was touched, but reluctant.

Using the French skills of Mrs. Ivan Vaughan (wife of an old Quarryman bandmate), Paul's lyrics for "Michelle" included some of his little girl's native language. Based on the picture he had received of his five-year-old daughter, he wrote, "Michelle." As is evidenced by the lyrics, Paul absolutely intended to connect with her later. If you read the words, you will see that the whole song directly acknowledges her as his own: "**Michelle**, ma belle. . . . My Michelle." The song suggests his belief that they would someday connect. It **is** sad to imagine the impact of **his French daughter** eventually learning this song of hope. "Michelle, . . . I'll get to you somehow. Until I do **I'm telling you** so you'll understand. Michelle, ma belle, Sont les mots qui vont tres bien ensemble." **The hard rub** is that we never know when life will slow down enough to deal with all of those things on our "To Do" lists. He received the photograph in the mail in late April. In May, he was working on French tunes.

Early on, Paul saw his friend, the French teacher, to get words to sing in Michelle's language so that she would understand. Paul began recording the song at EMI Studios on 17 June. It was only two months from the letter's postmark. They did more with the song on 12 October and 11 November, to include it on their *Rubber Soul* album released 3 December 1965. As far as I can tell, Paul still could not make room in his busy life for his daughter by the time he died on 11 September 1966. I have heard that Michelle McCartney is a fine bass player in Los Angeles. She has tried to contact me.

NOTE: On 14 June 1965, Paul meet with George Martin at Studio Two to do preliminary work on "Yesterday," followed by recording "I'm Down" and "I've Just Seen A Face." While there, Paul showed George the photograph of Michelle, and recited these lines: "Michelle, ma belle / These are words that go together well / My Michelle." On 3 November, a few minutes before Paul recorded it, George provided the song in its entirety.

Even though **I feel** for her, what could I say? In this novel, **I say quite a bit** that I cannot in the legally troublesome world **of nonfiction.** If I were to meet her, I could not admit that her father had been laid to rest. And yet, **I cannot** say that I am her father either. That would **be** a terrible lie. If she ever wants to meet **someone who** knew her father, the best choice would be Mike, Paul's brother.

Are you understanding, Michelle? Mike also cannot admit that Paul **has died**, but can tell you nice things about him if that is what you would like to know. However, Michelle, if what you want to do is to find out how Paul felt about you, replay your song. It is what he left to you. He said the song had been written years earlier because everyone knew he was in love with Jane. The child was hush-hush.

Erika Hübers was a young girl Paul met in Hamburg, Germany. Her father owned a club on the Grosse Freiheit, and so had connections. Erika became employed as a server in one of the clubs in that area. That is where she met Paul in August 1960. They hit it off right away and were sexually intimate. She believed that they would be married. With the Beatles' intense performance schedule not leaving much time to socialize, **Paul was glad** to have a steady date. Paul dated Erika **for about a year** and a half, off and on. They conceived their only child together in March 1962.

Saying again, as always, that it would interfere with his career, but wanting to continue getting it on with Erika, Paul urged her to abort the child. She refused. **She urged him**, if he loved her, to marry her **to raise their child together**. When he refused, she felt that he did not love her, **even though** he had told her that he did. She felt that **he had used her**. The hurtful break-up that ensued resembled that of Monique, and was the same pattern with others who would not abort.

On 19 December 1962, Bettina Hübers was born twelve days before the Beatles last Hamburg gig. Under pressure later from the government in West Germany, Paul agreed to pay child support. Bettina, reared without a father in the home, was not told her father's identity until her confirmation as a teenager. It was a very exciting revelation to her. She adored **the Beatles**, and especially loved Paul. She had **never imagined that she was** his daughter. Of course, by the time Bettina found **out**, he was long gone. Now, in her mind, **I am** her father. She too wants contact, which is **clearly a** bad idea.

Paul could have willed **part of his** fortune to his children, but did not. He wrote out a **whole** list of everyone he wanted to receive an inheritance. Sadly, Bettina was not one of them. He did not say why. The reason can only be guessed. Here is my shot at it. He did not know her—or any of his children. He funded her child-support needs against his own will. Those payments that he agreed to, I became legally obligated to complete. Those who handled my funds assured me that all such obligations were met. I did not renege on anything that Paul agreed to pay. I, or my people, honored all of his commitments. Paul did not mean harm or benefit to children who were strangers to him. To be a father, in the best sense, it is not enough to have merely donated the DNA. A true father goes on fathering for as many years as he remains a father. There was no bonding there at all. Beyond conception, Paul never fathered Bettina. She wanted a father. When she was told of Paul, she pursued me, wanting me to be her father, mistakenly assuming that I was he. That is an easy mistake to make. It happens all the time.

Finally, when Bettina turned twenty years old, back in 1982, she filed a paternity suit to get money. That put me in quite a predicament. I did not want to be a part of it, but had no choice. All of the enormously negative consequences for me breaking the non-disclosure agreement are worse than ridiculous. **Without going into it,** there is no way I would possibly break that agreement. That is exactly why **I am** cautious to preserve the novel status of this **revealing** book. In fiction, such as a song, poem, or novel, I can say anything. That does not violate **the agreement.** Yet, in straight communication, however formal, in an interview, or in court, **I am obligated to be** silent about having any knowledge of **Paul's** death. I cannot say, "I know nothing of Paul's death." Instead, I am committed to speak of it only as though it were my own. "No," I say, "I am not dead."

Owing to that extraordinary obligation for me to remain silent about Paul's death, as well as to the negative consequences for breaking that agreement, I am in an awkward position when it comes to his children. When hauled into court to respond to Bettina's claim that I was her father, I was enormously frustrated. I wanted to explain it all, but could not. Some people say I should pay up out of

Billy's Back!

respect for Paul; but it was **Paul** who set it up as it is. He set my course. He **is the one that** agreed only to the required support payments. **I honor** him by doing exactly as he instructed.

Subpoenaing me **for the paternal suit** left me no choice. **Playing along**, I provided the evidence required by their court, **I submitted**. I allowed a blood draw to prove **the DNA** from my left arm. At the court appearance **to identify Bettina's** father, I proved that it could not be **me**.

Even with that irrefutable DNA evidence, Paul and Erika's long-term relationship had been so **clearly established**, and Erika's fidelity to Paul so **well known**, that the court ruled that I must be the **father** of Bettina. Plainly, Erika was no slut. She **was** not sleeping with other guys while giving her all to **Paul**. The court could see that was true. I had to be the father.

No matter how many character witnesses lined up and swore that faithful Erika had never been with another man, it should not have mattered since my **DNA does not have** a parental match. It was under **that** argument that I appealed the decision and finally won. Erika and Bettina were shocked. The decision seemed **impossible** to them. Erika looked again at the drawn blood **evidence**. Besides the insistence that I had proof **of identification**, they also, as an added precaution, took my picture and enclosed it with the blood sample. Erika got her hands on that picture and stared at it. "Es ist nicht er!" she shouted. "It is not him!" She said that **I looked a lot like** Paul, but claimed the court was conned by **an imposter.** The head shape was not as she remembered him. Mine is longer.

Erika recalled that Paul was a lefty. However, when they examined my signature, they could tell that my name was signed by someone right-handed. They took my signature to a Beatles museum where each of the Beatles' autographs was on display. Again, there was a big fuss because they did not match. To Erika and Bettina, that proved that Paul fraudulently sent an imposter to go and donate his blood for him. That is how she made sense of the whole thing—knowing Paul was the father.

Erika and Bettina were both positive Paul was the father. Now, with my wrongly shaped head, the right-handed signatures, and with their confirmation that **Paul's** autograph in the museum could not be by the same **hand** as my signature on the blood-draw sheet, Bettina **says she has proof** of my fraud. She only has begun to fight. She is **now** in her forties and is attempting to sue me for fraud. **I cannot** make her understand—unless Bettina reads this underground book—because I cannot **tell her** about her father's death. **If she wants McCartney** DNA, she would have to **get it from Mike.** As kind-hearted as I am, **I would love to tell her** all about it; but cannot. **On the other hand, Mike is not** eager to become **involved either.** Why should he be? He is not the one being accused. I am.

NOTE: To safeguard the McCartney name, Michael McCartney's support in the entertainment industry was conditioned on him using a non-McCartney stage name. As Mike McGear, he had doors opened to him that never would have opened otherwise.

Mike played no part in his brother's replacement, but was well acquainted with William before the switch, and was glad that William accepted Paul's role. Mike worked directly with William, especially after the Beatles years. Mike and William have a lot in common. Most notably, they both enjoyed creating musical comedy. Despite William's superior station, they consider themselves friends and colleagues.

Billy's Back!

It is between Bettina and me now. I will let DNA do the talking. I could bring a hundred people to the court who would swear that I am Sir James Paul McCartney. Then, in front of everyone, I could wield my arm and let them draw another vile of blood. I would bet all of my wealth and reputation that it would match the sample that I gave the last time. My DNA has not changed one bit since then. That theatrical appearance should settle it all at last. With whom the fine people of Germany are messing, they have no idea. **This is not the only** paternity test that my DNA has cleared for **Paul.**

NOTE: Most people fail to comprehend the connection between the global military industrial complex and the global entertainment industry. Both descend from the same elite group that presides over the organizations that also control the world's money supply, and which endeavor to control all other industries that significantly impact human attitudes and behaviors.

EMI's exchanges with German government intelligence resulted in, and were in return strengthened by, EMI hiring many Nazis after WWII. High-ranking German officials operating within the cultic inner-circle, as well as many other people of Western European prominence, were aware of EMI's switch to the illuminated Paul who would facilitate the social revolution in preparation for the New World Order.

Erika's legal case provided a predicament for the German government. Germany is a key player in the coming one world government. Without compromising shared global agendas, and undermining affiliations, they could not allow Erika's court case to prove that William is not Paul. However, based on the submitted DNA, the court also could not prove that William is Paul. The only solution was to eventually dismiss the case on a technicality without ever allowing it to go to trial.

5

Drive My Car Backwards.

"Drive My Car" was written after one of Paul's nightmares about a girl, alone in the rain, wanting a ride in his car. In this song, he would cheat death by saying, "You drive! **I'm not your** driver!"

I have raised a glass to **Paul** by doing a number of songs dealing with cars or with driving. I use virtually any excuse to work a word in with such a Paul reference. I could pick several albums for examples. However, being in the album title, I will use *Driving Rain,* named for the rainy night that he met Donna and ended their lives. Although no song **on the album** is entirely about Paul dying, you can **see how I** wove in the driving image. For example, **notice** the title "Lonely Road;" and consider how **every line** has a double meaning with reference to both Paul and to Linda. **It is** about both. "I hear your music and it's **driving me** wild / Familiar rhythms **in a different style**" is repeated throughout the song, but is true of the rest of the song as well.

In the song, "**From a Lover** to a Friend," which I sing about **needing Linda** to let go, to let me love another, **I use the driving image** with

BILLY'S BACK!

"It's far too easy ride to see," and then again as "Despite too easy ride to see." The title song, "Driving Rain," brings to my mind an emotional storm, driving, and severe loneliness. It is my broken heart driving me sad. There is plenty in there about Linda; but the entire song is of driving. I sing, "Why don't we drive in the rain . . . Go for a ride in the driving rain." **Then, of course, there** is "Riding Into Jaipur" which **is** all about me riding through the night in **a car with my babe**, meaning Linda, **who had passed away.**

Those songs above, and many others, pull in the driving idea, but are not specifically about the crash. Here are some Beatles songs about Paul's collision: In "Don't Pass Me By," Ringo sings, "You were in a car crash, and you lost your hair," suggesting that he lost his head, but also being an inside joke since **Paul really was** losing his hair. In fact, his baldness gave investigators cause to doubt it was Paul when they **found** him. His hair was pushed back and held there, **matted with blood**, so that all his baldness was shown to the top of his head. His line, "When I get older losing my hair," was a serious concern; but he hid his balding well with his combed forward mop-top cover-up.

Showing exactly where Paul "blew his mind out in a car," the *Magical Mystery Tour* takes you there. In the movie and album booklet, we refer you to "ten miles north on the Dewsbury Road," Paul's death site. We filmed this trip on the first anniversary of his death. In the title song, you hear a car skidding and crashing, representing both Paul's Aston-Martin and our tour bus. **The trip was** a magical tour group **mystically experiencing the decapitation of the "Magical Mystical Boy"** (as he is called).

"A Day in the Life" and "Revolution 9," to name songs of other albums, have backward recordings of sounds of car crashes. You would need to play them backwards to hear them.

During their work on *Revolver*, the first Paul's last album, while high on marijuana, and working on "Rain," John accidentally played a tape of that song in reverse. In that instance, John's pot-induced impaired judgment led to a discovery that impacted our Beatles music for the better. We then impacted various other bands who imitated us. **The Beatles**, most especially John, had avidly **used Preludin** to enliven his stage performances **in Hamburg**, and sometimes to keep them awake, but most often to ignite maniacal stage antics. By the time I came along, they were heavily into many other drugs that occasionally brought on creative benefits, such as in this instance with "Rain," but that far more often brought down performance standards. For example, it was his drug-induced impairment that made John act as though his song, "What's the New Mary

NOTE: Later, when enlisted by EMI, the Beatles were initially marketed to a somewhat conservative demographic. The public personas created for John, Paul, George, and Ringo were to start as naive and innocent Liverpool lads. Evolving while the world watches and sings along, the boys would gradually mature into broad-thinking men of the world. All would see them outgrow their childish inhibitions, embrace enlightenment, and expand their wealth and world power. As intended by the social engineering experiment, all who followed them would likewise mature in those ways. Initially, when the boys played the innocent card, the public could not know they used Preludin or any other drugs. Later, as their personas awakened into broader thinking (when William stepped in), they were required to be open about using many drugs.

Jane," **had** any merit at all. "Mary Jane," which is commonly **understood** to mean marijuana, is fine, but not while on **the job**. I could not get John to kick his habit of using drugs while recording. Once I left **the Beatles**, I demanded that everyone working on my material were to do so while thinking clearly. We **could party** and have a good time all we wanted later, **but not** while working. I do not want pothead quality **on my records.**

Reversing the recording of "Rain," playing it backwards, sounded interesting. George Martin did some experimenting with it that night after John left. Adding a clip of John's vocals and guitar to the song in the reversed direction, he made the world's first backward masking. **Backmasking** is a Beatles invention in that it **began with that Beatles song.** We then did it in others. It was **George Martin**, not John, who thought of it and **first tried it**. The next day, George Martin shared it **with John, who** thought it was great, and **was happy to keep it** in there. The text of that first of many **backmasked** overlays for the Beatles was "When the rain comes, they run and hide their heads." In this first instance, the sound of the backward message did not at all resemble that of the forward sound, but did not have an adverse distraction from it either. Very often in the backmasked songs that followed, we employed backmasking where the sounds were more similar, being less obvious going forward.

Delighted by that hidden enhancement in "Rain," and realizing that it was historically significant as a recording first, they released it as the B-side of Paul's "Paperback Writer" single rather than on

Drive My Car Backwards.

Revolver as had been intended. On *Revolver,* they then used backward recording in "Tomorrow Never Knows" in a reversed guitar solo, and again in "I'm Only Sleeping." They released *Revolver* just a little more than one month before Paul crossed over. Starting when **I** took his place, and thus from then on, we **used reversed messages** to tell the world **of Paul's death**. Backmasking became a new way to for us **to tell the secret.** However, we were not the first to listen to recordings backward.

Going all the way back to 1877, when Thomas Edison invented the phonograph, he began—at least as early as the next year—to play recordings backward. He wrote about it. Although Edison never played them backward as much as forward, he was fascinated by the "novel, but altogether different [sound] from the song reproduced in the right way." Many years later, Aleister Crowley had me listen to phonograph records reversed, attempting to train me, in my early childhood, to think backwards.

Once as **Yoko played** Beethoven's "Moonlight Sonata" on **the piano**, John wondered aloud how nice it would sound **backward.** He challenged her

NOTE: William's training to "think backwards," as he put it, included, with great practice early on, learning to write backward and even to talk backward. When it came time to create backmasking, he took to it naturally with an unusual ability to anticipate what kind of a sound a reversed word would produce. In his youth, he also became proficient at swiftly walking backward.

William also notices what a word spelt backward might mean, such as in the case or RAM and MAR. For a subconscious suggestion, or to bring focus to one, he might reverse the word order, or say the opposite of something.

Checking or chasing such clues causes confusion and creates counter-clues. Here is an example of a false clue to cause confusion. If this note were to tell the reader to find Paul's corpse indexed as "Paul J-Something," rather than as "J. Paul McCartney," that reversal would be a false clue or counter-clue. The reader is not meant to find the body. Do not ask for such clues. None are real. This will also add confusion: Juxtaposing every riddle ventures into subtleties.

to play it that way. **She did it.** He used the melody that emerged to write "**Because**." With that help from Beethoven, **it was the best song** on the *Abbey Road* LP **from a musical perspective.** We were great, but were not up to the sophistication of Beethoven.

You will read in this book about many more songs with backmasked Paul messages. A few were revealed in 1969. From then on, countless other bands used that new Beatles method to hide their own secret messages. For example, The Doors, in "Break On Through," backmasked, "**I am** Satan." All my Beatles backmasking was **of Paul or his death.** In some of my other roles, such as The Fireman, I do it with other content. Backward and forward, I still drive Paul; and he still drives me.

NOTE: When William created backmasking in various songs, it was nearly always to say, in so many words, that "Paul is dead." John and George also concealed such Paul messages. "Revolution 9," which is weighed down with backward recording throughout, includes representations of Paul's demise.

However, more aligned with the above referenced Doors backmasked message about Satan, and consistent with countless songs by numerous other artists seeking to affirm their Satanic affiliation, when we play "Revolution 9" backward, we hear Yoko say such things as, "Satan, look at me please." "Satan, look at me. Come on, Satan, now." "Satan, is he great?"

Recording artists have their own reasons for making such recordings. The motivational and literary contexts are usually more significant than the actual content. In Yoko's case, although listeners may guess at why she included Satan in her witchcraft, the context of the song, when played backward in its entirety, is about Paul's life and death. In his final years, he had increasing anxiety over his Satanic compact, which many see as tied to his sacrifice.

Global governing methods succeed by controlling information. Beliefs determine attitudes, values, perceptions, and behavior. One way to control information is comparable to sleight of hand. If a leader holds hard facts in one hand, and softer ideas in the other, followers blindly favor the ideas that support their own paradigms. Most people avoid seeing, comprehending, or considering, anything that would disprove their own biases.

Yoko's sleight of hand drew attention from the martyr to the witch. By calling on Satan, those who were unaware of Paul's similar words could not see how they seemed to lead to his death. The lines confirm that part of Paul's story for the initiated while directing others to look away. Since the public could not want that to be a death clue, they could not see it in that context. It was much easier to believe that the Satanic lines were about Yoko, and that they did not reflect the views or practices of the band or its management.

6 (Chapter 7 in *the Memoirs*)

"Born a Poor Young Country Boy"

I thought this clue was more obvious. James Paul McCartney was born in Walton Hospital in Liverpool, where his mother, Mary, had worked as a nurse in the maternity ward. **Paul was raised** in Liverpool. The population **there** has grown tremendously over the past two centuries. It is a very old city, dating back to King John (1166 – 1216), but was not heavily populated until the early 19th century when 40% of the world's trade passed through its port. It should have been a dead giveaway. That place is urban. I sang that I was "born a poor young country boy."

If it is **Paul you are** looking for, he is buried in a field of grass **pushing up rhododendrons.** I am not him. You can **"Find me** in my field of grass" or sitting **"beside a mountain stream"** watching the "waters rise" ("Mother Nature's Son"). The peaceful country is my heritage.

Having McCartney wealth is far better than being "a poor young country boy." For me, the most excellent possession is my farm far from the urban

BILLY'S BACK!

insanity. It is **in Scotland**, in the "Heart of the country where **the holy people** grow, Heart of the country, **smell the grass** in the meadow." On our farm in the heart of the country, I have what I want: "Want a horse, **I want** a sheep," and I usually "wanna get me **a good** night's sleep, Livin' in a home in the **heart** of the country." Those nice rural lyrics are from "Heart of the Country" on my *Ram* album.

The country living has influenced my music. Before I joined the Beatles, at a time when my records were made with fellow session musicians rather than with real bands, I made albums that you have most likely never heard. One was called "Cowboy Favourites," by the Maple Leaf Four: Bill Shepherd & the Ranch Hands. That was a good cowboy sounding band for a country collection of songs. If you ever hear it, you will recognize the American cowboy voice I used in "Rocky Raccoon." Not wanting to be left out, Ringo made his own country sound in "Don't Pass Me By." That was good country-style fiddling George added in too. He too had country potential.

NOTE: Because every aspect creates our nuances, singing from inaccurate experience (Liverpool domiciled) reveals outstanding additional details. When William sang of Penny Lane, it sounded as if it were a street of significance in some quaint village. To those who knew that obscure street in the old congested city of Liverpool, the song felt inauthentic. By contrast, Wings' "Mull of Kintyre" was very well received in the UK, being the first single to sell over two million copies there. The difference was that William only pretended to be from Liverpool, but actually loved living in Kintyre.

Three months before Paul died, he was advised to purchase High Park Farm in Campbeltown near the Mull of Kintyre, Scotland, as a tax shelter. He bought that three-bedroom farmhouse, on 183 acres, on 17 June 1966, but hardly saw it.

William inherited that property, but mostly neglected it until he and Linda began renovations in 1969. It was their primary abode until her passing. To reduce the number of sightseers, they also purchased the nearby Low Park Farm. Now, in Linda's absence, William rarely goes there anymore.

Speaking of "Rocky Raccoon," the antagonist in that song was Daniel, whose name was derived from the song, "Danny Boy." That song, although written by an Englishman while living in America, is outstandingly popular with the Irish here and also beyond. Irish families, including McCartneys, found refuge in Liverpool during the potato famine in the 1840's. Tens of thousands of Irish immigrants filled the city. The swelling was permanent. They are still there. By popular interpretation, **the song begins** having a reference to funeral pipes: **"Oh Danny boy,** the pipes, the pipes are calling." **Later,** near the end of the song, it goes on to say, **"If I am dead,** as dead I well may be, Then if **you bend and tell me** that you love me, **I'll** sleep in peace **until you come** to me." If you **have** ever noticed the pipes line sung on the *Let It Be* album, and wondered what it has to do with Paul, now **you know**.

With all my hints **about me** being from the country, and with your understanding that Paul was not, consider the difference. Our music was mostly for city-dwellers. The Beatles were Liverpudlians.

7 (8)

I Was a Session Musician.

I had been in a few bands that never made it commercially. I sang and played with hopes of the big time. **I also participated** in some groups more for fun than **for profit.** Making music has always been fun for me. Most of the time, I worked as a session musician. That was my Paul training. I tinkered with many bands, small ones mostly.

When I became Paul, his Beatle name opened all the other doors. I went on to fiddle behind the scenes with bigger bands. **I became** friends with really great artists. Most of **that work**, just like before as a session musician, went on entirely anonymously. For me, it was a delight to be involved with those bands. **As Paul, I** did not need compensation. I just **had good times** that I could relive whenever **I heard the songs replayed** on the radio or **on records.** As Paul McCartney, I could crash most any EMI recording session.

Everyone was delighted to have a Beatle drop in to play with them. Sometimes the bands would stop doing whatever they were up to so that they could jam with me. Other times, I helped various artists make their records—either as a non-credited backup musician, or by offering timely advice or ideas. **You can imagine** what it meant to a lot of them to have **Paul McCartney** drop by and lend a hand.

All along, I was interested in having my hands in as many bands as I could. **I helped them out**; but they helped me too. I learned **a lot** from them. I especially hung out **in Abbey Road's Studio Two.**

The years of session work had taught me a lot about the music business. Most of all, the range of experience was beneficial. I would be hired to help record a rock and roll album one day, and to sit in a nice and proper orchestra the next. Sometimes legitimate bands would need a little extra sound that I could provide. Other times, albums were put together for bands that only existed for the hour. We invented them, or somebody did. Someone would put up the money to hire a group of young models or actors to jump around and pretend to be a band for a photo shoot. Having a look of the cover, some no-name musicians, like me, would be hired to cover someone else's music. Occasionally, I was fortunate enough to include some of my own original material. Recording songs I wrote was especially satisfying.

Now, another thing **I was** learning at this time was that it was **big business**, and all for show. Oh, sure, it was **for the love of music** as well. But what we created was **much more than mere** music. Ultimately, it was all an **illusion.** We created sounds and images that would sell. If it sounded and looked good, it made money. It was not about reality any more than most shows are. For the show, as Brian Hines had done, we invented our own identities.

Professionally, I generally used one set identity to attract business, and another for any particular group. My business name was for the agents or others to call me and hook up my next gig. Usually, that was the only name **I needed**. Normally, names did not go on album covers, and were ignored on orchestra programs. Whenever **a name** was needed on an album, one would be selected or created specifically for each group. Having already adopted identities in order to work with bands before, it was not as outlandish as you might imagine for me to adopt the persona of Paul. Like an actor in film, the character name is part of the show.

For my *Cowboy Favorites* album, which used the same Western cowboy style as in a few of my other songs, such as "Rocky Raccoon," I used my boy howdy rootin' tootin' name, Bill Shepherd & the Ranch Hands, aka The Maple Leaf Four.

As Billy Pepper & The Pepperpots, I covered one Beatles song for each side of an album, followed mostly by my songs. (A friend, Jimmy Fraser, wrote two songs—one for each side.) I called it *Merseymania* (Labels: Allegro Records, with the identical album on Hurrah Records). The band and the same album was also called *The Liverpool Beats!* (Rondo), with the exact same record. Then, I shortened that band name to Beats!!!!! for *The Merseyside Sound!* (Design Records). Those were all the same record.

Billy Pepper & The Pepperpots then made the sequel, *Beat!!!!! More Merseymania*. Like before, I **did a Beatles song** to begin each side. Jimmy and

I Was a Session Musician.

I wrote the rest. He did three then. The Beatles songs that we used were "I Saw Her Standing There" and "I Want To Hold Your Hand" for *Merseymania*, and, for *Beat!!!!! More Merseymania,* "She Loves You" and "Please Please Me."

Even though I did not live in Liverpool, or in the surrounding boroughs that are also part of Merseyside (near River Mersey), I sought for identification with the Beatles, and thus with their community, to sell records. Something plainly told me that it would pay off to be identified with them, to pretend to be one of them. That was the only way that I could think of doing it.

Living and making a living **as Bill Shepherd** (Shepard, Sheppard, etc.), **I never made it big, but** loved what I was doing, and **never lost the dream of** somehow someday hitting **the big time.** This was

NOTE: After their Tony Sheridan single, the Beatles first two A-Side songs from singles were "Love Me Do" and "Please Please Me."

From the Decca recordings on 1 January 1962, Brian Epstein created a demo, which Sid Coleman arranged for Brian to share with George Martin on 13 February. Upon hearing the samples, George considered them rubbish. However, after declining the offer, he was overruled by a superior.

Shocked to be ordered to take them on, George had the band come to EMI Studios on 6 June. After working with them for three hours in Studio Two, he determined that further recording would have to wait until suitable songs were written for them. The first song offered to them, which George planned to be their first hit, was "How Do You Do It." To teach the song to the lads before their next recording session, George made a demo and had it delivered to them. It was recorded by Barry Mason, backed by the Dave Clark Five.

On 4 September, the band returned to EMI. They rehearsed for three hours in the afternoon with Ron Richards in Studio Three. Ron taught them five new songs including "Love Me Do," and "Please Please Me." Afterward, George took them to dinner, and then returned them to Ron for their recording session scheduled from 7:00 to 10:00. Struggling, it lasted until 11:15.

In the morning, George and Brian listened together to the recordings. The vocals were weak. The guitars lacked precision. The inventive drumming was distracting. And "How Do You Do It" could not measure up to the demo.

George was ordered to work with the band directly, to proceed as if Ron's recordings never existed, and to record their first hit single on 11 September. Besides that date already having historical military significance, it was also Teddy Adorno's birthday, and was exactly one month before the opening of the Second Vatican Council, giving the Beatles a one month head start.

yet one of many small steps, seemingly one of many meaningless steps, that ultimately trained me in preparation for where I am today. It is like what I wrote of synchronicity in the "Let It Be" chapter. **Everything works out** for the best. I referred to these albums when Brian interviewed me for the Paul position. The albums did not make any meaningful money **for me** directly, but did help impress the person who mattered more than a fan base. My role as **Billy Pepper** made a positive impression on Brian Epstein who considered the plausibility of having me **fill Paul's shoes**. That is figurative, of course. In reality, **with** his small shoes, I would have to "Cut **my toes** off to spite my feet" ("Flaming Pie").

When I did my session work, I would play a tuba one day, then a piano or clarinet the next, whatever instrument was needed. Clients also often used me for backup vocals. **In a pinch**, they appreciated my talent in voice-matching. **They would play a taped** recording of a **voice for me to imitate**. I would have it quickly **by singing along**, and then would keep it for the rest of **the recording** session. The average listener would assume that the guy credited on the album cover was in fact the man **they were hearing**. That is when I was known as **"The man with a thousand voices."** I did not have a thousand voices; but **it was my reputation** and often my best contribution **that clients valued** over and above my instrument playing. Imagine a band ready for a six hour recording session, but unable to do it because a backup singer's throat is

I Was a Session Musician.

sore or scratchy. When **you** book the time in the studio, that is it. You **cannot wait** until a throat is feeling better. Unless you have big Beatles bucks, all must go as planned. **You must pay** for the time whether you use it or not. And **the studio** may not have another opening until it is too late. There are also often contracts with strict completion deadlines that cannot be put off. That was when they really appreciated "the man with a thousand voices." It paid my bills.

When I first joined the Beatles, I imitated Paul. Owing to his scratchy worn-out voice quality, it is easy to imitate, but harsh on the throat. When it was time to record, I went with a clearer sound, and varied my voice for each song for effect. You can hear John and me using a variety of voices in "You Know My Name." **I use my Vivian voice** for enough of it that I expected **to be recognized** as a match with how I sing **as Vivian Stanshall on the** strip stage in the *Magical Mystery Tour* **film.** As I sing in "The Fool on the Hill," I am "the man of a thousand voices, talking perfectly loud. But nobody ever hears him." I played as Viv until the mid-90's.

Having the right appearance is all that matters. When **I look like Paul**, fans hear him. If I look like another, that is who people hear. Even, as in Viv's case, when it is obvious that the hair, mustache, teeth, nose, and ears are not real, it does not matter. People will still only hear what they believe they see. My Viv costumes were a running gag with beards and foam latex. The fixed blindness of fans

---

NOTE: While dressed up as Vivian, William often wore fake teeth that were usually over-sized as part of the humor. That was fun and easy. Matching Paul, however, required shifting some teeth, and filing others.

made it easy for me to play as Paul once my looks were close enough. **Appearances** are subject to the environment. Being **on album covers** as Paul, the Beatles context **proved I was him.**

Since my role as the fool, Vivian Stanshall, was my most successful gig other than Paul, it is also one that is easy to find online. As Viv in the *Magical Mystery Tour* film, I look like my son, James, does now. If you compare images of James and Vivian, you will see that my son looks exactly like me.

Paul, having never been taught to sing properly, sang from his throat. That throaty sound we hear in all of his songs may have endeared him to some. I do not know. Maybe **Paul's lack of voice quality** ultimately worked for him in that it **made him sound** more youthful and innocent **like an untrained teen** in love for the first time. **But he was not as innocent** as he sounded—just untrained. One of the first things singers are taught is to breathe from the diaphragm. Proper air-flow gives a smoother flowing sound.

Another reason to sing from the diaphragm, and not from the throat, is that it preserves the voice. Now, even in my last stretch of life, I can still out-sing Paul. His years of singing improperly gave him a chronically irritated throat. He wore it out in Hamburg. **I hear his** voice cracking even from studio **recordings** where a more aware artist would have re-tracked it later when the voice returned. However, for Paul, it was always going hoarse. It was part of his sound. I heard that early on, and used it to imitate him, but never made an actual habit of it. If I had, it would have ruined my voice just as it had ruined his. Once it is ruined, that is it. It does not recover.

Here is a tip for you. When you sing along with my songs, or when you sing anything else, consider it an investment in your own voice quality to breath from down deep. In your talking as well as in your singing, breathing deeply will add decades of longevity to the quality of your voice. Likewise, the importance of drinking water cannot be stressed enough. You can avoid voice strain by staying hydrated, and by breathing from your diaphragm whenever using your voice. You may consider this report on voice-care one of my many free public service announcements. **You can count on** more outstanding tips for wellness in **this** book. In this case, besides giving useful **personal information**, it also provides an obvious contrast between myself and Paul. Learn to hear those differences, and to practice breathing deeply whenever you use your voice—and keep drinking water!

8[(9)]

Playing with the Bonzos

I, a little bit like the Paul before me, have always enjoyed playing and experimenting with avant-garde art, music, theater, and ideas. More than the early Paul, I like pushing the conventionality boundaries of modern society. That's what **I'm talking about** when I say "I'm not conservative." **The public** viewed the Beatles as being unconventional; but take note of the sharp turn from conventionality that I brought to the band. Look how their style changed when I came on board. By comparison, they were very normal. They had the mop-top hair, but wore suits, ties, and Beatle boots. Most people tend to imagine that the Beatles invented their Beatle haircuts; but they did not. They copied the London art students, who were the real pioneers.

I was among that trend-setting crowd. It was the new **look**, the **new** sound, and the new way of seeing and shifting the world. From a conservative view, silliness was all that we stood for. However, from our perspective, and according to the intentions of the social engineers who secretly promoted us in the media, normal was not good enough.

As a precursor to the avant-garde movement, Dada, or Dadaism, got started in Switzerland. Not wanting the culture that was a part of the First World War, the most creative people set all new standards of art, literature, and theater as a rejection of the prevailing rigid standards. This rebellion had spread on its own accord, but was spurred on by the gross absurdities of war. Artistic avant-garde anti-art again grew together with the anti-war response to the Vietnam conflict. Fighting is absurd.

Let us add some boxing context. The World heavyweight boxing champion, Floyd Patterson, like the plot of some Rocky movies, was accused of only fighting the people that he knew he could win. He was being protected. Finally, in 1962, he foolishly agreed to fight Sonny Liston. It was a big event. The fight was scheduled to be held in New York, but the New York Boxing Commission denied them a license because of Liston's criminal record. **The event was** then moved to Chicago, Illinois, and **viewed in England** by transatlantic broadcast. Liston (who was murdered years later) dethroned the champion, knocking Patterson out in the first round, making Sonny Liston the new world champion. In a rematch the next year (1963), Liston won again, taking him two seconds longer. A year later (1964), Liston lost the title to Cassius Clay, who was later known as Muhammad Ali.

Rodney Slater and "Vivian Stanshall," both art students, while meeting to watch the fight that had only one round before the new champion was named on 25 September 1962, were playing one of six word games that amused them that night. The game involved cutting up sentences and letting the fragments form **new** ones. One of the combinations that "**Vivian" came up with** was an instant laugh: **"Bonzo Dog/Dada."** From that line, they named the band that Rodney had already been nudging Roger Wilkes to start with him. They called it "The Bonzo Dog Dada Band." However, much to their annoyance, the general public was not aware enough of the Dada movement, and supposed undesirable paternal meanings that had to be explained away so frequently that the band was soon renamed **"The Bonzo Dog Doo-Dah Band,"** which then **evolved** into "The Bonzo Dog Band," in an effort **to** simplify, which was finally further abbreviated to **"The Bonzos."**

Call them what you want. They were a whole lot of fun. I'd say the Bonzos were to music what Andy Warhol was to visual arts. The Bonzos stretched and pushed the boundaries of musical entertainment. I had been involved in that group as long as anyone. The Bonzo Dog Dada Band had begun four years to the month before Paul died. Chris Jennings and Tom Parkinson joined in, as did several others here and there who were loosely affiliated. It was never about who was a member and who was not.

The whole thing was more about who was open to having **a good** time. Each one of us took part in heralding an **escape from reality**. The band was anything but real. I, as Vivian, had disguises evolving, or rather revolving, from false teeth overlays, and any one of several rubber noses and big pink rubber ears, along with a blond wig, to diverse costumes, such as my gorilla suit, that were only recognizable by my mannerisms. Altering or concealing identities was part of our ongoing fun. Names too were distorted or disguised. For instance, I thought the name Vernon Dudley was plain—not zany enough for our group. Vernon was a lecturer at Goldsmiths College. I christened him our very own Vernon Dudley Bohay-Nowell. The extended name stuck well, unlike the name that I tried to stick to Neil Innes when he joined us. Neil later created the Beatles' parody band, the Rutles.

I always enjoyed playing with the Bonzos. I had fun and felt alive with them. As Viv, **I was more** free to be myself than when stuck **in this Paul** McCartney role. The Bonzos were not **about making** enough money or fame. I had plenty of **all that**. It was about laughing it up, having a **good old time**. I loved it before, and still loved it after I became **Paul**.

I never intended to earn a living from it. It was the kind of thing that we did for our **entertainment.** Later, when **I had a lot** more resources, I could put a bit of money **into** it. As the millions came pouring in from **my Paul role**, I did not in the least mind letting a tiny fraction go to the Bonzos. Expenses for disguises never bothered me at all. In fact, I enjoyed dressing up as much as the music.

I made up the spacey pseudonym of "Apollo C. Vermouth" to suit the Bonzo song, "I'm the Urban

Spaceman." As Apollo, I co-produced the song that ended up making money for us; but it took my Beatle funds to get it there.

As was expedient, I would go back and forth between playing the Paul and Vivian roles, making a network between them. As Vivian, I co-wrote "Death Cab for Cutie" with my friend, Neil Innes. "Death Cab," as **I will explain** elsewhere, refers to Paul's car. Then, **networking** myselves, I, as Paul, welcomed the Bonzos to play "Death Cab for Cutie" in my *Magical Mystery Tour* film with me, now as Vivian, singing it as one of the last performances of the movie. The point was to give clues about me standing in for Paul, and to show who I really am. I am a cross between them and others.

I take on separate personalities with each role; but there is a good deal of overlapping too. The type of music that the Bonzos did which I enjoyed the most was their fun British music hall style, which Americans would call vaudeville. It is mostly mindless entertainment, a mix of rousing songs and burlesque comic acts. **It is not serious music**, but rather an escape from it. **I love** all the more serious stuff too; but playing with **the Bonzos** was just about having a good time. **It was play.**

My fun with the Bonzos lasted decades—up until I learned that Linda, my love, was slowly dying of cancer. Then my priorities shifted. I wanted to spend whatever time with her that I could. The sense of losing her took all the fun out of pretending to be Vivian Stanshall. All of the personal history that I made up for him had to reach its conclusion in his own death.

Linda was compassionate to the end, as I will discuss in a chapter about her. Our family had three years notice. It was more than we gave the world. First **we** sought to beat it naturally. Now I have **found ways that** were less known then, ways that could have **added years.** When we finally gave up on herbs, we turned to a more traditional Western

NOTE: This note will be clearer after reading the note in this book's chapter 33 (*Memoirs* chapter 39). William remained active in his Vivian Stanshall role until Linda's doctor discovered her cancer. With her condition on his mind, he felt that he could no longer do the Viv role, which was all about zany fun. In light of Linda's impending death, William decided to retire the Vivian role, to kill off that fictional persona. He met with the actor who had lived as Viv for all those years, and offered him a retirement package that would keep him on the payroll, but would have him mildly alter his appearance, relocate, return to his original name, and agree to cease all further appearances as that ginger geezer, and from all further acting and musical performances.

The 51-year-old actor living as Vivian flatly refused William's offered retirement package, saying, "Over my dead body!" He said that he had built his life and family around that character and would never give it up, with or without William's money. He had so integrated his own life-story into his Vivian role that giving up that position would have felt like a death to him.

Vivian, who had frequently turned to excessive drinking to battle anxiety or depression, predictably drank until he passed out on 5 March 1995, hours after receiving another message about the retirement proposal. In his drunken stupor, he could not awaken himself later that evening when an electrical fire broke out in his top floor flat in Muswell Hill, North London. To William's astonishment, the next morning (on 6 March), before resolving the retirement matter, the Vivian actor was found dead.

Honoring the Vivian role (by William and the double) a memorial plaque was unveiled in the Poets' Corner of Golders Green Crematorium on 13 December 2015, opposite that of the actor's widow Ki Longfellow-Stanshall, and daughter Silky Longfellow-Stanshall, along with one of William's close friends from the Who: Keith Moon. Keith had spent his last evening out with "Paul and Linda" a few hours before his death on 7 September 1978.

On 26 January 2018, Ki wrote Vivian's biography, comparing his life-story, or the quality of her innovation, to a fairytale by the Brothers Grimm: *The Illustrated Vivian Stanshall, a Fairytale of Grimm Art.*

Medicine approach. **That is when it** was time to tell reporters. Cancer **attacks people** in many different ways. **What cures one person may kill another.**

Vivian Stanshall was known to wear flamboyant hats. The strange name came from a word game in which we produced the phrase, "Hats in villa vans." Scrambling the letters, I soon produced "Vivian Stanshall," which, when scrambled further, produced "Van villains' hats," "Vanish all in vats," "Vat, vanish all sin," "In lavish salt van," and "Halt vial van sins!" Years later, I saw a bumper sticker that reminded me of that last one. It was on an old hand-painted van, presumably, I now realize, by someone most ignorant of love. It said, "If this van's a-rockin', don't come a-knockin'."

Stanshall and Vivian were names I had heard before, but never together. They are both good for the wordplays **I was looking for**. The persona would do **the most outrageous performances.**

Anyone may ask, "Who shall do such a thing?"

They answer it, "Stan shall!" Stan shall do the nasty salacious musical comedy, and any other undignified thing that my father forbade. Not I, but Stan is the man for all such things. Whatever I will that I, Will, dare not, Stan shall do twice as well.

Having fun with dice as a child, there was a game **I played** in which the higher rolls had the advantage. **Rolling sixes** on the cubes were the best. In Roman numerals, two sixes are VI VI. Putting it in language, it is Vivi, the root of Vivian. That game of Sixes actually used three dice; but in the English language, what name begins with Vivivi? I used Vivi as a nickname, but it shortened to Viv.

9(10)

The Last Song of Phase Two

Peter Fonda inspired the last Beatles song that Paul took part in recording. **The Beatles,** wanting entertainment while **on a touring break** in Los Angeles, back in August 1965, **ended up partying** together with Peter Fonda, among several others. Peter freaked out John. They were both high enough to be impressionable. John's acid added to the freaky impact. Also setting the stage for really making an impact, all of the Beatles were nervous about the distinct possibility of them being killed while touring. Security was a concern.

NOTE: Fundamentalists of all religions receive media support because they help to destroy not only society, but also the mainstream religions of their own roots. Fundamentalist Christians sent death threats to the Beatles throughout the tour. John's remarks that the Beatles were more popular than Jesus, and that Christianity would go, intentionally alarmed the Fundamentalists who feared that John was correct. In their minds, there was a spiritual war between the Christians and the evil Beatles. In the fearfully egoic minds of so-called Christian soldiers, the attack on their faith justified defensive murder for Jesus.

Incited by their own fundamentalists, Christians everywhere verbally attacked the Beatles in churches, community meetings, and in the media. To that extent, to follow Jesus, one would stop following the Beatles. By the Christians' energy used to fight the Beatles, they enlarged the band to their own hurt. Many fans, loving their idols as programmed, left Christianity. If the Christians had stayed in love-energy, rather than dropping to fear, they would have increased.

79

There were perils and attempts on their lives. **No one talked much** about it publicly because they did not want **to encourage it.** Even so, it spooked everyone. After landing, they would see bullet holes in their planes. In some of their concerts, Ringo would turn his cymbals to shield him from possible bullets flying at the band. On top of all that stress, what made them all the more nervous about dying was Paul's horrific dreams. **Paul had begun** all his horrible death dreams early that year. **Dying** was never far from their thoughts.

As they partied with Peter Fonda, the drugs brought out his own death issues. From what I am told, when he was just a young lad, his depressed mother committed suicide. **When he found out,** it destroyed him spiritually. **He could not deal with** that pain, and shot himself in **the stomach.** He tried to end his own life that way. **It was too much grief** for that ten year old.

With that issue unresolved, **it needed to pop out** again later in his adult years. Sure enough, when on a bad LSD trip, he experienced his own idea of death. Recalling it, he was going up to John and saying, "I know what it's like to be dead." John, already taken by acid, could not deal with that lingering "I know what it's like to be dead." John could not purge it from his head until he wrote it out in his song, "She Said She Said." As always, he changed "He" (Peter Fonda) to "She," in order to keep fans believing our songs were all about romantic encounters. We often made that change. As another example, "Maharishi" became "Sexy Sadie."

The Last Song of Phase Two

Likewise, songs about Paul or me were made to sound like love songs. The Stones did the same with "Ruby Tuesday," changing "He" to "She." Their other Paul songs are gender-neutral, using "you," as I will show in the chapter about them [*Memoirs* ch 37]. Becoming the last Beatles song that Paul helped lay down tracks for, being at Studio Three of the EMI Studios, "She Said She Said" was coincidently, or providentially, about John's death anxiety. It was done in four takes from 7:00 pm, 21 June 1966, to 3:45 am. It became the last song recorded for the ending of that second Beatles phase, being the last song made for *Revolver*. The Beatles then revolved again with new personnel, a new sound along with it, a new public image, a new message, and a new soul. Death songs continued woven in throughout the last Beatles revolution.

The *Revolver* album cover sketch shows Paul on his way out. **His face** is turned away on account of his belief that he **would die** soon. The album included "Eleanor Rigby," "Yellow Submarine," and other songs foretelling his death.

NOTE: Part of the illusion of the Beatles is that they are thought of as the same four-member band from 1960 to 1970. In reality, however, only John and George were in the band for all of those years. Although it may be argued that they were actually three distinct bands, it helps to see them as only one band with three phases.

Phase One (1960-1962), consisting of John, Paul, George, Stuart, and Pete, was a club band that generally only performed covers of other artists. Aside from backing Tony Sheridan, they did not do studio recordings.

Phase Two (1962-1966), consisting of John, Paul, George, and Ringo, with intensive assistance from George Martin and others who acted as if they were a part of the Lennon-McCartney partnership, became a global sensation, breaking records in both album sales and concert performances. For the first time in history, they had an audience that was large enough to use a stadium.

Phase Three (1966-1970), consisting of John, William ("Paul"), George, and Ringo, with continued assistance from George Martin and others, was the world's greatest studio band.

Paul understood that **his position** would revolve so that society **could revolve with** the band. His view of **the global revolution** was not the same opinion as was held by John, who had joked about it. However, after **I stepped in**, when Paul's position did revolve, I was able **to** give John much more information. To those who **push the New World** Order, he sang, "You say you want a **revolution.**" As he better understood the global social engineers' intentions to help themselves by helping us, he had mixed feelings.

NOTE: John, like most everyone, could at least temporarily be swayed either way about the good or evil that would come by destroying the old social order in favor of the New World Order. He originally wrote and sang, "But when you talk about destruction / Don't you know that you can count me out." However, as was again explained to him, the Beatles were not permitted to oppose the NWO—or the destruction required for it. Hence, on "Revolution 1," he added "in" after "out," meaning, "You can count me in." Having the "in" on one version, and not on the other, drew attention to John re-thinking it.

Many people wonder if the NWO will succeed. For the most part, it has already. The power has already been transferred behind the scenes with only a charade of national sovereignty remaining. Global organizations already work through governments to the point that the governmental facades are quickly becoming obsolete. The NWO continues to increase in scope as it gradually comes out of obscurity. Those controlling the media are careful to pace that disclosure. If the public learns too much too soon, they could reverse the NWO progress that has been made. The coup must be revealed little by little as the public accepts one point at a time. Too much public awareness now could still overturn the cabal's global overthrow, and could spark court action everywhere for treason and other capital crimes. Ironically for this information age, the global takeover is only possible by controlling and withholding information.

10[11]

Masonic Checkmate

In *Through The Looking Glass,* Alice goes through the changes and becomes a queen. I told Mike (Paul's brother) that I am as Queen Alice in becoming Paul. Later, Mike gave me several small *Alice in Wonderland* figures **for my back yard** as a house-warming gift as **I settled into** Paul's house. That inspired me to redo **Paul's garden, putting in** a tarot zigzag path with the **statues at the nodes.**

We pinched ideas from many sources, and incorporated them into our lyrics and artwork; but we were especially enamored with Lewis Carroll. His *Through The Looking Glass* and *Alice in Wonderland* imagery was used **extensively**. If you are familiar with those works, **you can see** how they brought us to an awareness of **tarot and chess.** You may recall the talking cards and chess pieces.

In turn, those images, each rich in their own symbolism, turned us on to other symbols found in literature from around the world.

BILLY'S BACK!

love

checkmate

Whenever possible, we combined the symbols. Looking **for symbolism** in this drawing that John drew in 1967, **see** how the images all work together. You can see **the tarot** heart, spade, diamond, and club, each **assigned to** a different band member, as set into **the Biblical four-headed beast**, with each

NOTE: A quality tarot reading can be illuminating. If you do not have a deck of tarot cards, we recommend that you get one. Meanwhile, ordinary playing cards will suffice. For insights about emotions, feelings, or relationships, hearts in playing cards = cups in tarot. Corresponding to your thinking or communication, spades = swords. For practicalities in the material world, diamonds = pentacles. For insights about creativity and action, clubs = wands. Whether reading tarot, a book, or anything else, embrace whatever resonates with your soul. Whatever does not resonate, let it slip away without resisting it. Whatever we resist sticks to us, increasing whatever we find objectionable.

head saying something about that Beatle, and each having a chess piece representation, and also a letter. As four heads of one creature united in **Paul**, we are each distinct, but together playing Paul's **left**-handed bass guitar. In cards, we are four suits of one deck.

Ace of spades is a card that has for centuries symbolized secrets or secret societies. It also represents personal transformation, and/or death. It is the Dead Man's card, or Death card. As such, cards sold with the *Yellow Submarine* storybook in 2004 featured Paul as the ace of spades. **That is** why **the** cards were included. As with all of our **products**, it was to show the world our Beatles **secret, which is** our hidden message to the world, namely, **that Paul** is the Dead Man, and that I was **transformed** to mend the broken band.

As in John's hat in his drawing above, he is of diamonds. To connect him to that suit, think of him singing his "Lucy in the Sky with Diamonds."

On the first sketch, clubs hung around George's neck on a long ribbon. The word "LOVE" in that version was written in capital letters. John drew the original on one of the days we worked on "A Day in the Life." I got him to make the more polished version later. I bought it from him for twenty quid, a slice of lemon meringue pie (which I would have

NOTE: In the Beatles Yellow Submarine playing cards, the fab four each dominate one suit, and are featured as its king and ace. The suits are the same as in John's picture: George is the king and ace of clubs (wands), Paul is of spades (swords), John is of diamonds (pentacles), and Ringo is of hearts (cups). Know your four kings and aces.

given to him anyway), and a large plant grown illegally on my farm in Scotland. We were both happy with the transaction.

The four heads in John's Beatle beast sketch **show us as a** horse, man, lion, and eagle, which were based on **Revelation** 4:7, except that John drew a horse **for** George instead of a calf to tie it in with other **prophetic passages**, and to fill the chess role in the band. George is the dark horse or the black knight of our game. That identification grew in meaning for him as he rose in prominence. He reinforced his dark horse image later by naming a song, album, and recording label after it.

Uniting the symbols, George is the dark horse of clubs. Clubs are fitting for George who was in the set of Beatles that began it all. **He was** the **only one** of us last four who was with John **in the beginning** when the Beatles were only known for playing at clubs. If you cannot see the clubs in this picture that is reduced in size to fit this book, look George in the eyes and think of the clubs where they had played.

NOTE: William sold the plant to John in 1967, the year of *Sgt. Peppers.* That same year, the four Beatles, along with 60 other Brits of influence, placed an advertisement in *the London Times* calling for the legalization of marijuana.

In 1970, after a complaint that "Paul McCartney" was growing his own pot, police came and confiscated his plants. Although publicly familiar with the herb, William said he did not recognize it. According to his masterful plea, he received the seeds in the mail, and planted them without knowing what they were. He used the technicality that he could not know each seed's gender.

Adding plausibility to William's claimed ignorance, he had failed to top or prune the plants, and had not removed the males, resulting in the five females becoming pollinated. On the news, police could be seen carrying away the male plants. Neglect lowered the quality that year, but strengthened his claim in court that he did not know the gender. Had they all been male, they would have all been low in the forbidden tetrahydrocannabinol (THC).

Masonic Checkmate

The suit of hearts goes to Ringo. John never did see him as the brains of the outfit, but always loved his heart. Ringo has a good heart. The R and O, in Ringo also ties to the rook in chess. Besides being a castle in chess, a rook is a bird. The beast bird is an eagle; but both agree in one for our fowl symbolic needs. Ringo kept the heart in our castle.

John is the magical wizard whose vision became your reality, creating the Beatles. Just as he gave himself the most spiritually advanced role on the cover of *Abbey Road,* he did the same here, making himself the bishop—the most Godly.

Our ace of spades is Paul. I am the queen of lonely hearts. My queen role in chess makes me the most powerful piece on the chessboard. I, queen, rule the Beatle beast through my power from the most valued piece, the king. **As long as the king** goes on, the queen has power. It **is still the same** even now. As Paul continues, **I have power in his** name. Paul's discontinuance would bring an **end to** nearly all of my work as well. It would **be my own** retirement. The gender issue comes up now and then. **I am** straight. I do not mind having female roles **in symbolism**. I am secure enough in my sexual identity to not be threatened by them, or by any of the humor that goes along with them. On the cover of *Sgt. Pepper's*, we have Tarzan (played by Johnny Weissmuller) looking at my butt. It is a joke about my role as the queen of hearts, standing in for Paul, in the heart of that album cover.

BILLY'S BACK!

Notice that the letters above the beast correspond to those made by our hands on *Pepper's* back cover. We discuss why you cannot see my letter "O" in another chapter. For now, just take my word for it. **Envision my** "O" filling in the gap of the word "**LOVE**." Correspondence of those letters with the pieces we represent on the chess board are clearer on the album. John's final drawing concealed it with lower-case letters. However, if you look at his picture and imagine capital letters, you will be made aware of simulated chess movements. The dark knight moves in an "L" pattern. **The queen**, who **is** your darling, moves **all around the board**, circumnavigating, represented **as Paul's halo**, or an "O." John, our bishop, makes a "V" with his hands. In his case, he is pointing into his pants for his own added venereal significance ("of or pertaining to sexual desire or intercourse"). In chess terms, "V" represents the two diagonal paths that each bishop may travel. Ringo's "E" illustrates each way that a rook may go: vertical or horizontal.

Looking now to the front cover, the hat that Ringo is wearing is flat to resemble the rook or castle. Looking a bit like that of a cowboy, the hat worn by George suggests horse riding. And as a knight wearing a little box says to Alice, "You're admiring my little box," now George wears one.

You can see us as the queen, bishop, knight, rook, and at their right, disposable (wax) pawns. But why is no king among them? Alas, "The king is dead." That is the commonly held meaning of

"Checkmate," and is why John wrote it below his picture. It is not etymologically accurate, but works perfectly for the symbolism—and agrees with Paul as the ace of spades, the Dead Man. We learned how to play the game without him.

Under the "O" in John's picture, you can see that my hat is pointing right to it, as if connecting to it, linking their meanings. My hat, connecting to the "O" that allows me to circumnavigate the board, is the hat of a wizard (being one of the five Beatle wizards in the *Magical Mystery Tour* movie), and is significantly higher than the rest, demonstrating (as in the game of chess) higher authority. Only the king is taller and higher in authority. **I outranked** the bishop and all others, but not **our dead king**. He is over all. All that we did was **to preserve** his life. That is how we stayed in **the game.**

Now, John's mitre resembles the bishop's traditional ceremonial head-dress in the old game. It is split, like the "V" above it, resembling the bishop's diagonal paths. The letter "V" also makes a compass, correlating with the knight's square (L). These carpenter tools, necessary for building temples and other buildings anciently, were preserved as holy symbols devised to carry spiritual meaning. Those meanings and applications are explained behind closed doors quite often as part of the regulated instruction that is

---

NOTE: Along with the more standard meanings, the compass and square also suggests the idea of inclusion and exclusion based on one's degree of enlightenment. Just as one uses a compass to draw a circle, the Beatles (a Master's compass) encompassed all who had the ears to hear them. Outsiders, who were not fab enough to be drawn into their circle, were called "squares."

Billy's Back!

handed down by **the Masons** and their religions in under-wraps **codified observances**. I have heard it countless times. Initiates **have** regular reminders of each of their **hidden meanings**. While it might be a worthwhile read **to discover** what those symbols each mean, consider for **now** that they have become representations that bring to mind not only their nested sacred connotations, but also institutions.

Over the centuries, they have become symbolic of the fraternities or religions that perpetuated them as symbols. Most recognizably, it has the "G" for God, Gnosis, Generation, Geometry, Great Architect, or Gatekeeper. Emblematic of their secret fraternity, all Freemasons

NOTE: Freemasons of the lowest degrees know that the G represents God (the Great (or Grand) Architect of the Universe) and Geometry (applied with the compass and square, the measurement of the earth and of all things in it). In this way, the G represents the connection between the earthly and spiritual aspects of existence. God and Geometry are somewhat alike. As Saint Bernard of Clairvaux states, "What is God? Length, breadth, height, and depth."

The G may remind some of Gates, and that the fraternity is a Gateway that one must pass through for some of the world's most significant positions.

Advancing by degrees, moving from darkness into Masonic light, one gradually places less relative significance on either God or on Geometry, and lose interest in the various lesser meanings. Growing in Ha Qabala (light and knowledge) degree by degree, moving only as close to illumination as we are prepared, the thing we learn to value the most—which is central to the upper levels—is Gnosis, secret spiritual truth. That is the big G to the Illuminated.

The doctrine of the illuminated is a body of ancient secret knowledge. It is said to have originated with Enki's teachings to the Brotherhood of the Snake (Earth's first secret society) in Sumer at the dawn of recorded history. While concealed from the profane, the teachings were passed down, and adjusted, through esoteric organizations. These groups intermingled, spreading their own influence, sometimes by the same individuals that were concurrently affiliated with multiple secret societies in parallel or in concentric circles.

For example, through overlapping memberships, Freemasons received the secrets of the Knights Templar and of other organizations. Contrary to their myths, Freemasonry only goes back a few centuries. It is not a literal continuation of any ancient order, but is illuminated with some of the same teachings, and promulgates some of the same ancient symbols.

well know the compass and square. When we see a compass and square, we more readily think of them than of what those symbols actually mean.

Our own **secret hand gestures**, veiled meanings, and all else on the album **suggest that we too have** made a fraternity or religion to convey **hidden truths**. In our case, it is all of Paul, and is **centered in me**, as Paul's representative. Having been **revealed only in** cryptic symbolism until now, it is **time to expose it** as plainly as possible **in this tell-all book**. This book is not intended to recruit you to freemasonry, but to simply increase your awareness **of Paulism**, and of all that it entails. We now welcome you to our own secret society, the fraternity and sorority of believers in Paul, complete with our music, images, mysteries, and secret knowledge. Did you notice any degree of Masonic meaning in our 33 *Past Masters* tracks?

Notice the symmetry on the *Sgt. Pepper's* cover. **All of it passes right through** me, representing the departed **Paul**. Seeing me as him, consider how all is **centered in his heart**. All is in the heart of Paul. Seeing it that way, get out your compass and square to see how everything lines up through me, the new queen or king of the game. **I am** there as the queen standing in for the king. Rather than seeing me as under Paul, think of us as **one in** the same since the one represents the other. That is Paulism for you. At first you learn that I am not **Paul** since he is a dead man. Then you learn that I am Paul since he, residing in a spirit world, continues on through me. It sounds paradoxical, but is merely progressive.

BILLY'S BACK!

Everything crosses through Paul's heart—which is represented by my own heart. For example, use a square or other straight edge to see that the top of all three of the heads of Shirley Temple form a line right through my heart. There are several other such parallels. Things at one end correspond with things elsewhere, again and again, crossing exactly through the same point revealing the heart of Paul.

Another of many examples of corresponding images crossing through me is from the wax John. Look at all of their wax eyes. Everyone is looking down at the grave site below them except for John. What **John is looking at** can be brought into your focus by placing **your** square across the cover for a straight line that intersects all the others crossing through my **chest.** Continuing that line through me, you will be looking directly at the breasts of Diana Dors (born Diana Mary Fluck), Great Britain's sex symbol, comparable to Playboy's first centerfold, John's "pornographic priestess," Marilyn Monroe.

Until you understand that pattern, **it all appears** random, but is not. A straight line **from William** S. Burroughs crosses my heart and goes to my fingers. He wrote, *Dead Fingers Talk.* Sounding enough like "burrows," we decided to use that imagery also. Continuing that same burrow line directs you down to the name of Paul in yellow hyacinth flowers as if to say that Paul is burrowed in the ground below the flowers, as though the flowers were on his grave.

Next, consider Carl Jung's famous religious and mystical **approach** to psychology and personality. From **the shadow** of his glasses that rest on his forehead, **it looks as though** he has a third eye. A ray from **his third** eye through my heart points to the third **eye** on a statue from John's house.

Everyone **took notice** of the ruby slippers on the Shirley Temple doll. First off, visually, the slippers emphasize the redness of the blood dripping down Shirley's clothes, and of her bloody driving glove. Moreover, some people have correctly recognized that it is an allusion to *The Wizard of Oz*. That story assuredly matches our theme. The protagonist, Dorothy, enters another dimension to be aided by a sensational wizard who helps her dealings at home.

I have already alluded to our mystical roles of wizardry. **Paul goes** to another dimension, and helps us **back here** at home. The wizard in Oz needs **to use false appearances** for his audience to believe **he is** the great and powerful one when he is really just **another guy** from Kansas. We too used false appearances to seduce our audience, and even you, into thinking that I was a great and powerful teen idol. That wizard and I have a lot in common.

The ruby slippers were Dorothy's means of returning to reality. If you follow them through my heart, which is the way of discerning all reality on that album, you will discover that the straight line enters into W. C. Fields. That actor was the original wizard choice for the 1939 version of the classic film. Again, you only get the full picture if you look through me to see it.

Billy's Back!

In cards again, **a "wild card"** is one card that substitutes for another. **I am the** wild card with the likeness of the **ace of spades**, being the substitute for Paul. Hold a ruler to Oscar Wilde's head, and then make a line through my heart to see where it goes. You will see that it leads you straight to a car that's gone wild on Shirley Temple's lap. Putting it all together, as Oscar Wilde, look through the heart of the wild card to see the wild car. Extending that line, it takes you directly to the driving glove.

Extending a line from Lawrence of Arabia (**T. E.** Lawrence) right through my heart to the far side, **you may see** a hookah. It does not connect to **Thomas E.** Lawrence per se, but to Arabia. Our first choice was Gandhi, being from India. He would have pointed to it perfectly. However, so as not to offend any of our Indian fans, we simply put Lawrence there, and ended up removing Gandhi. We only wanted him out of respect, but understood that others would see it differently and be offended. It was the same story with **Jesus**. It was out of respect for him that we **wanted him in** the crowd.

This pattern occurs **through me** many more times, making connections, some weighty, some

---

NOTE: William is truthful, but deceptive, to say that they only wanted Jesus on Sgt. Peppers "out of respect, but understood that others would see it differently and be offended." They wanted Jesus in the crowd out of respect for Paul. All present give their honor to Paul. However, with this album overtly launching the drug revolution, the Christian issue was to remain covert.

With Jesus on the pro-drug album, fans might see things differently than intended, and find the drug revolution compatible with Christianity. The intention was to make them entirely incompatible so that when fans sided with either drugs or with the Beatles, they would naturally distance themselves from Christianity, and perhaps from all organized religion.

humorous. Now that I have shown you the pattern, you can find them. Some of them you would only find if you were familiar with Lewis Carroll's *Through The Looking Glass*. Some of our lyrics are understandable only in that same literary context. Edgar Allan Poe's *Gold Bug* also serves to provide the needed context. Carroll and Poe are each among the crowd on the cover.

Understand, however, that when you discover an allusion to Carroll, Poe, or others, that is never the sum total of the story. For example, in a direct response to lyrics by Donovan, I used a line from *Through the Looking Glass*. **I'll explain**, in a chapter on Donovan, how he "gave me **the word**, I finally heard." Carroll writes: "**The Queen said**, 'that would have been **better** still; **better**, and **better**, and **better**!'" Even the increasing tone came from Lewis Carroll. He says, "Her voice went higher with each '**better**,'" Remember, I am the Queen based on that same story that gives us all of the chess imagery. I used emphasis from Carroll: "'Oh, much **better**!' cried the Queen, her voice rising to a squeak as she went on. 'Much be-etter! Be-etter! Be-e-e-etter!" I sing practically the same thing in "Getting Better."

Undermining my role as queen a bit, you can also **see** me as another character in that story. Alice says, "**If I'm** not the same, the next question is, Who **in the world** am I?" Well, that is the grand question that has puzzled the world about me since 1969. Alice agrees, "Ah, *that's* the great puzzle!"

Billy's Back!

"Be what you would seem to be" is advice I received from that same story. You can see how everything fits the *Alice in Wonderland* theme so well that Mike gave me all those *Alice* figurines. Mike and I had opposite attitudes about using the McCartney name for gain and fame; yet he still openly welcomed me to it. Mike too has made records, but did not want to capitalize on Paul's reputation. Rather than using his McCartney name to help his career, he went by Mike McGear. Even before **I got Paul's name**, I tried to create the illusion of being **associated** with him in order to sell records. **It did not work until it** was a reality. Mike, however, **connected to Paul** for brotherhood only, not for profits. It is commendable. "Let's all cheer for Mike McGear!" ("Lika Mika Macca")

In making allusions to Carroll's work, and layering our lyrics and art with ancient symbols, the mind (being connected to the universal grid) recognizes that there is more to it than meets the ear. That is an idea that John got from Stu Suttcliff. They both understood it on a very basic level, but did not have any idea how it worked. I did not either until much later. Although **each** brain occupies only a small amount of space, the **mind expands** outward and on beyond the **mortal limitations.** We create new associations as we go. Whenever one work makes **allusions** to another, the associative link works to **connect us** to the second work even if we do not **consciously** understand it all. While the entire work is **too** much to be fully absorbed, we sense the connection to something beyond what we hear. **We feel** that connection to something deeper.

On **an intuitive** level of awareness, the hidden encoded **message** feels good. The connection to other works **through** the warm universal grid of light and **knowledge** feels good in the same way that love feels good. **On some levels**, there is no difference. Receptivity **to spiritual awareness** can make us love a song without **understanding** any of it.

Allusions, **more** importantly, allow people to connect to the **literature** that they already know, signaling a link to **connections** that are already established. In the case of Carroll's Alice, or any kind of story woven into the fabric of society, when our generational consciousness triggers greater awareness, it is even better. But linking to any text at all combines the present work with all of the links already established to the alluded literature. **One** of the things that makes Lewis Carroll an **intriguing choice** is that it is already so thoroughly **entrenched culturally**. My favorite line from Lewis Carroll **is** from *Alice's Adventures in Wonderland:* **"'That's Bill,'** thought Alice." Alice again had it **exactly right**. The world can learn a lot from her.

In 1966, when my uncle was a higher ranking Mason than I was, he called upon George Martin on 12 September. My uncle told George that a fatal automobile crash occurred in the night, and ordered him to have me replace the late Paul. He said I was selected because of my long qualifying lineage, and because of my musical talent. That same uncle had ordered me to acquire that talent in anticipation of that day. With John in Germany, George felt that the

BILLY'S BACK!

next best person to talk to would be Brian Epstein, the Beatles' manager, who could not be reached for several hours. **When at last they talked,** Brian informed him that **I had already been selected.**

NOTE: In 1961, Before Brian Epstein became their manager, the Beatles (John Lennon, Paul McCartney, George Harrison, Stuart Sutcliffe, and Pete Best) mostly performed in or near Liverpool. However, to perform at the Top Ten Club, they were in Hamburg, West Germany, from 27 March to 2 July.

While in Hamburg, on 22 June, the Beatles backed Tony Sheridan to record their first single, "My Bonnie." The B-side was the song, "The Saints" ("When the Saints Go Marching In"). That single, as released in West Germany in October, was credited to Tony Sheridan and the Beat Brothers.

While the boys were back in Liverpool, the single sold well there, supported by their local performances. When word got to Brian Epstein that a local band had a single, he spent a lunchbreak at the Cavern Club to see them perform, and then proposed managing them. In December, he met with them a few times at his family's business, North End Music Stores (NEMS), from which Jim McCartney had years before purchased a piano.

That same month, Brian persuaded Mike Smith of Decca Records to travel some 222 miles to see the Beatles perform at the Cavern Club in Liverpool. Upon seeing them, he agreed (some say he was bribed) to give them just a test run in Decca's recording studios. On New Year's Eve, Neil Aspinall drove the Beatles (at that time John, Paul, George, and Pete) to London. The next day, Brian helped them select their best songs that they had performed in clubs. They recorded all twelve of those cover songs, and also recorded these three original songs by John and Paul: "Hello Little Girl," "Love of the Loved," and "Like Dreamers Do." Of the three, none were considered memorable.

Upon evaluating the Beatles' recordings, Decca turned them down. The cover songs were uneventful. Their originals were not catchy. The band demonstrated unsophisticated guitar playing and drums. The poor quality was unmarketable. The world later ignorantly laughed at Decca for rejecting them, not understanding that Decca was right. The Beatles were too noisy for hits until, under George Martin, they had quality songs, precise session musicians, and unprecedented media support. It was hardly the same band. To experience the contrast, play *Anthology 1*, which includes five of their Decca recordings.

Failing to get a recording contract with Decca, or a positive response from others that Brian contacted, he secured a British release of their "My Bonnie" single on 5 January 1962. He credited it to Tony Sheridan and the Beatles.

As Brian continued to share the reel-to-reel Decca recordings, the HMV record store manager suggested transferring them to disc to make them easier to play. Brian then took the tapes upstairs to a studio and pressing plant where he met Engineer Jim Foy, who, in turn, contacted Sid Coleman, of Ardmore & Beechwood (a subsidiary of EMI). Sid arranged for Brian to meet George Martin. By that meeting, and by EMI receiving reports from others describing what Brian was doing, it became time for EMI to act before Brian interfered with EMI's plans. Although the project was not yet to that point, EMI assigned the Beatles to George Martin. George eventually agreed to use their voices.

11[(12)]

Billy Shakespeare

Shakespeare, another extraordinary **William, was** one source from which we gleaned lines **to make** hidden death clues. I pinched **a line from him for** "With a Little Help from **My Friends.**" As if answering questions by the press of how it feels to be **the new Paul**, the song flows as an interview. It **keeps** asking questions that the newcomer, Billy **Shears**, must answer. Later, another interview went essentially the same way in "Baby, You're A Rich Man." The first of these songs uses the well-known Shakespeare line, "Lend me your ears."

You likely knew that those words come from the play, *Julius Caesar.* I allude to this speech to establish **the *Sgt. Pepper's* scene**. Have you ever considered the context? It **is** Mark Antony standing over Caesar's corpse **to share** words appropriate for the burial, **a funeral oration.** That is why the new persona, Billy Shears, when first revealed, says, "Lend me your ears and I'll sing you a song." As shocked Romans gather for Caesar (as each of the *Pepper's* mass gather for Paul), we hear, "Friends, Romans, countrymen, lend me your ears."

Inserting Paul's name where Shakespeare penned Caesar, Antony continues, "**I come to** bury Paul, not to praise him. The evil that men **do** lives after them; The good is oft interred with **their** bones; So let it be with Paul." In Shakespeare's **work**, Antony intentionally speaks negatively enough of Caesar to trigger a strong resistance to such negativity, prompting a revolt. If I were to speak negatively of Paul, saying that he were some Satan worshipper, most of you would also angrily resist it. Going too far in any direction provokes others to push back. That is what Antony intended for Caesar.

So let it be with Paul. Imagine the resistance you might feel if I wrote, "The evil that Paul did lives on still. The good that he did is interred with his bones." You may ask, "What lives on; and what did Paul take to the grave?" And then, "What was evil or good about each?" **Antony's speech** goes on exemplifying all that **is wonderful** of rhetoric—and works perfectly **for Paul.**

Antony says, "You all did love him once, not without cause." Again, consider his words as though kindly spoken of Paul. "What cause withholds you then, to mourn for him?" Do you see how Antony sets the funeral stage—and thus the *Sgt. Pepper's* album theme?

"O judgment! thou art fled to brutish beasts, And men have lost their reason. Bear with me; for my heart is in the coffin there with Paul, And I must pause till it come back to me." (See if that part changes in meaning for you the second or third time you read this layered book.)

Another contribution by Billy Shakespeare is a scene from King Lear. An excerpt was included to underpin the death message of the song, "I Am the Walrus." You can hear these solemn death scene lines in the song's fadeout. In the play, Oswald speaks these words to Edgar who defeated him, "Slave, thou hast slain me: villain, take my purse . . . bury my body . . . seek him . . . O, untimely death!" Then Oswald dies. "**I know** thee well: a serviceable villain." He's talking to **the dead man.** Edgar is saying this. "As duteous to the vices of thy mistress As badness would desire." Lest we miss it, at this point that Gloucester shows up, he says, "What, is he dead?" Edgar gives the old man this answer, "Sit you down, father; rest you." All of that dialogue (and parts skipped here to fit the code) heard at the end provides the rich death context, and points back to me, the slave who receives Paul's purse.

BILLY'S BACK!

12[(13)]

What's in a Name?

"O, be some other name!" Juliet says wistfully to Romeo. "What's in a name? that which we call a rose By any other name would smell as sweet" (William Shakespeare). Now, **I have** been William for long enough to know that **my own name** did not serve me as well as the name **of** Paul. As myself, I am still William, Will, **Billy, or Bill.** But my stage name, Sir Paul McCartney, takes the bill, and pays our bills well too. But whether Bill, Phil, or Paul, it is the same. For example, when Mel Gibson's movie said he was William Wallace, everyone understood that it was just for that show, and that every night when he went home to his family, he was still Mel. Even on the set, between takes, obviously, he answered to both names. Whether they wanted Gibson or Wallace, it was the same.

NOTE: What's in a name? William used many names for himself, and also encoded his father's name in this book. His father's role needs to come to light. Networking with the global elite, William's father inadvertently positioned William for greatness practically by birthright.

A woman of renown within the cultic elite (one who revered William's father) identified William as a three-year-old musical prodigy. She selected him for initiation and training, and shared her plan to use William's service to music to transform the world. The plan that evolved over time, as William grew within the inner circle, began out of respect for his father. Eventually, before the Beatles' last tour, the faction pulling for William prevailed over a plan to do Paul's work by many without granting anyone the full position.

That is how it always is in showbiz. The same actor who is Romeo in Billy's play one day could have a different role the next, and still be himself when he goes home at night. It is the same with each of my roles. **I play the** part of Paul McCartney for this fine **long-running show**, but am still Bill. Rightly so, **all performances require** performers to adopt personas fitting **each** specific show. It is not dishonest **to have one role with a name** in one film, and another of each **in some other show**. It is all showbiz. **Every role has its own name.** Playing **the part of Paul is the same.** For the Beatles, my name was Paul. My solo Paul work is a spin-off of the Beatles act. In other roles, **I go by** other names.

Early pre-Beatles tried on **several names**. They were the Black Jacks before the Quarry Men. They were Johnny and the Moondogs, Silver Beetles, Silver Beatles, Silver Beats, Beat Brothers, and Beatals Having many nearly-Beatle names, it was all in flux until they finally made it. Once the Beatles did arrive, the name became fixed; but the personnel continued **to evolve—covertly** in my case.

They also each **play**ed **with** their own names, as did I. While The Silver Beatles were on tour in Scotland with **Tommy** Moore, John, Paul, George, and Stu went by Johnny Silver (emphasizing that it was his own Silver band), Paul Ramon (an alias I used again later), Carl Harrison, and Stu DeStael.

Not wanting to use my own name in the Bonzo Dog Band, I invented a character (along with a name and family history) that I played up until "he died" in 1995. That eccentric Bonzo Band character's name was Vivian (Viv) Stanshall. Before and after "he died," others also wore my Vivian costumes. I, as Apollo C. Vermouth, produced the Bonzo Dog song, "**I'm** The Urban Spaceman." Helping to make **something for** Jackie Lomax, one of our many Apple **artists**, I also produced his song "New Day" entering the same Apollo alias. Ringo added drums. George also produced some of his songs.

To explore wider avenues in music without diluting the Sir Paul McCartney name, sometimes I have done projects as though I were a part of other bands. For example, in The Fireman (named after the "Penny Lane" fellow with paper money in his pocket), at first, no one knew it was me. Now that we have done a few albums under that name, it is seen more of a subsidiary of Paul McCartney, which is also a collaboration with Youth who contributed a lot. It is a more danciful sound than I have in my standard McCartney line. I still do my McCartney bit; but The Fireman is something I may do now and then on the side, just as **I now** and then put out more classical music. I **find pleasure** in cutting into other music markets—or even **in making** new paths outside of the music world.

Having the freedom to use a variety of **personas** helps me break out of my Beatle typecast music role. With my personas created before playing Paul, they all fit session gigs or albums. Once I could begin entertaining and recording as Paul McCartney, the studio doors were ever left open to me. When I could lend a hand, it was nearly always uncredited work. When **they wanted to use** my name, apparently to help their sales, I would invent an alias, or recycle one, rather than dilute **the McCartney** label on another performer's product. The **name** Ramon(e) was used now and then that way.

Letting go of the Paul McCartney name long enough to do other albums has allowed me to do a few things that I could not do as Paul McCartney. In 1970, when my first "McCartney" solo album was released, fans felt that it was below my established McCartney standard. Some of them expressed the opinion that my "Singalong Junk" was just a filler. That instrumental version of "Junk" on the other side of the album as "Junk," was for karaoke kind of amusement. However, it was not what my devotees expected. I never did that again. However, over the years, some people have said they liked it. I have bounced the idea around of having an entire album of instrumental tracks, and might as a bonus CD one year. I would make it a two CD set: one having everything on it, the other with all but the vocals.

As I write about this new idea, I realize that it may result in some other recording artists doing it now before **I get** around to it. If that happens, just remember that **you**, and they, read it here first. If you **want to copy** that idea, just as you copied my idea of including **the lyrics** with an album, it is okay with me. **Go right ahead.** We might start another new trend.

The idea of including instrumental versions so that you can be your own lead singers (or perhaps have it as a backing sound for your own back yard band) is one thing, having a fully orchestrated exchange for the regular versions is an entirely different idea. Seeing the common practice of rearranging other people's material for use with orchestras, another idea that **I had** was to make a new orchestrated version of **my own material.** That way, when I hear a school marching band doing a song that I wrote, there are better odds that I will like the arrangement. It is not something I would make a habit of doing, but decided to try it once. It took time, but I arranged and orchestrated my entire Ram album. As you might assume by now, I did it under a pseudonym. I released it decades ago, way back in 1977, using the name Percy 'Thrills' Thrillington. In case you are wondering, that outstandingly thrilling name was used five years before Michael Jackson's *Thriller*.

Using the services of Roy Kerr (The Freelance Hellraiser), I took some of my old under-finished, lesser-known material, and had it all remixed. I knew he was quite the wizard of remixery. Those ditties were remixed into something really worth hearing. I commissioned the work to play it for sound entertainment before the concerts of my 2004 tour. Being impressed by how it turned out, **I added** more tracks and released the whole **collaborative** remix album under the band name Twin **Freaks.** Early on, John and Paul, as a duo act, had been the Nurk Twins. Now I am one of the Twin Freaks, leaving you to wonder whether the other twin freak is John, Roy, or Paul.

What's in a Name?

Living on through others, sometimes my own inventions spawn new creativity in other artists. As Vivian Stanshall, I co-wrote "Death Cab for Cutie" with Neil Innes. Ben Gibbard liked the song well enough when he heard me sing it, as Viv, in our *Magical Mystery Tour* movie, that he started up a band by that name. Along with their good music, **they have** raised a meaningful voice to wean people off of **their** addictions to meat. They are doing some **good in the world.**

Even though I am not the one to first use the Ramon(e) alias, it was my use of it—when I added enough to one of the Steve Miller Band's albums to be credited for it—that inspired the band name for the Ramones, the world's first highly popular punk rock group. One's destiny is written in his name.

When Brian Jones died in July 1969, we decided it was time to let our fans in on our Paul secret (as **I discuss** in *Memoirs*). Once Russ Gibb broadcasted **the clues** three months later, the world began to find **lots of hints that** had been hidden until then. **People began writing about** them. One writer, Fred LaBour, **not only reported** on clues we provided, **but also embellished** a bit, making up material.

It was LaBour who named me William Campbell. My first name is easily deduced from "Billy Shears," as announced in the *Sgt. Pepper's* title song. Yet, he seemed to know that "Billy Shears" was merely my stage name. (I meant it to sound like "Billy's Here.") Arbitrarily (after Glen Campbell), LaBour set Campbell as my family name. The surname stuck. Coincidentally, I have Campbell relatives.

13⁽¹⁴⁾

I ONE IX HE ◊ DIE

"Paul is Dead" enthusiasts say that Paul died on "Stupid bloody Tuesday," late on 9 November 1966, and was officially pronounced dead on "Wednesday morning at 5:00." That story is partly true, but more untrue. Looking at a **1966** calendar will prove, first of all, that 9 November **was** not on a Tuesday.

Legal action was **a constant concern.** We wanted to tell all, but also feared the courts, not to mention incurring bad press for the band. **At first,** we feared we would be ruined when the world learned our big secret. At the same time, **I was anxious to say,** "Hey everyone, look at me! **I'm a Beatle now!"**

Devising clues to put into many of our songs and our album cover art was a fairly safe way to tell everyone as much as they had ears to hear and eyes to see. I wished to tell all. The fact that fans were all deaf and blind came as a striking surprise, urging us to make the next album even more obvious.

During my early Beatles days, we feared being too clear. The object was to say all, yet nothing. Having that as a goal, we intentionally threw people off with information and concepts that completely encompassed truth, but not with the most apparent analyses. We let them willfully reject painful truth.

I ONE IX HE ◊ DIE

Let me show in the Stones chapter all the work required on **our part** to reveal clues that had been too obscure **for the public** to find on their own. But for now, **I'll explain the** misunderstood drum date. The *Sgt. Pepper's* **cover** depicts a funeral gathering with several symbolically significant characters there to bid farewell, or welcome, to Paul McCartney.

The focal point is the drum. We let it out that we hid a date on the drum-skin. You can hold a mirror or CD up to the words, "LONELY HEARTS" to indicate the date. Holding up a mirror half way down those words makes it possible for you to see how I, the other half, live as Paul ("looking through the bent back tulips"). It reveals the once hidden, "I ONE IX HE ◊ DIE" with the ◊ pointing up at me, Paul's stand-in. The Roman numeral IX is easily understood as a nine. The "I ONE" had the potential of being mistaken as a Roman two (II). To avoid that error, we leaked the fact that it was an 11 early on. Since then in 1969, it was known that the date was 11-9. However, we could not very well go back and tell you how to read 11-9.

In 1951, a movie came out called *The Guy Who Came Back*. The title brings to mind Paul or maybe Jesus, "he that lives, and was dead." Each came back better than before—except that in Paul's case, others stood in for him. The movie starred Paul Douglas. That **Paul died on 11 September** 1959. It was exactly seven years before the death of Paul McCartney. Here **in Great Britain**, the date is

---

NOTE: The elite intended to make Paul a Christ-figure, "he that lives, and was dead," but also the Biblical beast that deceives the world, making all wonder at him, and worship the image of the beast whose head had been slain and yet is (from Revelation). In order to work subconsciously, to bypass conscious objection, the symbolism is too subtle to grasp without the "Paul is Dead" context. For example, the big "T" at the center of the Beatles logo **BEATLES** secretly represents Paul's cross replacing the cross of Jesus.

BILLY'S BACK!

not abbreviated the same way that it is in the States. **We would write** it 11-9-1959. Paul McCartney's expiration date, **11 September 1966**, is expressed numerically **as 11-9-66 or 11-9**. We left years off dates in casual writing then. I wanted to add the year to the drum-skin, but could not make it look right.

NOTE: Some people argue that the global cultic elite premeditated Paul's death date because they hold 11 September as a significant date for conquest.

On 11 September 2007, Russia tested their "Father of All Bombs," the world's most powerful non-nuclear bomb, with an explosion equaling 44 tons of TNT.

The US military–industrial complex selected 11 September 2001 to launch a "War on Terror" by a controlled demolition of the Twin Towers, and a missile strike on the Pentagon. With media support, officials pretended that the US was attacked by foreign terrorists, panicking citizens into giving up rights with the passage of the Patriot Act (a 300+ page document ready for Congress that same month, based on the German "Enabling Act" of 1933). The Homeland Security Act of 2002 leveraged that same false flag to further diminish human rights.

11 September 1962 was the date that the Illuminati selected to launch its war on Christianity. They predetermined that the media would spin whatever song the Beatles record on that date to become their first number one hit.

11 September 1941 was selected for the groundbreaking of the Pentagon, the headquarters of the United States Department of Defense.

On 11 September 1857, in Utah's Mountain Meadows Massacre, about 120 people were killed—mostly by men who (in Mormon temples) had taken Masonic Vengeance Oaths. They had sworn to avenge the blood of Joseph and Hyrum Smith (their prophet and his brother) who had died in a gunfight (killing Freemasons on both sides) in Carthage Jail. Joseph Smith's death was a loss to the Mormon (LDS) church that he founded, and to the global cabal's "Council of Fifty," which had secretly crowned Smith king, and plotted a Native American uprising (fulfilling Book of Mormon prophecy) to help Smith conquer the Americas as a step toward a one-world government and religion.

On 11 September 1831, the prophet Joseph Smith (before becoming a 32 degree Freemason) had a revelation that "the rebellious shall be cut off out of the land of Zion," which Smith identifies as the Americas. They "shall be plucked out," and his LDS church would "judge the nations" (D&C 64:35-37).

11 September 1708 was a turning point in the Great Northern War when Sweden's Charles XII stopped his march to conquer Moscow outside Smolensk.

On 11 September 1697, in the Battle of Zenta, forces of Prince Eugen of Savoye defeated the Turks, ending Ottoman control of much of Central Europe.

On 11 September 1645, Thomas Fairfax's Army occupied Bristol.

On 11 September 1609, an expulsion order was announced against the Moriscos of Valencia, beginning the expulsion of all of Spain's Moriscos.

On 11 September 1557, Catholics and Lutherans debated in Worms.

On 11 September 1541, Santiago, Chile was destroyed by Michimalonko and his army of indigenous warriors.

On 11 September 1390, the joint forces of Vytautas and the Teutonic Knights launched a five-week siege of Vilnius in the a Lithuanian Civil War.

And finally, on 11 September 1297, at the Battle at Stirling Bridge, our hero, William's hardy warrior ancestor, William Wallace, beat the English.

The epigraph in the drum skin came soon before the song and album title, as I will explain shortly. Hiding a message that is seen when divided through the center with a mirror (or now a CD) took time and effort. **I will tell you** how we did it. It was not merely **a happy accident.**

By the focus on "LONELY HEARTS" (the words containing that clue) we are saying we are each lonely—from missing Paul. I, now as Sgt. Billy Pepper, did not miss Paul at all, but was of all the most lonely. I missed my face and loved ones.

The drum-skin numbers had two meanings. The date he died is "I ONE IX," or 11/9, as I have explained. Nevertheless, we also anticipated the likelihood of confusion that the date 11/9 could bring due to our dissimilar date writing. Using England's system of date abbreviation, 11/9 is the 11th of September. Just as we Brit's drive on the side of the street opposite of Americans, our months and days are also on the other side of the divider.

Americans showed their egocentric tendencies by assuming that we went by their dating format. November 9, 1966, was not the death date, but was significant as the night that **John** met Yoko. That date could have been seen as the death date of the band for those people who **blamed** Yoko for the band's demise. Nevertheless, it was not Yoko who broke up the band. It was **me.** Or, rather, it was each of us, but mostly the absence of Paul.

John and Paul wrote songs together and had their Cavern Club days that bonded them. They went all the way back as Liverpool mates. I was an outsider always masquerading as his old chum, but never connecting to him as fully. My pathetic Liverpool mimicking was never quite right. I took the Beatles to new creative heights, better than Paul could have ever done, but could not give them the same old Paul mood. I forever raised the bar of pop music with my *Lonely Hearts Club Band.* **I was** the greatest Paul for the public world, but not **for the** private hearts of the band members.

To me, our albums were **serious business**, but not so much for them. It had been for them; but their steam had all run out.

Each of them was of their same old low-quality mentality. As before, they wanted to be in the studio long enough to record their songs, and then go off and forget about it for another season. Sometimes I yelled at them to get themselves into gear. They weren't accustomed to being bossed around. It made them all miss Paul even more, which made me all the more lonely. That loneliness drove me on to higher achievement because **I used** work to take my mind off of my pain. However, **my** incessant work isolated me further from my **bandmates.** It made me stand out as not one of them.

Saying that Yoko broke up the band concealed Paul's death, but was never the real issue. It was not Yoko who split John and Paul; it was Paul's death. Paul had been John's writing partner before entering the spirit world, but mine afterward. It is true that Yoko was a nuisance because she interfered with our work, but was more evidence of the loss of band cohesion than a cause of it.

Returning now to the "I ONE IX HE ◊ DIE" drum skin, consider how the drum message continued on our next album. Another way to perceive the *Pepper* drum, before the words "HE DIE," is that I, the last Beatle, am an unknown variable. There had been three known ones, "I + one + I" and one more excluded, X'ed out, replaced with the new Beatle X, the unknown Beatle. Now, with one X'ed out, there were three Beatles left. Thus, the writing on the wall of the *Magical Mystery Tour* drum gives you yet another verification saying "Love the 3 Beatles." Then again, on our *Abbey Road* Album, we have that same idea sung by John. Doing the math for those who thought the drum-skin message did not add up, he sings, "One and one and one is three." On the *Pepper's* drum, that is 1 and one and 1.

All right then, the point was to explain the death **clues** in the drum's date; but it ties together. Having **revealed** all that, I'll explain the smooth transition. **Paul's** "early warning," that he received from his **death** nightmares, moved him to work it all out. He was sure of his death. **He told his family** and some of his closest friends **that he would die**, be replaced, and live on in and through his coming impersonator. Now, having explained all of that to everyone, once he did die, they were all at least half-expecting to see me show up as his continuance. They did not at all resist the switch of form because Paul had prepped everyone for it. Some of them were in denial saying that he was not dead at all, just transformed.

Some skeptics have questioned why all those close to him would go along with such a charade.

Billy's Back!

People close to him did receive some compensation; but that was not their primary motivation for silence. I represented Paul to them. I became **Paul** to them. Their only way to not lose Paul was to accept me. Recognizing Paul in me, they **welcomed me** with overwhelming gratitude. If I could truly be Paul, **I** would keep him there among them. Jane especially **felt** his presence in me. Any paid compensations they received, officially to buy their silence, were **more like going-away** presents from Paul. However, since he was not really gone, it was all more of an acknowledgement of his love for them.

Conspiratorial silence was not for the money, and was hardly ever enforced by violent threats as some out there have suggested. They were silent out of love for Paul. They did not want to lose him again. Now that I was Paul, exposing me as anything else would betray Paul and risk losing that man all together. They believed that he would carry on in and through me. I honor Paul by using his name.

It was not until the 20 January 1964 release, *Meet the Beatles*, launched by *The Ed Sullivan Show* the next month, that the Beatles entered the world stage with their first of several number 1 albums on the US Billboard Top LPs. LPs are played at thirty-three and a third (33⅓ or 33.3) rpm. From that release until the end of Paul's life, was only 2 years, 33 weeks, and 3

NOTE: Ed Sullivan was flown to London for special training to create this historical event. Setting a record for the largest audience for an American television program, on 9 February 1964, approximately 73 million viewers in over 23 million households (over a third of the American population) watched the Ed Sullivan Show, featuring the Beatles. That show, and other publicity, gave their American tour an enormous boost, and made sales soar. During the week of 4 April 1964, they held 12 positions on the Billboard Hot 100 singles chart, including the top 5. Beatlemania became an unprecedented reality.

days (2.33.3) = (Phase 2. LP rpm). My tour as Paul on the world stage has gone strong for generations. Beyond **Paul's** 962 days on the world stage, none of **the Paul** McCartney that the whole world knows was him. I have been Paul much longer.

Singing "**One and one and one is** three" was a multiple message. "Love **the 3 Beatles**," and all of that, told the world different things. First of all, like all of our Paul clues, it said that Paul had died. Making the point obsessively from *Sgt. Pepper's* on, including all of the allusions in every album **I have** ever made since that time, I also showed **the world** that we were not okay with that loss. **We wanted** sympathy for Paul's loss, and mine; and we showed in endless ways that I, the new Paul, was not one of them. I was a Beatle in the sense that it became my band. I was also one of the Beatles in the sense that **I was their** creative force, the one who, as their **new leader**, made writing assignments and album concepts. I was always the band's prominent focus ever since Paul died. All of my Beatles work was my karma. No one can say I was not a Beatle. Even so, I was never fully one of them.

All that I did for them was appreciated eventually. They did not like being bossed around, but did realize that they could never have reached such great

---

NOTE: When George Martin signed on the Beatles, he appreciated their wit and their voices. However, their limited skills and ignorance about music theory created extra work for him. Because the band did not read music, and did not speak the language of music, communication was labored.

William, the band's new de facto producer, on the other hand, joined as George Martin's equal. They traded off roles. When either was playing an instrument or conducting the musicians, the other was usually in the control booth. False perceptions aside, the Lennon-McCartney team never held a candle to Martin-Shepherd. William, whose skills surpassed everyone in their own instruments, often had them re-do their work after showing them how.

heights without me. **I also needed** them. Obviously, if I did not need **their launch pad**, I would have already done it **for my own** career. Until I had the Paul persona, I could not **take off** on my own. I lacked fans. I had the talent that I needed to do *Sgt. Pepper's*, but did not have the fan-driven funds required for the endless studio hours that I dedicated for it. Even if I had attempted it on my own, it was much better with help from "the 3 Beatles."

Before doing the *Sgt. Pepper's* title song, Mal Evans, Peter Blake and I worked together with the year as part of the drum clue. **We had** the idea of revealing it with a mirror, but had **to massage** it enough to make it work. First, I wrote "**11-9-1966**" which, depending on how we held the mirror, was made to resemble "II B 1BEE" or "II 3 I3BB." One of us suggested that we use Roman numerals or all written numbers. I combined them both with Arabic as "I ONE 1X 1966." In the mirror, it looked like "LONELY IBEE." I said, "Lonely Hearts!"

We wrote it out in capital letters and could see that it resembled "I ONE IX HE ◊ DIE." That is how I then came up with the full title, and decided to have myself on the cover stand above the pointer. I later said Joe Ephgrave (Epitaph-grave) designed all of the drumskin. It is a clue. Peter also helped John, George, Robert Fraser, and me make our needed guest list for the funeral. In reality, only Paul's family and Jane came. But for the album, all kinds of people were included. It took months for Peter and his wife, Jann, to collect the photos.

Sending Paul off to the world of spirits was one thing, but welcoming him *into* that spirit world was another. My original plan was for our stand-up cardboard photographs to all be of those who had already died (become spirits) who would welcome Paul into their spirit world. That was the main idea. **It was** a gathering on the other side. They were there **to greet Paul**, who had now become one of them.

Then we decided to add to our list of heroes. We decided to include some fictional movie characters who had died, and thus the actors who played them. Six weeks before Paul died, Bob Dylan had an accident on his motorcycle. The newspapers had called it a near-death experience. With the great influence that Dylan had had on John's writing, John insisted on also including the hero who almost died.

The reason that former Beatle Stuart Sutcliffe was in the crowd and not former Beatle Pete Best, is because Stu had already died by then; Pete had not. There was no slight intended against Peter. **It was** only a matter who was in Hades to welcome **Paul.** Marilyn Monroe was there because she had already been murdered by then—apparently by government operatives. It was not a suicide as they claimed.

Dylan said he would have died by then too if the accident had not slowed him down, making all the years that followed more sane with clearer values. Most vitally, he had six weeks to detoxify **at last**. Long addictions were killing him. Almost all of **our** cardboard guests were associated with **death**.

Adolf Hitler was invited to the **party** for a time. John loyally wanted Hitler there **to greet Paul**. "It is not about who is in heaven and **who is in hell!**" John said. "How do you know where **Paul is?**"

In what would have reopened Christian wounds caused by John's comment in the *London Evening*

BILLY'S BACK!

Standard in March 1966, that the Beatles were "more popular than **Jesus**," a cardboard Jesus being nestled into the crowd **was also intended**. Without question, many record-buyers would have been offended. Others might have been glad to see Jesus there in that *Pepper's* context. Paul would have liked to meet him for sure. That interview published in March came and went without anyone making a big deal of it. *TIME* magazine republished those same words four months later, still without stirring any evidence of offence. The public was not manipulated to panic from it until *Datebook* magazine reprinted it and plastered the Jesus quote on their front cover. That presentation made it a big deal, stirring outrage

NOTE: Before contracting the Beatles with EMI, George Martin attempted to explain to John and Paul that they would become a famous writing team, greater than Rodgers and Hammerstein. When John corrected him, saying that they practically never play their own material, Martin said, "Mark my words. Lennon and McCartney will be the most famous writing team in the world!"

Martin went on to say that the media would make the Beatles big enough to topple Christianity. (See the second note in "Paulism," chapter 61 of *the Memoirs*.) John did not believe it. The Beatles were, after all, just a rock band that played in clubs. Still, the proposed level of support delighted him. Not understanding how social engineers could use the power of music to break down old power structures, John imagined the media backing the band in a contest of sorts with Jesus to see who could win the most followers.

By 1966, to John's delight and dismay, he could see that by the global elite's control of the media, they were accomplishing all they had set out to do. They built the Beatles into something much bigger than life that was overthrowing Christianity. John was delighted by the band's success, but disillusioned that even Christianity was too weak to stand up to an Illuminati assault. Although he had grown up with disdain and contempt for nuns, he had believed that Christianity was too powerful for conspirators to conquer.

Using Beatle images as if they led the engineered movement, with added anti-Christian support from the Rolling Stones and others, Christianity made a stark downward turn from Beatlemania onward, making more room for New Age philosophy and paganism.

John was neither prophetic nor arrogant, but simply informed when he said, "Christianity will go. It will vanish and shrink. I needn't argue about that. I'm right and will be proved right. We're more popular than Jesus now. I don't know which will go first–rock 'n roll or Christianity. Jesus was all right, but his disciples were thick and ordinary. It's them twisting it that ruins it for me."

days before the tour, giving the band a political mess to deal with before they could put on a show.

On *Sgt. Pepper's,* our first album since John's press conference to cool his inflaming Jesus remark, the idea of setting off a new wave of album-burning seemed unwise. There was an active anti-Beatles hullabaloo going on the whole time that the band was on their last tour. Some people were saying everyone should be anti-Beatles because Beatles were all anti-Christ. **John** clarified himself to set it all right, but **was** only believed by those who loved him. John **being anti-Christ** was not his point.

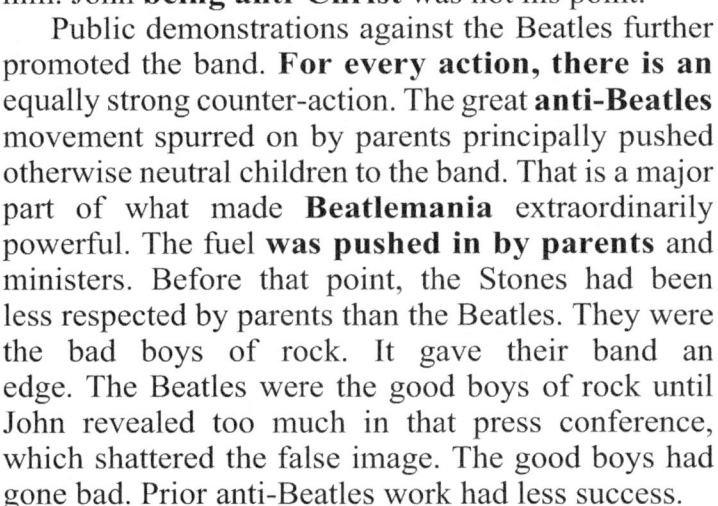

Public demonstrations against the Beatles further promoted the band. **For every action, there is an** equally strong counter-action. The great **anti-Beatles** movement spurred on by parents principally pushed otherwise neutral children to the band. That is a major part of what made **Beatlemania** extraordinarily powerful. The fuel **was pushed in by parents** and ministers. Before that point, the Stones had been less respected by parents than the Beatles. They were the bad boys of rock. It gave their band an edge. The Beatles were the good boys of rock until John revealed too much in that press conference, which shattered the false image. The good boys had gone bad. Prior anti-Beatles work had less success.

Engulfing images or symbols in flames has always been an effective way of stirring people to revolt, riot, or to reel out of control. The large bonfires of Beatles albums across the United States enticed many more teens by the appeal of the

---
NOTE: Anti-Beatles album-burning demonstrations were the most prevalent in the United States, Mexico, Spain, and South Africa.

forbidden. The heat of it all was felt everywhere with fanatics claiming that **the Beatles** were all of the devil. Energized by the egoic emotional appeal induced by the idea that Jesus **needed** to be defended against the Beatle beast, **Americans** and others were lining up, choosing sides: "Choose ye this day whom ye shall serve: The Lord, or the Beatles!"

Later, **after the frenzy** ran its course, most of the burned **albums were repurchased.** At last, when it was clear that the group posed no real threat, fans who missed their favorite records bought them all again. It was good for sales. Those sales helped us in the charts, encouraging others to buy as well.

Making the Phase Two Beatles band look more dead than the assembly standing behind them, their line-up of **gloomy wax figures** beside the New Fab Four made them **look dark**, down, and out of date. Instilling the idea that **the old** band belonged to the past, and that the new **band had** arrived for the bright vivacious present, the **old drab suits** are faded into indistinguishable darkness, while the album's most effulgent colors are from the new band that now belongs to Sgt. Pepper. The idea of making that set of Beatles of wax is from Tweedledum's lines to Alice. He says, "If you think we're wax-works, you ought to pay, you know. Wax-works weren't made to be looked at for nothing." While you are looking, notice the shape of the old **Paul's** head. Being a realistically sculptured **figure** from photographs of all the Beatles, it **shows the old Paul**, and others, looking as they **had** looked before.

Notice **the small head** on Paul, fitting his small frame. The others were rather small too. I don't point that out to belittle them, but so you will recognize it. My skull-shape is more elongated, more oval. Contrasting the old Beatles here with the new band, it is observable that this Sgt. Pepper band is new and living, whiles the old band, the Beatles Phase Two, is dead—even though John, George, and Ringo continue on. The newness of my Pepper's band concealed the fact (shown by the contrasting images) that a new player has taken Paul's part.

We all resist seeing what does not fit our beliefs. **Generally, people find** it hard to comprehend that **one player** can replace another without us ever **having the** public made aware of it. As a case in **point**, consider *Bewitched*, a popular show on US television from 1964 to 1972. Due to Dick York's debilitating back injury, the Darrin Stephens role (the leading male) was given to Dick Sargent in the fifth season. What most viewers missed in all those years of watching it every week was that other roles on the show were also replaced. By comparison, our switching Pauls was relatively easy—with much fewer images of us available to the public back then. Our free access to images now would make it harder.

NOTE: The best way to know how Paul looks is to refer to his photographs. However, one complication is that many pictures said to be of Paul are of his doubles. Before and after Paul's death, all four Beatle positions had doubles that were used far more than most fans would imagine. William still uses his. For appearance, the elite favored one of doubles used by Paul and William above the others, sometimes preferring him to Paul or William. His gift was to raise his right eyebrow remarkably high to create the Eye of Providence image. They intended their "cute" Beatle to promote that subliminal message.

Paul did not, however, use doubles for album covers. They are Paul's most dependable photos. Furthermore, since the advent of Photoshop, there has been a flood of photographs of Paul with morphed in elements of William. Some such images look real. Others are sloppy. Upon finding such pictures, some people compare them to images entirely of William as if to prove that they are the same person. Don't be fooled. Stay with album covers.

The part of Tabitha, the daughter, was played week after week by alternating twins. **The role of** Darrin's father was also played by **two actors**. For each of the two appearances of Tate's **partner in** the ad agency, each was played by **a different actor**.

When Alice Pearce died (before Paul), she was replaced by Sandra Gould for Gladys' role. They ended up using four different people to play Darrin's own secretary. Samantha's Aunt Hagatha was Reta Shaw for some episodes, but was Ysabel MacCloskey for others. With all of this being well established for a show that millions of people watched closely without ever noticing, it should be beyond reason to suppose that the world would notice me suddenly playing Paul's Beatle role even though our album showed the two sets of players standing side by side for contrast.

Without going into details that are available all over, the *Sgt. Pepper's* cover is loaded with symbols illustrating the fatal car crash (represented by the car rolling off of Shirley Temple) that had caused the head injury (as shown by the split-headed doll). The news blackout was a turned off television. Carefully hinting at lies we told to conceal Paul's death, we have his rugby trophy, looking like a higher than perfect "I," placed after the "L" in BEATLES to form the words "BEAT LIES." Exactly below "Lies," we have the word "Paul" spelt out in yellow hyacinth flowers since "Paul lies" dead, and we lie to cover it up. As is common in my songs, and in this book, it is a play on words.

It has been well noticed that there is an open hand over my head, which is a sign of death; but that is also a wordplay. **The palm is exposed**, or, spelling palm another way, we expose **Paul-M**. It is above my head since I too represent **Paul-M**. Off to the side, there stands another **Paul-M** substitute. **It is a palm (Paul-M) tree.** There is a wax substitute **of Paul M** at the other side of the album. **The palm is above my head** also in two images in the *Magical Mystery Tour* booklet, two more times on the original *Yellow Submarine* album cover (one on the front, one on the back), and is on a photograph in the *Yellow Submarine* movie press pack. It is on for several seconds in the *Yellow Submarine* movie, and is also in our *Magical Mystery Tour* movie. The palm repeatedly brings to mind the death and replacement of Paul-M.

Paul's name is in the flowers, shaped into a four string **bass guitar**; but one of our four strings is missing. The front cover is loaded with images attesting to the loss of Paul M., the "late Paul," or "Late of Pablo" ("Being For Benefit of Mister Kite!").

During the writing stages, some of the lyrics had to be adjusted a little to fit perfectly on the album. Before *Pepper's*, no one put lyrics on album covers. We were the first ever to provide them. We had unusual motivations for it, but started something new. The next time you read lyrics printed with that CD you just bought, remember that we did that on LPs first. **I'll tell you our** reasons for it. One that has been noticed is that we, standing behind those words, add **meaning** to them. Besides the rest of the clues that many of you know by now, here is the reason that had never become an issue until February while doing "Fixing a Hole" and "A Day in the Life," each with conflicting lyrics.

Each of us heard what we expected. Following Aleister Crowley's advice to "Say two things at once," John's "Nobody was really sure if he was from the House of Lords" overdubbed in that spot, **"Nobody was** really sure if he was from the House of **Paul.**" Like my Beatle/People, we could only consciously hear whichever one we expected while hearing the other subconsciously. I was concerned that people would hear the wrong tracks. It was to conceal "Paul" and "Beatles," that lyrics were provided, allowing fans to read along in order to hear the correct track consciously.

Let us try an experiment. Play John's song expecting to hear "Lords." It is the word you will always hear when it is what you expect. Then play it again, but listen for **"Paul."** You will only hear that word as long as it **is what you** expect. Still, we cannot expect and **hear** both at once because our intelligence is limited to focusing on only one thing at a time. The best that any of us can ever do is to oscillate back and forth, from one focus to another.

Try that same experiment on my "Fixing a Hole." Notice with full expectation the word "Beatle" in place of the word "people."

Please recall this paragraph five chapters from now when I discuss "See how they run." Those lyrics, and what I am explaining now, are of the same context of us Beatles, but **mostly** of Brian, each running about doing our parts **to save the band** by preserving the fantastic illusion that **Paul is me.** As was just suggested, just as John recorded "Paul" in the same place as "Lords," so too I dubbed "Silly Beatle" over "Silly people" for "Silly Beatle running round that worry me."

Explaining further the "Fixing a Hole" meaning, by overdubbing "Beatle" over "people" I subtly referenced the wax Beatles standing beside my *Sgt. Pepper's* band. Those wax figures, I should probably explain, were made by Madame Tussauds, which is a wax museum in London with museum branches in many major cities of the world. When **I sing**, "See the Beatles standing there," I mean **the dead** wax effigies. It is in the same place that **I sing**, "See the people standing there," which refers **to the crowd** we made behind us. John describes some members of that crowd, standing in a row, in "**I Am the Walrus**." But that song covers other clues too. **All throughout**, it gives disjointed Paul clues from here, there, and everywhere. The few people mentioned from the *Pepper's* crowd are only small parts of the song.

Reading on the back cover the words we want you to expect and hear, also notice "Love" spelt with our hands, except that you cannot **see** my letter "O" because I am turned around. **The absence of** seeing Paul there left a hole in the Beatle "love" that I must fix, along with the hole in **Paul's head** causing everyone's mind to wonder about **Paul's brains** wandering from his skull. Some fans **knew it was** not Paul's back shown in the picture, since **I** am larger. It is "Billy's Back." And yes, I am back.

Until the historical *Sgt. Pepper's Lonely Hearts Club Band,* we had worked on, but not launched, Phase Three of the Beatles. With that kick-off, everything changed for me as Paul McCartney.

Billy's Back!

The thing **I like** best about being Paul McCartney is that **this role** gives me the power to do good. I not only change the world with my music, but also with the potent influence of my position. I have adopted causes to support rigorously, but also **like** to step in to do some good in many other charitable **ways that** I have not made my own primary humanitarian **focus**. There is no point of mentioning most of **them**. I am only bringing up a particular charitable concert I was in because it relates to this chapter. We broke a record with it and had a good time.

"Sgt. Pepper's Lonely Hearts Club Band," which I sang with U2, opened the *Live 8* show in London, and was quickly uploaded. Before the show was a third over, downloads were breaking records. With all the proceeds going to charity, the song was on the Internet within forty-five minutes of its performance. The line, "It was twenty years ago today," helped us emphasize that *Live 8* was twenty years (almost to the week) after we did *Live Aid.* They were great shows, and raised a lot of money to help provide relief in Africa.

NOTE: Jimi Hendrix (having been trained in Laurel Canyon) said, "If there is something to be changed in this world, then it can only happen through music." Repetitious sounds and messages are key to mind-control. Frequencies impact our energy fields. Rhythm directs brainwave, pulse, and mood, which impacts hormone levels. Lyrics with catchy tunes carry precise messages to the conscious and subconscious as we consciously and subconsciously sing along. Enthusiastically receiving that repetitious mental programming from an adored superstar multiplies the impact.

Nothing directs human consciousness as effectively as music, especially when combined with drugs. Many people are brain-washed by giving them hallucinogens, and then subjecting them to repetitious audio messages. When the audio message is to take drugs, which the hearers do, the drugs then make the hearer more receptive to the continually repeated message to take more drugs, which the hearers do.

14⁽¹⁶⁾

The One and Only Billy Shears Rams On.

In our *Sgt. Pepper's* title song, I sing, "Let me introduce to you The one and only Billy Shears And Sgt. Pepper's Lonely Hearts Club Band." That introduction is to tell you that Billy Shears is Sgt. Pepper, and that the Beatles is now his band. On the cover, we contrast the old drab Fab four with the entirely fresh and new Fab few. It is my new band. **I am Billy** Shears. I am that one and only Sgt. **Pepper**. Bill or Billy are my nicknames. **I am** William, Will, Billy, or Bill. The song, "I **Will**," plainly about a longing for some elusive romantic love, is actually me, Will, singing to Paul. As is exposed eventually, there is a double meaning. I sing, "Who knows how long I've loved you," relating to the idea that no one knows how far back I go as Paul, or, for that matter, as admiring him from a safe distance. I saw a Beatles show at the Plaza Ballroom in Old Hill. The Diplomats opened that concert. Once I actually met Paul at a party; but we

NOTE: William is playing down the significance of seeing the Beatles at the Plaza Ballroom in 1963. He, as part of the Diplomats, had an arranged meeting with the Beatles backstage before the show. Although William was being groomed for the possibility, it was still years before the proposal to have him replace Paul was firmly set. Other options were being considered.

did not talk. No one knows how long I've loved any of the Beatles. Certainly, I love Paul still, as the song suggests. **His death** is what ultimately brought us together. It **did not end** my love for him. In some of these chapters I speak of the ongoing loneliness I suffered by taking on **his role**. "Will I wait a lonely lifetime?" Yes, I am willing; as long as I feel Paul's energy flowing inside of me continuing on, I will. Whether we're together or apart, we are connected "forever and forever." If that verse seems strange as a Paul song, it is more nonsensical as a love song.

On the next verse, Paul sings it to me. He says if he saw me, he didn't catch my name; but it never really mattered. He will always feel the same. He actually did see me at the spring party, and did not catch my name. But it didn't matter. **I am** here the same. When at last he finds me, **his replacement**, our combined song from my mouth will fill the air. Paul wants me to sing it loudly so that he can hear it now in the spirit world. **He wants me** to honor his name I bear, making it easy **for him** to be near me. 'Cause the things I do in his name endear me to him. Now you all know I am Will.

Even though I am Paul now, **I say "I, Will."** I, Will, shall love him forever and forever. **It is not** romantic; but is love nonetheless. I love **him** as

---

NOTE: William says, "I feel Paul's energy flowing inside of me." When he performs as Paul, that Paul-energy is so strong in him that he has no qualms about saying that Paul McCartney is performing. Although William brings a great deal of himself into every performance, the more a song is in Paul's own style, the more the spirit of Paul comes through. When William performs as Paul, intending to be Paul, he sometimes feels that he actually is him.

Similarly, when Gregory Paul Martin (son of George Martin) recorded *the Memoirs of Billy Shears,* while sitting at that same equipment to record the book that the Beatles (with his father) had used for their songs, he felt as if he had actually become Paul. Paul sings, and tells this story, in and through others.

myself. By the way, all the bass in this song was not played left-handed or right-handed. I sang it. This song has no bass guitar.

Now, as I was saying before being carried off in another fine song, the name Will, William, Billy, or Bill naturally surfaces. A growing number of people have exposed my role as William Shepherd. The most obvious clues are commonly known. I will point out one of my more obscure William roles. In preparation for leaving the Beatles, I went back to my own name of Billy in order to record and engineer my solo McCartney album. Honoring my good friend, George Martin, who taught me a lot about how to mix the sounds and all of that, I booked all of my studio time for that album, and listed everything for that project, under the name of Billy Martin. **I had no** idea how many other artists landed that same **name.** William Martin was Billy Joel's birth name, and is also the name of others you can read about, but not here. Billy Joel and I, two former William Martins, did a concert together.

Speaking of Billy albums, for a time, our only working title of *Abbey Road* was *Billy's Left Boot.* Each of us liked it, especially Ringo; but *Abbey Road*, being the name of the street the studio is on, elicits mystical meaning. Our procession crosses that Abbey for Paul's burial.

NOTE: We might imagine William being entirely alone, sneaking in and out of the studio to secretly record his first solo McCartney album. However, although he did spend much of that studio time alone, he was not in hiding. As always, bandmates and other recording artists were aware of his presence there. He often dropped in on others, sometimes providing assistance, and was likewise visited by others. Most notably while William worked on that album, Donovan (recording his *Open Road* album in a studio directly above him) was fully aware of "Billy Martin's" McCartney project.

BILLY'S BACK!

Giving my name, Bill Shepherd, on albums where **I am Billy Pepper** of Billy Pepper and the Pepperpots, I tried to show three years later that Billy Pepper is Billy Shears, who is called Sgt. Pepper. I thought I was virtually saying, "Billy Shears is Sgt. Pepper, who is Billy Pepper." All who knew Billy Pepper's records easily could have checked to identify the Pepper's band leader. On Sgt. Pepper's back cover, I stand with my back to the audience because I am the conductor, Sgt. Billy Pepper, leading my band. With both bands, you can see that Pepper is the leader's stage name.

Maybe the old William gravestone (of Paul's replacement) in the *Yellow Submarine* movie was too cryptic. But it should be obvious why we did not edit out the part where I am introduced as William, accidentally said, automatically, out of habit, in my *Give My Regards to Broad Street* movie.

John, George, Ringo, and others, when they were annoyed with me, used to refer to me as "Beatle Bill." Some acquaintances still do. George let that ridicule about me, "Beatle Bill," slip out in a live video recording once. The slip ended up in John's documentary, *Imagine,* released in 1988. John and George were being rather rude talking about me in saying that and other such things. When John refers to "The Fab Four," George quickly corrects him, "**The Fab Three**." John agrees. While it is fine to **miss Paul**, no one was more fab than I was.

Our *Magical Mystery Tour* album, as I have mentioned, had a photograph of the four of us Beatles. On Ringo's drums, it says, "Love the 3 Beatles." It showed that only three of the four remained. But there I was too. How fab was Paul compared to me? If you would compare my work over the years since 1966 to his before that point, you would see that from that point on we went in a much more creative direction. Nothing before *Sgt. Pepper's* compares to it. And I have it; as the Paul-driven senior, **I am still** more fab then the old Paul was. I, **Beatle Bill**, reinvented fab!

Some Bill clues are subtle. I sing, "got the bill, and Rita paid it." John has "Bungalow Bill," and "Tonight Mr. Kite is topping the bill." Others are blatant, such as "Billy Shears." The above *Give My Regards to Broad Street* reference brings up a key question. In a scene at the BBC building, when I enter the room and am greeted by my good old friend who introduces me to the other, he says, earnestly, "Do you know William?" Well, that is a question you need to ask yourselves. Do any of you tell yourselves that **I am that** same old Paul who had inches less height, far less **musical talent,** much less administrative ability, and less focus for the band? Or, "Do you know William?"

Let us move on to Shears, shall we? Since 1969, rumors have circulated about "Billy Shears." We let the world know that "Billy's here." I use it as a wordplay. Shears are also used as a Shepherd's tool. Really, **I am** a Shepherd, but not of sheep (unless that is **what** you think of my followers). Shepherd is **my name**, or one of them. When something is **concealed** from you, or if it can be said that you got deceived, a saying is that "The wool has been pulled over your eyes." It blocks your vision. It has the same meaning in both directions.

The ram can't see us with wool over his eyes; and that wool also keeps us from seeing the ram. We cannot look it in the eye. A lot can be concealed beneath the wool. Wool may conceal any blemishes in the flesh. A rash or wound, for instance, might be indistinguishable. **Sometimes** one cannot tell the quality of the ram until the **shears** are employed. Losing the wool **removes the deception.** With *Sgt. Pepper*, I, the fab Shepherd, pull out the Shears. Letting all know that "Billy's here" is what the Shears are all about. The opening song suggests you are about to have the wool removed from your eyes, or from hiding the ram.

Shearing the ram removes the blinders from both directions. Whenever someone cuts the wool from his eyes, letting the sun shine in, the ram can both see and be seen. Then you will see that Paul is gone. **Everyone sees** in the bright light of day. "Look for **the girl with** the sun in her eyes," or she who sees **reality unveiled.** When you do, you will see "she's gone" ("Lucy In The Sky With Diamonds").

Enough about that. Some of you are wondering about the ram. I will explain.

With all the Bible fans who buy our albums, I would think that more would catch the Ram symbol. Here it is. Abraham's chosen son was replaced by a

---

NOTE: Abraham (originally Abram) is said to have been born in Ur of the Chaldeans (Urs Kaśdim), where Sumerians had their civilization at the dawn of history. It is now part of Iraq. In the Biblical account, God changed the name of Abram (Hebrew: "exalted father") to Abraham ("father of multitude"). The name is shown to be prophetic since Abraham became the common patriarch of Christianity, Islam, and Judaism, and a literal ancestor of multitudes who live in regions dominated by those religions.

Followers of Abrahamic religions belong to one of three concentric circles. The outer-circle receives exoteric tenets from those of the middle. Those in the middle circle acquire teachings from the scriptures as guided by their leaders. Those of the inner circle use the same scriptures to instruct those of the outer circles, but are more interested in esoteric texts and secret teachings that remain concealed from the uninitiated. Secret oral traditions unlock those hidden texts, and completely reinterpret the scriptures. Those who understand layered meaning may use the same verse to teach a lower level concept to the masses that is then used in quite a different way to train illuminated mystics. Such layered meaning is found in the name of Abram.

ram caught by his horns in a thicket. That story is explained in Genesis 22. Abraham took the ram by the horns, and offered him in his son's place. My *Ram* album cover shows a ram caught by his horns. That ram is me, offered up in Paul's place, being entreated to suffer for Paul. However, **I am** also the one holding the horns. See me as **the Shepherd** holding the ram. It is another reversal. The son has died, and the ram lives on in his place. **I am** both the animal and the man. I am the replacing **ram**; and I am the [Billy] Shepherd. I, the man, have maintained steady control over the beast. I have the beast by the horns, but also am that beast.

NOTE: In addition to the common meaning of the names, Abram and Abraham, shown in the previous footnote, there are also secret Kabbalistic meanings that have special significance to William, our man of RAM.

The Kabbalah, the essential text of Jewish mysticism, was adapted in Western esotericism as the Hermetic Qabalah and Christian Kabbalah. The Hermetic Qabalah is foundational to the philosophy and framework of magical societies (such as the Thelemic orders), mystical-religious societies (such as the Builders of the Adytum and the Fellowship of the Rosy Cross), and of Wiccan, Neopagan, and New Age movements. It is also the basis for the Qliphothic Qabala as studied by left hand path orders (such as the Typhonian Order).

According to a secret ancient tradition, the Kabbalah was passed down among the Sumerians until possessed by Abram. When he left Sumer, he took the sacred tablets with him. In the oldest Kabbalistic circles, following the tradition of hiding our greatest secrets in plain sight, Abram (Ab-Ram) means "He who possesses Ram." Ram signifies the highest expression of cosmic awareness. From that very old tradition, we have the saying, "Whomever possesses Kabbalah, also possesses Ram."

Going from Abram to Abraham magnifies the meaning. Although it might be seen as an advance in degrees, such as progressing in ritual from the left shoulder to the right, it is much more than that. He is not merely going from being Abram to being very Abram. He progresses from illumination to exaltation.

Ram Dass reminds us of a more humble Ram meaning. His new name, he says, means "Servant of God" (compare Matthew 23:11).

133

The name, ***RAM** (**R**adical **A**ppearance **M**odification to **R**eplace **A** McCartney),* reverses as *MAR* for a hidden sacrificial meaning. The sacrificial substitute for the man is marred by the holy offering. The essentially plain song, "Ram On," repeatedly telling me to do my ram work, furthers this idea of some religious sacrifice. In ancient sacrificial rituals, they cut out the heart. In a symbolic shadow, Paul's heart, as all else taken from him, was given to me, his heir. Remember, **it is a** reversal. Instead of the ram being made the **sacrifice**, it is the man, the dead Paul, whose heart is given away to the surviving ram.

Goats Head Soup, released by the Rolling Stones two years after *Ram,* was a darker version after they observed the sacrificial meaning of the ram in me. Their satanic meaning is well established, and is not the focus here.

Liking the Ram picture that Linda took, I found an excuse to use it: I wrote "Ram on." I did not name the album for the song. I named the song for the album.

In the Zodiac, the word for ram is Aries. The word, Aries is derived from the Latin *aris,* meaning "altars." The animal has always been associated with sacrifice. This ancient association is found in many traditions and religions. It is used in both sacred and profane contexts. If you say it is Satanic, have it your way. If to you it is a Christian or Jewish symbol, have it your way. It means anything and everything you bring to it. The common thread throughout is its sacrificial association whether religiously holy or sacrilegious. **I use the symbol** in no sacred or profane context, but only **to represent** or exemplify the death of **Paul**. He has crossed over; I, the ram, remain; **and** I am **the Shepherd.**

Perhaps some of you have noticed how closely Shears resembles Shepard. Look at the letters. Almost all of the Shears letters come from it.

Sgt. Pepper's Lonely Hearts Club Band needn't be unfamiliar to those few who remember "Billy Pepper and the Pepperpots". As the Pepperpots album label makes plain, Billy Pepper is Billy Shepherd. Billy Pepper is the one and only Sgt. Pepper.

In the open album jacket, my Sgt. Pepper uniform has an arm patch that reads "OPD," an abbreviation for "Officially Pronounced Dead," or "Omitting P and D." Omitting P and D from my name as "Shepard" leaves "Shear." In the States, the equivalent of OPD is DOA, "Dead On Arrival."

Here I should also mention that the name, Billy Shears, has produced a fine resurrection tradition. Exactly twenty years before *Sgt. Pepper's Lonely Hearts Club Band* was released, as the story goes, another "Billy Shears" is said to have passed away (the year that Aleister Crowley died), but promised to return in twenty years. Introducing "the one and only Billy Shears" suggests that the old magikal music man returned. If there is only one, he must have risen from the dead. **Alas, for him** and for Paul, each is still dead; and **I am the substitute**. I, Billy Shepherd, am now Paul. I am **the only Billy Shears**.

I should point out that even though I am "the one and only Billy Shears" in the Beatles act, it does not mean that I am the only Billy Shepherd in the music world. It would be very easy to get a few of us confused. Being a ram idol may also resemble many gods; but I am not those idols either.

"Ram on" was code for "Ramon." In Scotland in 1960, **Paul McCartney** used the alias, Paul Ramon. I am singing to Paul, "Ramon, give your heart to somebody soon right away." I am telling him to make his heart manifest in my own. I have also honored his Paul Ramon alias by using it myself on occasion, including on the Steve Miller Band's album, *Brave New World*. For a couple of his numbers, "Celebration Song" and "My Dark Hour," I do backing vocals, drums, and bass guitar.

By now, you probably feel that you understand the ram symbolism. There is one more thing that I want you to **know about** it. Remember, I am the Shepherd holding **the ram** by the horns, as if I were leading it **to be sacrificed**. I am also the ram held **in the hands of the Shepherd.** Strictly speaking, literally, a ram is a non-castrated adult male sheep. I am the ram shepherd. Do you follow me thus far? Yet, *ram* is often used generally to include male goats, a/k/a Billy goats. I am the Billy Shepherd.

15[(17)]

You Want Dates?

On 6 August 1966, Paul McCartney was featured on the BBC Light Programme radio show, *David Frost at the Phonograph.* Frost played records, and visited with Paul between songs. It would help if you could find a tape recording of that "live" broadcast (which was actually recorded **five days before**) or if you could find what **he and John recorded that** night at his house, **which aired at their tour's end.** Unless there is another recording of him that I was not told of, **you would have** a most current and reliable voice sampling of **the first Paul.**

To compare our voices, it is best to use a talking sample since it is not obstructed by multi-tracked harmonies, musical instruments, screaming fans, et cetera. *The Lennon and McCartney Songbook*, re-released under another title when I joined in, recorded 6 August, had the two of them discussing their songs that had been covered by various other entertainers. I had covered some of their songs as Billy Shepherd or Billy Pepper, but had not yet attracted enough success to be featured on their show. Now I cover the old Beatles songs quite a lot, along with my own material, whenever **I go on** tour. When **I** dissolved the Beatles, I wanted **to** let my fans **have** new material, and to let **my new** band spread **its wings** to fly from those **Beatles** years. However, one day I realized that the old Paul's material was pretty good too.

In two more days, 8 August, they released *Revolver,* the last of phase two. Three more days, now 11 August, they began their final tour, exactly one month before Paul crossed over. The timing is more intriguing now as we see the whole thing in perspective. To begin that last tour, they crossed over the Atlantic and landed in Boston, then took a connecting flight to Chicago, where they attempted reconciliation in a press conference that night for John's "more popular than Jesus" faux pas. Having explained it, they gave their first concert of that last tour the next night, 12 August, in Boston. They went to Detroit next where they did two shows, one in the afternoon, and one in the evening, on 13 August. Then they were bused to Cleveland where they did another concert on 14 August. There, yelling and screaming frenzied fans rushed the field.

John, George, and Ringo all said the hysterically screaming fans were bad enough from the audience; but when 2500 of them stormed the field in order to get to them, it was quite unnerving. The next day, they did a concert in Washington DC. There was hardly any time to spare for sightseeing, or breathing. The next day, 16 August, they did a concert in Pennsylvania. On 17 August, they did two shows up in Toronto, Canada. Then, the next day, 18 August, they did a show back in Boston.

The next day, 19 August, the Beatles put on two concerts in Memphis. On 20 August, the band was set to do their thirteenth concert in only nine consecutive days; but the show was rained out, compelling them to do the show the next day before ending up hundreds of miles away for a second performance that same day in St. Louis. Those two shows were on 21 August. **They went** from that second concert to the airport, **and then arrived** early in the morning, before sunrise, **in New York.**

Later that day, they met with the press. In the evening of 23 August, after their Shea Stadium show, they flew to California for a break in Beverly Hills. After a day of recuperation, they flew up north to Seattle for two concerts on 25 August, and then occupied their time with more celebratory play, rest, and diversion back in Beverly Hills. In Los Angeles, with an audience of about 45,000 people at Dodger Stadium, they performed on 28 August.

The Beatles last performance was in Candlestick Park in San Francisco. An elated audience of 25,000 heard them give that last concert on Monday, 29 August 1966. They returned to Los Angeles in the early hours of the morning, flying into LAX, and departed later that day, being 30 August. Arriving back in England the next day, 31 August, they were all exhausted. Besides the tour's grueling schedule endured, they all had serious jet lag. All four of them needed a break.

Billy's Back!

As was already arranged, and not because of Paul's death, as has been speculated, John and Neil took off for West Germany on 5 September to play parts in *How I Won the War,* directed by Richard Lester, and written by Charles Wood, the same guy who wrote the screenplay for *Help!*

Earnest "Paul is Dead" recitalists will tell you that **Paul** and John had argued on the night Paul **slammed the door** and ran off in a heated rage. It was not **like that.** First of all, John was with Neil in West Germany. Secondly, although Paul did rush out and slam the door, he was not in a rage.

Epstein, unable to meet with John, was with Paul and George in the studio. Brian said he scheduled their next studio session for when John returned from making his film. The Beatles would gather to record their next album from 7 to 14 November, and would have it released in time for Christmas. He in effect ordered Paul to have five songs written and ready to record by John's return from filming. That put Paul under great pressure. Paul rarely wrote anything without John's support. Brian said that he would tell John to have five songs ready too. He also gave George a writing assignment for two songs.

With the argument that ensued that evening of 11 September, **Paul did** leave in a huff, but was not in a rage. He did **slam the door**, but had vented against Brian, not **against band-mates.** George told me all about it. He was there. Ringo was with his family in Surrey at the time, but would not have been expected to write anything anyway. He rarely wrote his own material.

After Paul left the studio, he did pick up a girl; but her name was not Rita, as is almost universally believed. The name, Rita, was from a meter maid. I liked the "Rita Meter Maid" sound. John added, "Ahh [0:21], Paul [0:23]," to clarify the song's subject, and "You'd better believe it" at the end. Nuances were woven in: "Took her home, and nearly made it," had it not been for the crash, or, "Got the bill and Rita paid it." Those lines work together in connection with a song **I wrote in** collaboration with Neil Innes that we called, "**Death Cab for Cutie.**" I wrote **and performed it** as Vivian Stanshall. That's me, **wearing a disguise**, singing in an unnatural voice **at the end** of our *Magical Mystery Tour* film. While **I am** on the topic, in case some of you missed it, I am **wearing** yet another "disguise" as **my true self in** an earlier scene. The point was to resemble **my former life.**

Reading or hearing "Death Cab" lyrics in the "Lovely Rita" context puts it all together. **It** is about a cutie who calls for a cab; but it **is only** figurative. She was a young hitchhiker who, **in this book**, is Donna. She carried a suitcase in the rain. Paul, our taxi driver, pulls over for the pretty girl whose looks end up costing her life. "Don't you know, Baby, curves can kill" refers to her nice curves, not to the road's. The idea is that Paul could not keep his eyes off of her. John sings of that distraction in "A Day in the Life," "He didn't notice that **the lights had** changed." Paul's distraction was **their destruction.** Each must pay for the taxi. Cutie paid the fare with her life. The Death Cab lyrics are similar to those by

John's. As I sing mine, "The traffic lights changed from green to red . . . They both wound up dead." Owing something for the taxicab, the cutie is told, "Someone's gonna make you pay your fare." It is the same idea as, "Got the bill, and Rita paid it." However, the Rita line adds an extra little meaning needing clarification: the Beatles got the Bill. They got me, costing the lives Paul and Rita (Paul and the star-crazed Cutie, Donna). They both paid the fare for that fateful ride into the new Beatles phase.

Paul's dreams were contradictory, which make them a bit undependable. **We do** not always have every detail right. One of **the dreams** that impressed me was about the girl recognizing Paul and getting over-excited about it, searching each station up and down the radio dial for a Beatles song, hoping that Paul would sing along. In that dream, and in similar ones, the distraction was not about the girl's good looks, but about her going nuts in the car.

All we can say is based on the truck driver, and on evidence from the crash scene. The driver said Paul ran a red light. The yellow truck hit Paul broadside. That impact knocked them across the wet road into a pole, resulting in a partial decapitation, and a car fire, on Sunday, 11 September 1966, just minutes before midnight. One of our best decapitation clues is given in the *Magical Mystery Tour* movie where I wrote the words, "Magical Mystical Boy," (plainly enough with a permanent marker to be easily read) across the chest of what was intended to resemble the headless corpse of Paul.

You Want Dates?

In Ringo's song, "Don't Pass Me By," he tells his old friend, **Paul**, that he is sorry he doubted the death **dreams, and then** alludes to Paul's exit: "I'm sorry that I doubted **you**. I was so unfair. You were in a car crash and you **lost your** hair." It relates to John singing, "He blew his **mind** out in a car," and, "Here come ole' flat top." John had also doubted, which is partly why he had to laugh at **Paul's** photograph. It proved that all of Paul's **omens were** real. John flipped out. He became **horrifically hysterical.**

Until the corpses were "Officially Pronounced Dead," they were still legally alive. Even though both of them obviously died within seconds of the crash, Paul and Donna were both still officially living until pronounced otherwise several minutes after midnight on Monday, 12 September.

Identifying the burned and mutilated bodies was not as impossible as has been imagined. If they had needed facial detection, they could not have done it; but Paul's car quickly revealed his identity, and the girl's suitcase had a letter from her cousin staying with a friend on Leso in Mesocco, Switzerland. Apparently, Donna was headed there. Reaching her parents was not difficult, but time-consuming, with Swiss support. Police alerted her parents "Wednesday morning at five o'clock as the day begins."

Paul's father and stepmother, who had been notified Monday, saw his remains, but would not affirm that **it was** Paul. They did not recognize his clothes. **Nothing** about the messed up corpse looked undeniably **like Paul.** They finally admitted it could be him, but held the opinion that Paul had earlier loaned his Aston Martin to a friend. Investigators called Paul's dentist for x-rays; but they could not identity Paul conclusively because of how the injury smashed his mouth.

Searching for proof of **Paul's** identity continued quietly. The **investigator** assigned to the case had the decency to **keep his assumptions** from the press **until he had legal proof**—which he anxiously anticipated. Not imagining he could talk to a member of the band, he called others, without revealing why he wanted the information, to learn how to reach the Beatles' agent. When at last he did reach Brian Epstein, Brian immediately went to the morgue and said he did not think the corpse was Paul. **Brian** was permitted to take a few pictures. He **assured the** investigator he would have a positive answer **later** that day. That bought him a few hours to produce **Paul**. Meanwhile, **Jane too was** called in.

Under the circumstances **of Paul** predicting his own death and of attempting to find some talented look-alike **to replace** him, Brian had discussed possible **Paul** imitators with his brother and a few intimate **friends**. One **of** them who knew of my Billy **Pepper albums** (which covered Beatles songs), **recommended** me for the position. Having worked with **me**, Brian already knew me, but did not know if I was up to the role. Besides, I did not fully look the part. He called me and warmly extended an invitation to work on an album as a session musician, but did not yet say for whom. He asked me to meet him at the Abbey Road studio in an hour. He told me to bring my albums.

During that meeting, I showed him the albums I had cut. Brian asked me to play my cover of "She Loves You" from my *More Merseymania* album. Epstein said, "I had a hell of a time crossing the ocean with that song. **The Beatles were** unknown then. Capitol Records **refused the single**, as did Vee Jay." Brian said he finally convinced Swan to take it. They released "She Loves You" in the States exactly three years, to the week, before our meeting. It did not sell well at all until the Beatles' next single, "I Want to Hold Your Hand," was released

NOTE: The Capitol Records Building, at 1750 Vine Street in Hollywood, is only a couple of miles from Laurel Canyon. Once the Capitol executives became aware of the success of the Beatles' first album, *Please Please Me,* and being apprised of what the global scheme was creating right next to them in Laurel Canyon, Capitol Records finally agreed to accept their parent company's offer to be the Beatles' primary North American record label.

Parlophone Records, Odeon Records, and Capitol Records were all EMI subsidiaries. On 22 March 1963, the Beatles released their first album, *Please Please Me,* on Parlophone (their UK label). On 22 November, they released *With the Beatles* on Parlophone (for the UK), on Odeon (for the Western European continental market), and on Capitol (only in Canada). Capitol was not permitted to release *With the Beatles* in the US due to the trauma that would befall Americans on that day. EMI had been warned that releasing the album in the US on the day that John F. Kennedy would be assassinated would hurt record sales and give the Beatles a lasting negative association.

Instead, for the US, after given time to mourn, the tracks were divided into two Capitol albums: *Meet the Beatles!* (released 20 January 1964), and *The Beatles' Second Album* (10 April 1964). The latter, although the Beatles sixth album globally, was the second to be released on Capitol in the US. The first US Beatles album, *Introducing . . . The Beatles,* had been released on the Vee-Jay label on 10 January 1964.

The *With the Beatles* and *Meet the Beatles!* cover art used shadows to conceal the left eye for each emissary of the New Age. Now, representations of the Eye of Ra (right eye (sun)) or Eye of Horus (left eye (moon)) are often made by celebrities who conceal one eye (usually with a palm), or who show one eye darkened by bruising—perhaps sometimes consensually.

the following year. I played my cover version, which entertained him a little. Then **I** played parts of a few songs that I wrote. We **discussed** my session work, leading to explanations of **my musical abilities**, and so on. He seemed nervously abrupt at first; but that lessened gradually and was replaced with a growing excitement. Finally, before Brian had told me a single word about Paul's death, he asked, "How would you like to be **Paul** McCartney?"

I thought he **was asking me** to fill in for Paul to help with a particular recording session. I said, "I'd be delighted **to play on a Beatles album**!" I would help with a song or two, **or so I thought.**

"Even if it means you are not credited?" Brian asked, as if it mattered.

"Certainly," I said. "That is standard for most of us session musicians. I can play as anyone. I do it all the time."

Brian slowly nodded his head as he studied my eyes. He smiled. "Marvelous!" he said. Then he told me the whole story.

Everything became hurried. I dyed my hair. Brian took pictures, and then described many of

NOTE: This day began William's hair-dying practice, which would continue for most of his life. Dye concealed his reddish-blond hair, then grey hair, and now white hair. On at least three occasions, while sitting in a bathtub, William applied a protective coating of petroleum jelly to his penis and scrotum, and then used a washrag to apply ammonia-free hair dye to the rest of his body. On each occasion, he was delighted to show off his dyed body hair. He made a point of being seen entirely naked, and of having Linda take photographs intended to seem candid. Usually, he only dyed his hair in areas of his body that he expected the public to see.

Early on, preferring the freedom of an open shirt, he often dyed his chest hair. Later, for the freedom of not having to dye body hair, he choose to either wear crewneck shirts or to keep his shirts buttoned above the chest hairline. With this disclosure, he says he now might as well stop dying his hair entirely.

You Want Dates?

Paul's mannerisms while we drove to Paul's parents' home. All there welcomed me into their family, and took me to Paul's house. Jim located Paul's birth certificate, and other documents. Before long, using a picture of me taken earlier that day, Brian made an identification card. He had me write this line: "In Mark Twain's words, 'The reports of my death are greatly exaggerated.'" We met his friend, a notary. I signed my note, dated 12 September 1966. Brian dropped me off at the studio, and then rushed off with his new proof that Paul was alive.

We stopped at a payphone for Brian to call John. Emptying his pockets of change into the phone, he could not reach him. Instead, he sent this telegram: "PAUL WAS RIGHT [STOP] DREAMS CAME TRUE [STOP] HE IS A NEW MAN NOW [STOP] ORGANIZE YOUR SCHEDULE TO MEET ME AT 1:00 PM TOMORROW [STOP]"

Reaching a point in the filming that John and Neil would not be needed again until the next set, they went on leave in Hamburg. The telegram message reached their hotel while they were out.

Everyone seemed satisfied by my notarized avowal except for Samuel, a snooping Birmingham reporter who found the same facts that the police were forbidden to say: The fatally demolished vehicle was the property of **Paul McCartney**. He, and a female passenger, **was dead.** He had acquired the

---

NOTE: Although William had already noticed some of Paul's mannerisms before, he found it useful to hear Brian's observations. In William's Beatle years, he made a point of subtly working in Paul's idiosyncrasies to help others subconsciously accept Paul's identity. Those mannerisms are like passcodes for the subconscious mind. Currently, however, rather than using those mannerisms to fool his public, he uses them to give insiders a laugh. Without being subtle at all, he will make a Paul expression, and then touch his mouth, face, and hair as if to say, "Look at me! I am doing Paul mannerisms!"

Billy's Back!

Aston Martin DB6 only six months before. Now Paul and his car were no more. The news was sensational. It would have sold many papers, and could have been the reporter's career-making story. Papers live for such stories that do not come along often. Samuel sensed it. Unable to dissuade him, an officer referred the reporter to Brian Epstein. Brian was packing when **Samuel** called and agreed to meet in person. Brian **said Paul was** on holiday. Samuel persisted. Brian said that he and an associate would be driving to Paris **in the same car that** Samuel was then claiming **was destroyed.**

"Well, that's impossible!" Samuel said. "I have seen the vehicle. It's demolished!"

"Enough of what you think you saw!" Brian said. "I spoke to Paul this morning two hours before he left for Paris. Hold your story for a week or two, until he gets back, or you and your paper will be the laughing stock of Great Britain!"

"I'd be the laughing stock if I didn't print it!"

The meeting went on and on; but the determined reporter was not convinced. Brian tried to appeal to his sympathies by explaining that the Beatles had just returned from their exhausting American tour, and that they all needed a break from the public eye.

Without admitting anything at all about Paul's tragedy, Brian explained that their peace was worth considerable compensation and that McCartney, in particular, needed a long break before another press conference. When nothing else worked, Brian gave an ultimatum. **Samuel could** either take a cruise and large payment to **drop the story**, or spend years in court in an expensive libel suit. Brian said, "Even if you are right, you will lose. We have a lot more resources than you!" When that threat failed, Brian called a persuasive Tavistock agent who gave encouragement to Sam over the phone. Sam agreed.

Brian drafted a deal edited by Rex Makin, who negotiated with Samuel until it was signed. Then Samuel's payment and travel arrangements had to be made. By the time Brian left for Hamburg, he was nine hours behind schedule. Mal Evans agreed to let John know to change their 1:00 meeting to 10:00; and swore Brian would never hear from Sam again.

Although Mal swore he sent **John** a telegram in the morning, John had not **received** it. While it is not for me to say who dropped the ball, I will say that John not receiving **that** notice of Brian's long delay was a horrible **torment** to him. Although Mal was a good friend of Brian, of the band, and of everyone else close to them, John's anguish of not getting that telegram created a real rift that nearly destroyed their friendship, and almost cost Mal his job. Still, he was right about Sam never returning.

NOTE: Rothschild's Committee of 300 commissioned the Tavistock Institute of Human Relations to apply mass mind-control techniques for social conditioning that would break down all cultural and societal structures, and rebuild them according to NWO agendas. "The snitch," going by the name, John Coleman, was the first to go public with the Beatles' Tavistock project. He revealed that Tavistock directed Stanford Research to undertake the work under the direction of Professor Willis Harmon. This work, later known as the Aquarian Conspiracy, became the basis for creating what the world came to know (beyond their bar-band years) as the Beatles, and then for creating many other manufactured bands that sprang from England and California.

Most relevant for this book, the Beatles were a construct of the Tavistock Institute, conveniently located at 30 Tabernacle St, Shoreditch, London, five miles from Abbey Road Studios, at 3 Abbey Rd, St John's Wood, London.

Working with EMI and various media powerhouses, Tavistock made the Beatles one of their culture industry's highest priorities. Tavistock, funded and directed at first by the royal family, and then by the Rothschilds directly, is fully aligned with their globalist agendas, and cannot be stopped by any governmental jurisdiction without Rothschild consent.

Once Brian acquired contact information from George Martin, and called on Tavistock to protect their project, nothing on earth could shield Samuel.

16[(18)]

"Two of Us"

"Two of Us" is a song that I always officially say is about driving around with Linda. If you ask what it is about, that is what **I have to tell you**. It may be the closest thing to **a love song** that I originated and recorded as a Beatle; but it says nothing of love. It is **about two strangers** only united by the fact that they were **in the car** together at Paul's end, **who thus die together.**

Feeling as though I had the leverage to make any demands that I wanted, when John and Neil met with us in Paris to work out the new deal, I called their work trite, and said most people have had enough silly Beatles love songs. Having heard the name of their new *Revolver* release, I said I would help them revolve to new Beatles music, not only with new sounds, but with a new theme also. Rather than their insipid "She loves you, yeah, yeah, yeah, I wanna hold your hand," I would lead the band into a new direction entirely. Until then, the vast majority of their repertoire consisted of love songs. There was an indecisive part of me that was not sure **I should go** through with the radical makeover. **For me to lose** not only my looks, but also **my identity** would be hard, and harder **to adopt the identity** of some guy who is **already well established**. Doing it for a week **would be a blast**. Stepping into a role for a night would be more business as usual. We session musicians did that. However, committing to it for an ongoing duration, possibly for a lifetime, was most frightening. I was not sure I wanted to do that.

When **we met** to discuss what we each wanted out of the deal, **there** was a conflicted part of me that hoped I would ask **for** too much and blow the whole deal. Part of me wanted **it all to work out**; but I was equally undecided. I particularly did not want to start some new life just to do silly love songs. I really felt divided over it. When I said, "Okay, but no more love songs," I thought that condition would end our negotiations. After all, what would the Beatles be without silly love songs? I had not yet

---

NOTE: As designed from the start, the Beatles music would evolve from the most naive that their writers could imagine for them, to the most liberated. Their first number one hit in America (being their second in the UK), credited to Lennon-McCartney, though far beyond their writing skills, was "I Want to Hold Your Hand." Launching the engineered social transformation, that hit sold over 15 million copies worldwide.

Part of the genius of the song was its sophisticated musical composition coupled with simple childlike lyrics. As intended, that first impression in the States created the illusion of sexual inexperience. The group's pretended virginal naivety sharply contrasted the reality of each player.

George, the youngest of the group, was the last to lose his virginity. John and Paul watched without George knowing until their applause at the end. Well before their first recording session, all four Beatles were very active sexually, and, unfortunately, all four had contracted gonorrhea. Contrasting the song provided to them, they were far beyond hand-holding fantasies.

William stepped in after the virgin's sacrifice when it was time to outgrow the music of inhibited childhood infatuations to move into the adult world ruled by uninhibited will. William did not need to be specifically directed to end the Beatles' childish love songs. He had already been indoctrinated with the idea that their music would grow up, and occasionally contributed to it. With such training, his call to end their love-song era was fully anticipated by those in control. He realized later that in this instance, as in many others, he thought he was exercising free will, but was, in fact, doing exactly as trained.

spent the money to buy their *Revolver* album, and could not think of any big Beatles hits before it, except perhaps one, that was not a love song. That was their whole gig. All of their hits were of romance.

Erring in my thinking, that John was at that time of sound mind, or that he was then in any position to negotiate anything at all well, I was shocked that he, with a blank dazed stare, responded to my impulsive demand indifferently. **He said** the band would not survive without **love songs**, that selling love fantasies is what **made them big**, and that it defined them. However, he said, **some songs** on their new LP were not about love. "They **are pretty** good too," he added. Then he said, "**All right**, the Beatles can go on beyond love songs now." We had a deal. My mind raced for another demand that might kill it.

"Something," which George began recording on his 26th birthday, appeared to be a great exception to our ban on love songs. First, George pretended that he was not sure if the ban was merely for songs made by Lennon-McCartney, or if it would also

---

NOTE: As discussed in chapter 37 (51 in *the Memoirs*), the Beatles created Apple Corps to invest in new talent. Their first American artist (having ties to their Laurel Canyon associates) was James Taylor. When he auditioned for George and "Paul," James sang his favorite song that he had written thus far, "Something in the Way She Moves."

As JT sang it, George pictured the way his own wife moves, looks his way, or calls his name. That audition song, and George's adoration of his own wife, Pattie Boyd, inspired George's best Beatles song, "Something," which borrowed the first six words of the audition song. Pattie also inspired these Beatles songs, "If I Needed Someone," and "For You Blue."

Pattie also inspired some of Eric Clapton's best songs, "Layla" and "Wonderful Tonight." "Layla," written in 1970, draws the name from "The Story of Layla and Majnun," by Nizami Ganjavi (1141–1209), who based that poem on a 7th-century love story. Clapton wrote "Wonderful Tonight" in 1976 while waiting for Pattie to get ready to attend "Paul and Linda McCartney's" annual Buddy Holly party. Patty divorced George in 1977 and was married to Eric from 1979 to 1989.

include his songs. **I said he knew** it included the entire band and that **every song impacted** our Beatles image, which by **that** time had successfully gone on to more **interesting music** than all of the love songs of the band's second **phase**. However, I also now realized that George's new love song was of a higher quality than all of the childish ones sold on every Beatles album before I joined.

John and Paul had only allowed George one song for each side of each album. He was in the habit of recording more than that, and then saving his surplus. That stockpile paid off for him when he went solo. He already had a good stash of songs. John argued in his defense that "Something" was the best song that the Beatles had recorded in a long time.

Realizing that I would never make an exception otherwise, George had already hidden a big "**Paul is** Dead" message, which trumped the surface **love** message. Five months earlier, John's "Julia" had an encoded dream that he had had of his mother. The romantic suggestions are merely a cover for the actual story. Likewise, on that album, I had "Martha My Dear" about my large sheepdog, which Paul received as a puppy not long before I took over. I inherited Martha from him right off. Then it was not many months after my dog song came out that Bob Dylan made one of his own, following my example. His "Lay Lady Lay" was often mistaken for a sexually charged love song, which benefited Dylan considerably in sales. For the sake of the Paul message, **I allowed** George's "Something."

Paul's absence was a common theme. George, with Ken Scott's help in the control room, added our most sophisticated backmasked Paul message. **I** will quote it when we discuss Paulism. You **can hear it** consciously only if you play the song **backward.** Now that you know our rule, you can be sure that "Two of Us" is not entirely a love song—since Phase Three Beatles had none, with only that one exception for George. I am glad I did not insist on him saving that song for his solo years.

Understanding that "Two of Us" is not a **love** song, and that Paul died on Sunday, 11 September, adds considerable clarity to the song. I sing, "Two of us [Paul and Donna] riding nowhere," going to "nowhere land," as Paul describes it, foretelling his death that would make him a "Nowhere Man."

Donna was not spending her money for the ride. **Paul** picked up Donna because the poor girl had not **made** enough money to hire a real taxicab. Paul's **money** was from his fans who spent their hard earned pay on his Beatles records. They were both "spending someone's hard earned pay."

Singing as Paul to Donna, it goes, "You and me Sunday driving, not arriving." On that last drive, upset by their fatal crash Sunday night, they never arrived at their intended destination. Instead, that night they went home to God, so to speak. Thus, "We're on our way home. We're going home."

Donna's suitcase had postcards and letters from her cousin staying with their friend in Switzerland. A letter with the Swiss address led investigators on what one officer called "a wild goose chase" to find the young woman's parents. The police were "chasing papers," not chasing Paul and Donna.

Donna and her cousin had each been "sending postcards, writing letters," which investigators soon retrieved and pinned to an evidence board. They were all "on my wall," meaning that they were included with the collected evidence posted at the station to figure out and prove **Paul's** identity. Very suddenly, the car caught fire, **burning** them like matches. "You and me burning matches."

In a bit, when help arrived, the crew was "lifting latches" to remove the victims. I memorialized that night's wild and windy rainstorm by the song's line, "Two of us wearing raincoats." Donna was drenched. Going nowhere, they die alone "standing solo." I actually sing, "so low" (buried) "in the sun" (heaven).

Not arriving at their aim, "going nowhere," but home to God, their "long and winding road" went on without them. **Paul's** journey continued; only he is no longer **the driver.** I am. That is the reason that **I am the one** singing as though I were Paul doing the **driving.** The "two of us" became one and continued together on the road where he left off.

I care about Donna to a point, but do not wish to recall any of her memories. There was a certain curiosity to find out what she was all about, to read her life like some book. I looked and found enough; but my interest is in Paul. Joining our pasts, interwoven with our futures in the present, Paul's own past, his memories, become my own. Yet, my voyage down the road of life also includes my own memories from before Paul took over my life.

I, with Paul, have memories longer than the long, stormy, winding road that stretches out on and on to nowhere. "Two of us" (Paul and I now), like the two of them (Paul and Donna), are on this same road going home. Everyone goes home. You better believe it. Paul is driving me until I get there.

"Hello, Goodbye" begins where "**Two of Us**" ends. The last word of "Two of Us" **should be** enough to show the connection. Paul ends it **saying**, "Goodbye." In "Hello, Goodbye," I am high, but he is low again. He says "Goodbye," but I say **"Hello."** As he checks out on the street, I check in. On the long and winding road of his own life, at his fatally appointed time to stop, it was my time to "go, go, go, oh no." Neither of us could understand why. "You say why, and I say I don't know, oh no. You say goodbye, and I say hello."

"Hello, Goodbye," on that road of life stretching out ahead, is about coming and going. I came. Paul went. **I don't know why**, as I say. It is just how **our parts were written** for this stage of life. He says yes **for me to play his part**, but I had not decided for sure that I wanted it. Part of me still tells him no. **Paul tells me** to stop playing my own life, but **to play his**. I was not sure about making that permanent **life**-changing commitment. Paul says yes, **but I cannot commit.** Compromisingly, I say, "I can stay until it's time to go." This song evolved in its meaning for me, as I increasingly wanted out of the Beatles. It was time to go

I was stuck in the Beatles box. In "Band on the Run," I sing about back when I was, "Stuck inside these four walls, sent inside forever, Never seeing no one nice again like you, Mama you." I am still stuck. When I dissolved the band and got out of that box, I still felt forever locked behind the Paul McCartney appearance. If I were to shed this Paul McCartney role, I would lose much of its wealth. **I thought** I should give it to charity. I do not need **most of it** anyway. I have simple needs. It **would be fine** to live on less. "If I ever get out of here, thought of giving it all away to a registered charity. All I need is a pint a day, if I ever get out of here."

That feeling of being stuck in Paul was present in my song, "Golden Slumber." In the introduction where I lead into Dekker's poem, I sing of my earnest desire to leave McCartneyism, and to return home to my own authentic life. "Once there was a way to get back homeward. Once there was a way to get back home." In a song six months earlier, I was less obvious about whom I wanted to "Get back, get back, get back to where you once belonged" ("Get Back"). I go on naming others, and think about immigration generally; but most meaningfully sang to myself. If only I were free to be myself. I did not obscure that fact in "Golden Slumbers." I wanted to get back home.

Going back six months more, I added to the end of my "Cry Baby Cry," my plea to Paul, and his earnest plea to me, "Can you take me back where I came from? Can you take me back? Can you take me back where I came from? Brother, can you take me back? Can you take me back?"

Being at the song's conclusion was to help you reach your own conclusion about all of that crying. I am mostly crying to go back to my own peacefully simple life where **I came** from. Likewise, **Paul is** calling me, his figurative brother, to bring him **back** to where he came **from** as well. In this way, it is kind of a mutual yearning for us both to get back home to **where we once belonged.**

17[(19)]

"Tuesday Afternoon Is Never Ending."

After Brian's telegram was sent from England and printed in Hamburg Monday evening, hotel staff forwarded it to John's room, placing it on a side table that they tidied by John's bed. When it arrived, the two of them (**John with Neil** Aspinall) were out shopping. Before they **returned to** their hotel, they ended up back at **the Kaiserkeller**, the same club they had visited **two nights before** when Paul died.

Recalling how **things got going** there with Paul and the others, John had returned to reminisce about the Beatles' first phase, with Pete Best on drums and Stu Sutcliffe on bass. Starting with that club in Hamburg, it really took off. Back in 1960, the Indra Club and Kaiserkeller, their first German venues, emerged as the Beatles' boot camp, giving them hard training, and a crucial turning point. It was not deliberate timing; but there could not have been a more perfect place for John to be when Paul died (except maybe at Eleanor Rigby's grave). There John was, less than two weeks after his famous band had left the United States, finishing another successful tour, reflecting on how very far they had come since

"Tuesday Afternoon Is Never Ending."

all their long exhausting nights in Hamburg clubs where they each worked harder than in any other years of their lives, but with far less pay. The work they did there in Hamburg paid off well years later.

John received Brian's cryptic message when he returned to his hotel room at 3:45 in the morning of Tuesday, 13 September. **He shouted** obscenities, and yelled for Neil. Neil rushed to John to see what happened. John yelled, "He says **Paul died and is** already replaced! How was he **replaced?** He did not even talk to me first? I need to talk to Brian! How do I make an outside call?"

With Brian due to arrive in nine hours, Neil explained that he would already be on his way, and would be unreachable until he arrived. John could not calm himself. Other hotel guests began shouting for John to shut up. It quickly got ugly. Unable to say what was wrong, he became abusive. Some thought he went crazy. Others blamed the alcohol. Probably all of them were right. John hysterically laughed one moment, and then screamed the next. In that state, **John could not** care what others thought, and could not **come to grips with** his own thoughts. Memories of **Paul's dreams** kept coming into John's mind. John had laughed, and made jokes about them. Now he half expected this kind of a joke back from Brian. Yet, deep inside, he feared that it must be real. John assured himself that everything would be clear at 1:00 when Brian would arrive, and that if he could keep it together, and drink enough, he would make it until then. Neil got John away from the hotel until nine that morning.

Around noon, John thought he figured out what Brian was up to, and laughed even hardier with the notion that his questioning was over. Brian would show up at one o'clock and tell John that **Paul was** dead, and that the new Paul was waiting **in the car.** There, Paul would pretend to be his own imposter. Everyone would get a laugh out of it. John figured that Brian had some business to conduct, and that he maybe told Paul about it, who decided to come along for a visit. The telegram was actually one of Paul's outrageous jokes. Paul was getting even with John for making jokes about the death.

Time progressed more peacefully once John assured himself that he had figured it out. However, it became a source of agitation as the hours went by. 1:00 came and went, as did 2:00 and 3:00.

Over and over, John looked at his watch and slipped back into fear and anger. He thought every now and then that maybe the joke was that they were not coming at all. Or, what if **Paul** and Brian attempted to play that gag, but **got killed** in a car accident along the way? "Now wouldn't that be a laugh!" **John shouted** out loud, "That would teach you!" He stared **out the window** for Brian's car.

Long hours stretched on. That long Tuesday afternoon dragged on and on without a visit. John yelled, cried, laughed, worried, wondered, threw things, imagined, tried to write, kicked furniture, drank, smoked, and screamed. Still, Paul and Brian did not show. John stared out the window, waiting.

"Tuesday Afternoon Is Never Ending."

In his anxious state, **John became ill.** His alcohol-saturated **vomit** was better undigested. Eating something **would have** cushioned his stomach, bracing it for **the drinks.** He had not eaten anything since the Indra Club. He ached from stress, hunger, and vomit contractions, but could not eat.

Bursts of rage broke his intense silence. 4:00, 6:00, and 8:00 expired without visitors. The torment lasted until Brian arrived at 9:49. Or, maybe, that is when the torment began.

Even before Brian got out of his car, John ran out to him. "Where is he? Where is he?"

"Don't you want to know what happened?" Brian asked, stepping out of the car.

"Is he in the trunk?" **John** began pounding on it while shouting to Paul. **"Are you** in there?"

"Are you **out of your mind?"** Brian asked. He could see that he was.

"Make him come out! Open the trunk!" John again began banging on the trunk of Brian's car.

"Paul is dead," Brian said, opening the trunk. "And no, he is not here in my trunk."

Anything Brian could say meant nothing. **John** had indeed gone absolutely mad, and **would not stop** until Brian handed him the photograph. Brian told me that John, with enormous bulging eyes, burst out laughing hysterically, and continued so for several minutes. It was the hardest day of John's life.

Now you understand John's reference to "Stupid bloody Tuesday." It is not when Paul died. Paul died on Sunday, 11 September, a few minutes before

Monday, the day that Paul's family, Brian, and I, were each notified. **Tuesday was the day that John** got the news, and **agonized over it** while waiting for Brian. "Stupid bloody Tuesday" marks the end of John's world of hope. Something died in him then.

You have probably heard that the line, "Tuesday afternoon is never ending" refers to Paul McCartney ending his life that day before the day ended. That is a sensible guess, but is historically incorrect. You see, **P**aul's unfinished day had already been spent two days before. If John had been here in England as **a**ll of th**is** Paul **business** was happening, he would have played a major role in it. John would have **u**nderstood it all on Monday before I did; and, as for "Lady Madonna," I would be without a line of **l**yrics for Tuesday. The song's oft repeated line, "See how they run," explains it all. The three remaining Beatles, along with Brian and others, ran about frantically like the "Three Blind Mice" of the English nursery rhyme taught to children: "Three blind mice. Three blind mice. See how they run. See how they run. They all ran after the farmer's wife [the queen, "Bloody Mary"], Who cut off their tails with a carving knife. Did you ever see such a sight in your life, As three blind mice?" The mice were injured and all ran about in desperation.

Historically, the poem is about Queen Mary's years of conflict with Protestants. More particularly, the poem was about three troublesome bishops. Still, for our purposes, **see how** Brian and others ran around when **Paul was** cut off. Just as Mary's retaliations **killed** the Oxford Martyrs (Hugh

Latimer, Nicholas Ridley, and Thomas Cranmer) in hopes of putting down the beast of Protestantism, so too, **Paul's** loss of life threatened to put an end to the **Beatle beast**. Yet, just as others rose to take the place of the **lost** bishops, so too have I now taken the place of **Paul**. Although Bloody Mary had almost 300 dissenters burned at the stake, no death can ever stop anything that is really meant to go on. Fate is not so easily overturned.

When we all rushed about setting things up that week after Paul died, **the band was on the run** to ensure its survival **without Paul**. Swift action was required to save the band. Behind the scenes, many ran around like three blind mice that had lost their fourth. Silencing the informed once and for all, Mal had Ringo accompanied by one of Paul's best doubles for a Melody Maker Awards broadcast. It refuted all evidence of Paul's death, and still does. We still use it.

In "Band on the Run," **I sing of Paul's** crash: "The rain exploded with a **mighty crash as** we fell into the sun." Saying **he "fell into the sun"** means he died and went to heaven. He also "fell into the *son*," entering me, the brother. **He was the first**. His end launched my beginning. **I am the second** one in this role. When Paul died, which made my role begin, "the first one said to the second one there, I hope you're having fun." Well, yes, it was fun for a bit. It was a dream come true. It sounds fun, doesn't it?

Not to complain, or to detract from how great it was, but it became too painful to stay with that band. Doing it, in due course, became too burdensome.

"Band on the Run" begins with me longing to get out. I cover that longing in other chapters. Although I was groomed for this work, it took its toll on me.

Now, "the jailer man [the police investigator] and sailor Sam [the reporter whom Brian sent sailing to Rome on a cruise] were searching everyone" to either find Paul or to prove his death. As they were here running around London (which I call the town), **John flew off to** Carboneras in southern Spain, to **enact his role** in *How I Won the War*. That desert location had been selected for the film due to its resemblance of a North African desert. It is where and when "the night was falling as the desert world [under Lester's direction] began to settle down. In the town they're searching for us everywhere, but we never will be found." Neither will Sailor Sam ("Helen Wheels"). We're the band on the run. See how they run?

18[(20)]

"Wednesday Morning Papers Didn't Come."

Here, I will tell you about my song, "She's Leaving Home." Setting this song apart from nearly every other Beatles song, **I made it without** any of the Beatles doing any of **the instrument**ation. Like "Yesterday," and **only a** few others, the score was too far beyond **Beatle**s s**kills**.

The deal Brian Epstein made with the reporter Monday evening was conditioned on the man getting his first installment **by** cashing his first check on the following day. He would have **ca**shed his check immediately that night; but **b**anking hours had already expired for the day. Brian and **Samuel**'s stipulation was that if the first check **did not** cash by 5:00 Tuesday, the story would be **submit**ted that day and printed that night for **the** Wednesday morning delivery. There are **rumor**s that is was printed and nearly dispersed when the government stepped in and required all those papers to be gathered and destroyed. That is embellishment. The check was good. Samuel cashed it (or at least someone did) on Tuesday; and the story didn't appear on Wednesday. That is the significant half of the double meaning hidden in the line, "Wednesday morning papers didn't come." However anticlimactic compared to all with the press, Brian forgot some documents for his Wednesday morning meeting with John.

The song, "She's Leaving Home" also references early Wednesday morning. It is about a girl running away. **I am that girl, so to speak**, and so is Donna. It represents me **running** from my previous life to live a new one **as Paul.** Though I had tried to make it as a recording artist, it was "something inside that was always denied for so many years" until I left the security and familiarity of home. I may have seemed a bit thoughtless to turn my back on so many people who were close enough to feel abandoned by me, yet not close enough, or not good enough at secret-keeping, to be let in on my Paul transformation.

Some loved ones felt abandoned by my emotional or physical distance. **The song** recognizes the pain I caused them **for my own** sake. The conclusion, "She's having **fun" was about me** occupied with *Sgt. Pepper's*, **having a blast** working night and day **to create the greatest album ever**, while all too many of my relatives were grieving over my disappearance. I wanted to tell them I was having fun now. Later, I echoed that idea in "Band on the Run" as if Paul says to me, "Hope you're having fun."

Donna may or may not have been a runaway. I cannot say for sure. Still, hitchhiking with a suitcase at her age suggests the likelihood that her parents had not consented to it, and that she could not earn a living on her own. She was poor. "Lady Madonna" uses the poverty idea with lines of her not having the wherewithal to feed her children, et cetera. "She's Leaving Home" is about the runaway idea.

"Wednesday Morning Papers Didn't Come."

As she goes off to Mesocco, Switzerland, if that were her goal, I imagine her leaving a farewell note. You can **imagine how devastating** that would be to her parents **for her to write** them a goodbye letter stating all **the reasons why she does not want** to live with **them anymore**, only to go off and die with a stranger in a horrific collision.

Her loved ones could never know (unless they read it here) that the driver who died with her was Paul. The street that Donna appeared to be headed for was Leso. It was on the return address on her cousin's letters. The *Sgt. Pepper's* cover says, "BE AT LESO." Can you find it? "BEATLES" is written in large letters by red flowers on the ground as if that band had died along with Paul. But Paul did not die alone. There is an "O" at the end. The word doesn't end with the "S," but with an "O." It actually says, "BEATLESo." We are telling her to rest in peace at the place of her intended destination on Leso in Mesocco. Break it up to read: "BE AT LESo." The fact that we intended it to be able to be broken up into separate words is shown by our intentional and obvious misalignment of the first word. "BE" is noticeably not in line with the rest of the letters. Now, while the thought is fresh in your mind, **look** at the *Sgt. Pepper's* cover. Once you see it, you likely do not ever need to look for it again. **It is shown** plainly, and will always be plain now that you know.

NOTE: "BE AT LESO." Donna appears to have been headed to Leso, a street in Mesocco, Switzerland, about 666 miles South-East of London (or 600 miles from Staffordshire). "Leso" is an Italian word, meaning "Injured."

For more about Donna, read the lyrics of "She's Leaving Home." I am not going to go through them all here since they are so straightforward, referring to when the police notified her parents.

Remember, they got the word on "Wednesday morning at five o'clock as the day begins." The early hour was to reach them before they left for work. This notification for them occurred the same Wednesday, 14 September, that the newspaper story of **Paul and Donna** would have run, intending to **expose their deaths**, if Brian, or others, had not convinced Samuel to take the payment. Those who lost Donna could have read about the crash in the paper on that same morning. It is always hard to lose a loved one, but even harder without having the whole story—such as Donna's or mine.

19[21]

"Thursday Night Your Stockings Needed Mending."

Inspiration and serendipity always play a part in song writing. **My favorite songs**, those most worth recording, **come to me as gifts**, channeled from friends in other dimensions. Suddenly, **I get** the essence, as though a whole creation were **beamed** down. My talent or gift is to be open **to receive** fine music. I sit down at a piano, or pick up a guitar, and play a few chords. Then, often very **effortlessly**, everything comes together. As the tune comes into my head, **I plug in** some silly gibberish words to match the **rhythm**, and then keep playing until the words complete themselves. I started doing that at the beginning of my Beatle career.

John said that he and Paul had plugged in silly enough lyrics to be able to remember them, and in that way, remember their tunes. As John said Paul related it to him, the stranger the lyrics, the easier they would be to remember. So, I picked up on it.

My own writing came easier when I understood how Paul did it. Each stress must be just right. In "Yesterday," the stressed syllable is "Yes," with

"-terday" being swifter and softer. That is why Paul plugged in "Scrambled eggs." The "Scram" was emphasized where the "Yes" went later.

As another example of the rhythm of words, consider the name of James Paul McCartney. Do not imagine that it is a coincidence that it is an identical rhythm to the name Eleanor Rigby. It is intentional, no coincidence at all. **Paul wrote** that song back when he was having **his death premonitions.** At first, he used his own full name. Then Miss Daisy Hawkins replaced it, filling in the same rhythm. Until the name Eleanor Rigby occurred to him, it just wasn't right. Eleanor fit it perfectly and was like saying "Hello" to Eleanor Bron who was a co-star in *Help!* when all the death omens began.

Liverpool has St. Peter's Church; and there are people buried there in the yard. John told me that on days when their schools would be too boring, they would each ditch and meet in that churchyard. Now, it seems like an unlikely place for kids to hang out; but that made it all the better hideaway, a secret environment. They went there often. It was a quiet place where nobody ever bothered them as they lay on the grass near the headstones, talking about girls, or what they wanted to do with their lives, or inventing lyrics. Hanging out by the graves helped reinforce death as a reality, reminding them of it nearly every day. One of the graves John showed me there has the name, Eleanor Rigby.

Every now and then he returned to it after I joined him. **It was a secret** place that he went to for solace, a **way to reconnect with Paul.** They never

"Thursday Night Your Stockings Needed Mending."

knew the real Eleanor Rigby; but the name came to symbolize death to them both because all they knew of her was her tombstone. The next time you are in Liverpool, consider a stop at St. Peter's Church on Church Road. You can pay your respects to Paul at the gravesite of Eleanor Rigby, whom Paul chose to represent himself in the song. Meanwhile, if you have the desire to see it from your own home, I suppose you may also find it online.

Unless I cover it now while it relates to what I am writing about, I may not ever get around, round, round to discussing the rhythm of the words, "Dear Prudence" or "Sexy Sadie." Now, I will show you the bigger picture that comes by seeing how those rhythms relate to that of "Eleanor Rigby."

"Dear Prudence" is one of several songs where the identity of the subject woman had deliberately evolved from someone else. Likewise, John wrote "Sexy Sadie" as "Maharishi," as I have explained in another chapter. The name "Eleanor Rigby," as **I** said, had been "James Paul McCartney," which **was** replaced with "Miss Daisy Hawkins" for a time. As that song was first coming to life in him, the use of Paul's full formal name came to his mind as though he were hearing it in a somber eulogy, or perhaps

NOTE: With adjusted capitalization and punctuation, the gravestone says: In loving memory of my dear husband, John Rigby, who departed this life Oct 4th, 1915, aged 72 years. "At Rest." Also Frances, wife of the above, died April 3rd, 1928, aged 85 years. Also Doris W, daughter of F & E Rigby, died Dec 24th, 1927, aged 2 years & 3 months. Also Eleanor Rigby, the beloved wife of Thomas Woods, and granddaughter of the above, died 10th Oct 1939, aged 44 years. Asleep. Also Frances, daughter of the above, died 2nd November 1949, aged 71 years.

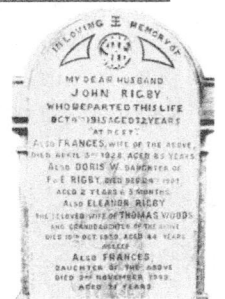

171

reading it in his obituary. The full legal name had a solemn terminal affect. It set the mood of gravely unhappy solitude. **The grave** loneliness of all the lonely people that he **would leave behind** was the driving force of **that sorrowful song.** It is how its profound **grief** was **set**. The morbid feelings evoked the **sad emotions that** sustained the song even after he **replaced "James Paul McCartney."**

Not all of the disguised identities were merely switched names. One of my own favorite concealed names is Donna. **Donna is** Italian for Lady. Paul's nickname, Macca, endures with me even now. I shortened **Macca's Lady**, or Macca's Donna, to "Madonna," like the Virgin, and went on to let her represent pretty much all women that struggle to feed their children. How do the ladies pay their bills? **Where do they find** so much money? **And, how does one handle** it? Eventually, you will appreciate **more** about "Lady Madonna." It is one of my favorite **Beatles** songs.

Notice any similarity between that melody and the tune of "Bad Penny Blues"**?** It was purely unintentional. It was not until later that I realized how that old recording had influenced me.

Prudence, as **I** said, was a name switch. Before our trip to **see** the Maharishi in India, John always yearned to see **Paul in dreams**, et cetera. That was a reasons **we went**. George, our guide, organized the trip partly **because of** our own desire for further **mystical awareness**, to unblock our minds **for access to Paul, and to get to know Krishna.** I may

"Thursday Night Your Stockings Needed Mending."

return to that point later to explain it better. Many of these chapters will overlap in order to explain the events in various contexts.

John first wrote this song seeking access to Paul. Yearning to commune with him, and stay connected, John wrote the simple-tuned line in India that later ended up as a natural precursor to "Dear Prudence." He sang, "McCartney, won't you come out to play?" So later, still in India, when some of us were bored out of our minds with much too much meditation, we became especially concerned about Prudence Farrow (Mia Farrow's younger sister) who became entranced to a point that she would not come out of her altered state. **John used his** lines about Paul and transformed them into a **song for Prudence** in order to lure her from her hut. John finished writing the rest of the song later, retaining the switch from "McCartney" to "Dear Prudence."

Although the Prudence Farrow incident made the song more about her than about Paul in the end, notice how easy it still is to see the rooted double meaning. In this simple little Paul and **Prudence** song, the publicly explained interpretation **is** only that we wanted Prudence to stop **meditating**, and to finally snap out of her trance. The underground meaning is that John was telling Paul to come out of his grave, to open up his eyes, and to look around. He wanted Paul to pick up his bass and really play it, not by me, but directly. "Come on, **Paul**," he thought, "keep playing, even if your music **is up in the clouds!**" The "Look around round round" backup represented the chanting

everyone was doing there, reminding us now of Prudence's meditation, but originally of John's **desires** to mystically call on, and somehow raise, **the deceased Paul McCartney.**

I should also mention here that John, when bored, liked to play with anagrams. Scrambling the letters of "Dear Prudence," he later came up with the words, "Run, Dead Creep."

In "Eleanor Rigby," Paul wrote about his own coming demise and of how sad and miserably lonely everyone would be without him. Mostly, he was emphasizing how sad his father would be having not believed him until it was too late to hang their name on another. Paul would be buried along with that name he received from his father, being named James after him. Paul imagined his father preparing everything for the funeral, but that no one could attend the service since all would be shrouded in restricted secrecy. He further imagined his father mending Paul's socks as a service, to his son, that had no point. Paul's father was always more inclined to mend socks than to replace them.

As Paul originally put **the song** together, as he conceived it, it **was about** how his father would inter James **Paul McCartney**, and have to deal with that loss alone. However, before it could be finished, new meanings developed. As another name-switch, Father McCartney grew into Father McKenzie, entertaining the empty church. James Paul McCartney became a lonely false-faced woman, dying to get on with her life, but never doing it, sweeping the rice away for others' weddings, but to her dying day never marrying. She dies there in

"Thursday Night Your Stockings Needed Mending."

the church where she had worked, and where her face was kept in a jar, preserved for the world. No one knows who she is when she is buried.

Eleanor/Paul dies unnoticed by the world. His father wipes the burial dirt from his hands as he walks from the grave. Very few people knew about it. "The undertaker drew a heavy sigh seeing no one else had come" ("Band on the Run"). As Paul foresaw it, his own **Father McCartney** would surely regret having **disbelieved him**, and interfering with Paul passing on his name. He prevented others from learning the truth until it was too late, when Paul and his name were dead and buried.

During a visit with Jim and Angie McCartney's family on Monday, 12 September 1966, when they all took me to Paul's St John's Wood home for documents, the thing that won them over was that I sang for them. Then they urged me to try on Paul's clothes. I objected, telling them that nothing of **Paul**'s **would** fit, but put on a shirt and pair of pants to **make the point.** He was inches shorter and had a smaller chest and waist. The cuffs went up my arms; the open pants stopped much too soon; and undershirts were out of the question. Nothing could button or snap. Paul was smaller than I thought. At last, Paul's dad, with teary-eyed earnestness, said, "You can wear his socks. I will mend them."

Can you imagine how I felt? They wanted me to fill Paul's shoes, and wanted to serve me for him, or do any last thing for Paul that they could, to have him continue on with me. Jim asked me to wear his underwear too. In my head, I thought, "Those most certainly won't fit me!" But I just smiled. Mike laughed as if he knew my thoughts, but nothing else was said. Three days later, Thursday evening, Paul's dad returned to Paul's house alone. He went through all of Paul's socks and mended as many of them as needed it. Paul sang, "**Look** at him working. Darning his socks in the night when **there's nobody there**." Or, as I wrote about it to Paul in "Lady Madonna," acknowledging the connection to "Eleanor Rigby," "Thursday night your stockings needed mending."

Paul predicted it. **I recognized its** fulfillment. Besides the "Eleanor Rigby" **socks line** showing the significance of his father's action, which I used, you should also know that in "Only A Northern Song" George got "there's nobody there" off the end of that same line of "Darning his socks in the night when there's nobody there."

Just as we were ready to leave Paul's house, Ruth (Paul's half-sister) excitedly telephoned Jane Asher. We waited for her at Paul's house. That first impression also went well. They had me sing again. Next, Jane and I went to her house. **She showed me** their guestroom that had become **Paul's own** for evenings that went on too late to drive **home.** We were there less than an hour before we went back again to Paul's. Jane wanted to collect her things.

The McCartneys had locked the door. Jane said that there was a ladder in the garden, and that she had used it before on one occasion. I followed her through the yard, retrieved the ladder, and set it up to the bathroom window. It was already open

"Thursday Night Your Stockings Needed Mending."

enough for Jane to reach her hands in to open it the rest of the way. **She climbed in** and then soon returned to the front door **to let me in.** That made her seem more fun than I had expected.

Having made it inside, **Jane** and I went through Paul's stuff. She took what she **wanted**. Since all of Paul's things were left to me, for **whatever** mattered to her, **I did** not stop her. Jane said she did not think **Paul** would mind her stealing a few memen**toes.** I didn't mind either. Paul and Jane loved each other very deeply. When I stepped into Paul's position, Jane and her kind family (just as Paul's) yielded **unreluctantly** to me taking over all of his roles. **Paul had** prepared them all well. I became Paul to **all of them**. They were instant family. To the utmost **amazed** astonishment of many onlooking insiders, there was an instant attraction between Jane and me. She was a bright, fun, and very beautiful entertainer, the perfect match for a Beatle. I did love Jane for quite a long time, it seemed. Paul still does.

20[22]

"Friday Night Arrives Without a Suitcase."

Brian's trip to Hamburg Tuesday was to work things out with John before presenting me, Paul's replacement, to him. Brian needed time with John without me there. He went hoping to have John invite me into the band the next day. Instead, Brian spent most of Wednesday helping John through his agony. **John had** not slept at all Monday night, and only a little **bit off** and on all throughout Tuesday night. His **grief** was intense. The best that Brian could do was to get John to the point of agreeing to meet with me on Friday. **That would give** John a little more time to clear **his head**. Brian returned to England Wednesday night with **the realization** that I might need more convincing than **John**.

Thursday, 15 September, Brian **met with me** again and explained John's collapsed mental state, as well as the itinerary for the next few days. As Brian outlined it for me, we would be meeting with John in the morning, and would be negotiating the new band deal over the weekend. Brian suggested then that I should be thinking about what I wanted out of the deal. **Brian** was a negotiator, a deal closer. He **prepared me well.** He reasoned that in John's distraught condition, he would agree to anything.

More than concerns about John going along with it, Brian's biggest anxiety was about me. If I got enough out of the Beatles deal, I would do whatever they wanted, and would keep the band together. All else meant little to Brian. Only his bottom line interested him at that point. His commissions would go on one way or another. His biggest obstacle, he thought, was selling me on it.

As I considered what I would want, I wrote it down, and asked, "What would be better than that?" I thought the best possible scenario would be for John to give me control of the band, to let me run it now however I thought best. I decided to begin at that point, and then make any concessions that we found necessary, perhaps eventually placing me on an even par with the rest of the band. With each refusal of my wish-list items, **I would ask** for something else to compensate **for** it. In that way, I would get more than **whatever** they had in mind. I had no idea how easy it **would be** for me to deal with John. I ended up with **more** than I could have expected.

As Brian mapped it all out for everyone, that night John and Neil took a train from Hamburg for yet another visit with Brian. This time, I would be there with him. We left London at the same hour to rendezvous in Paris. Our first stop was the hotel where we, along with John and Neil, would all be housed until Sunday. Then Brian had another stop to meet a courier who would bring the papers that evaded Brian Wednesday morning. I waited in the car. From there, we drove 30 minutes to a wrecking yard outside of Paris. We arrived at 9:00 and waited 50 minutes for a mechanic Mal found who could at length rebuild the Aston Martin. While in Hamburg on Wednesday, Brian had talked to John and Neil about the story of **Paul's** death being based on the destroyed car. It was **a dead giveaway.**

Until the reporter hassle on Monday, Brian had not considered that fans and reporters would quickly notice that the car—which still seemed new—was suddenly missing. Paul abruptly switching to my old car would prove that something was wrong. Brian contemplated it. Upon calculating odds of earning hundreds of thousand pounds sterling if he could maintain the band's appearances, he made calls to have either an identical car purchased, or that same one fully restored. **Mal Evans found** the gentleman who directed them to **the mechanic** we met near Paris. My new car was **in due course** fixed by this man.

My new car was exciting; but I made a point of not discussing it. I acted disinterested. What was years of my old income as a session musician was now an obvious business decision for Brian. My car, rebuilt as Paul's, was a very sporty DB6. It was finished in goodwood green with black leather seats, and had shiny chrome wheels. I had a reel-to-reel tape recorder installed in the dashboard to help me remember any spontaneously improvised songs. **It looked good** and became cost effective. Every **now and then**, while I was driving, I would sing a tune or lyrics into it, and would later on employ a guitar or piano to flush it out. It was a great

"Friday Night Arrives Without a Suitcase."

way to remember whatever **I thought** of. I recorded my first draft of "Hey Jude" **that** way while driving to see Julian. The built-in **tape recorder** also reminded me of who I **was. It** said I am Paul McCartney, a famous Beatle.

Now, after waiting almost an hour to talk to the man about repairing Paul's car, or (getting closer down to reality) about trading nearly all of it for nearly all of another, I was anxious to have the car rebuilt (or for Brian to have it done), but was late for our meeting with John. "She's Leaving Home" ends, almost, about that hour: "Friday morning at nine o'clock she is far away." **In fact,** Donna is buried, far away in that sense; but **I am literally** far away in France. The point there **in the song** is to understand that she is really gone. Nonetheless, there we were, "Waiting to keep the appointment she [or, I should say, Brian] made, Meeting a man from the motor trade" to trade Paul's car parts.

Looking at pictures of the demolished car, and further discussing the extent of the damage, he said that very little of the original could be salvaged, but that some of the parts could be used. After Brian's phone call to him days before, **he had** called around and found one like it with a **burned up** engine. That Aston Martin was in Nürburg. The oil plug came loose in a race. Although the engine quickly became utterly worthless, the **body** was fine. Between those cars and possibly **parts** from the factory, it would **look like Paul's original. The man** said it could legally be considered either car. "It **could be** the same car," he said, "but with mostly all **replaced** parts." It would be costly, but less than a new car. Whether Brian would pay for it himself or convince someone else to pick up that tab would all be decided the following day as our negotiations for replacing Paul progressed. Although I did really want the car, I played it cool because they felt it was urgent. I let it be their concern.

John and Neil met Brian and me at the Eiffel Tower at 11:00. We were very late. It seems like one in my position would be excited, nervous, and intimidated to meet John Lennon. Surprisingly, I hardly seemed worked up about it at all. John is the one that was a total mess. In my heart, I was nearly out of my mind, but kept my head for the negotiations, "playing hard to get" ("Here Today").

With all that had transpired, John was extremely depressed, and not at all enthusiastic about going on as if Paul were still with him. He said, "It's over. You don't know what it was like. The more that some devotees worshiped us, the more others wanted us crucified. **People shot at** our planes!"

"Don't turn **your back** on Paul," Brian said. "Not now! He worked this out!"

Everything John said suggested discouragement, depression, and growing apathy. It was only for Paul that he considered discussing the possibility of going on at all. John had had enough of making records and touring. With **Paul** dead, it seemed pointless. He said, "We **worked all those years,** each of us. For what? We **got all that fame, and** made all the money. **Now Paul isn't** with us to spend it. What good is it to **him** now? It's all for nothing, all for nowhere."

"Sounds hard to keep going, I know," I said, "but has Paul ever quit on you? I doubt it! Don't you ever quit on him. He worked it out to continue in me. Now that Paul has put me here in his position, don't let him down. Don't let me down. **Now I am** Paul McCartney." My boldness surprised everyone, myself included. As I said it, I felt **very powerful**. They felt that undeniable power in me **as well**. As I spoke, no one could deny what I was saying. I mean, they all knew **I was myself, William**; but none could deny that I was now **in Paul's place**. For John, I never needed any audition. It was not for anyone to decide if I should get the part at that point. Being beyond that, it was about comforting John and giving him the courage to keep the Beatles going without Paul. Brian, Neil, and I all gave John the encouragement he needed to go through with Paul's plan. We should have realized that it was beyond an issue that we needed to discuss. He would do it. How could he not? It was just hard for him to willingly take hold of the reigns at that point. That lack of leadership on his part was helpful.

Before he could express that concern, I relieved him of it. He said that neither he, nor George or Ringo, were ready to go back on tour again anytime soon. John said that even if they did, I could never impersonate **Paul** in front of a live audience. Even if Brian **taught me** Paul-mannerisms, our stage look and routine would be off. John, Paul, and George were all the same height, and had always stood next to each other, head to head. They all shared two microphones. Even if surgeries could make me look like Paul, **I could never be** shorter than I already was. **Paul**, at that age, could not instantly grow a few inches taller. Ten years earlier, they could have called it a growth spurt, but not at twenty-four years old. "Besides," he said, "our fans know our voices." It would not sound right.

I said we could give the world a new sound that no one could produce in live concerts. We could take sound samples and work them into our songs, along with large orchestrations, and some multi-tracked harmonies, instrumentations, and a barrage of sound that would provide a fuller resonance that is over and above anything that the Beatles, or anyone else for that matter, had ever done. With such a record, no one could possibly expect us to stand before live audiences with mere guitars and drums to exude the same multi-layered studio sound as our records. My Beatles direction excused the band from shows before live audiences; but, as John pointed out, would not keep us from doing press conferences that are always occurring, with album releases.

I said that after a few of our albums with our evolving photographs, **I would** only **have** to look like the current pictures of **Paul**, not like his old ones. Paul would become whoever I am. After a few albums with pictures **alter**ing our appearances, semblances of Paul would be in **me.** By the time we went on tour again, they would be expecting the Paul that they have all seen in current album pictures. Old differences will no longer matter.

"Ever play any instruments left-handed?" John said, "Whether or not we perform on stage, there is the matter of promotional pictures. Paul cannot suddenly play right-handed. Are you a lefty?"

"No," I said. "I play better right-handed, but can get better at it. Until then, we can flip the pictures.

"Friday Night Arrives Without a Suitcase."

Set the negative in upside-down. It will come out left-handed in the pictures until I can get it right." Everyone thought that would work for photographs of me without the others. All of us underestimated the speed at which I would learn to play the bass as Paul. It seemed impossible until it happened.

In the hours that followed, we discussed what we each **wanted** out of the deal. They wanted to turn me into **Paul**. We discussed the injections, surgeries, coaching, **and all that goes with it**—ups as well as downs. I said that as long as I had all the ups, I would not mind accepting the downs of Paul. They all looked at me as though they had already understood. They wanted to know what, for all of my extra sacrifices, I would want. It was a given that since I would play Paul McCartney's role, or, since I would become Paul, that I would have his house, his royalties, and all of his other assets.

"Right," I said, "but for losing my previous life, and my looks, and many of my friends, as well as many of my relations, I should get more. Paul never had to put his family outside of his magical circle!"

Everyone seemed to agree. I was thinking, "Stay cool, Bill! Don't blow this!" **I made** my case that with the change of music from what they had done that they could perform live, to **a new sound**, having new multi-tracked studio work, that they needed new leadership. I had much more studio experience than any of them did. I pointed out—from what Brian had told me—that they had recorded their songs and then left them in the hands of others to make it all work. The new band would evolve into a much higher quality sound. To that end, whatever amount of creative energy we would invest in our initial recordings, I would personally do months more work afterward, tinkering to develop our songs, going over them, making them perfect by adding layers of sound, tracks upon tracks.

John said, "We've actually got a good sound already, and have already done overdubbing."

Obviously, disrespecting the Beatles' sound was not going to win points with John. I realized that I had to show respect for his band to keep him open to dramatic changes, big enough expansions to require new leadership. I said, "Everyone knows that the Beatles are the best band in the world. There is no sound on this planet that measures up to it. Yes, you have a good sound already. **Let's take it** further!" I said I would take that sound **and make it better**. I told them I have an ear for **music**, and that they all underestimate their own potential. "**Yes,** you are great," I said, "but you can be **much greater!**" I explained how I would have fixed some of their songs. I surprised them by the many imperfections that I had noticed and could remember. Their acceptance of it all encouraged me to elaborate.

"Can you fix all of those sorts of things without doing more and more takes?" John asked.

"All that and much more," I said. "But more takes are also needed to get it right."

"Say you decide to fix everything, is that going to take all of us back in the studio? Or would it be enough for you and George Martin to go through it all and polish everything?"

"Friday Night Arrives Without a Suitcase."

"He can help too," I said, "but only if he can take direction. I mean, I can always use a talented hand. Everybody can give me ideas. **I would pinch** some ideas from him and from you and **the others,** but at last, it has to be up to me. **It is my band now.** We can all play it, talk about it, and knock around ideas; only someone has to make the final decisions. That would be me. For each album, **I will assign** the songs to be written. I will come up with **the album** themes or concepts for those **songs to fit**. I will tell you where we are going with **each album**, and have each of us come up with so many songs for it."

"Hell," Brian said, "they've never had concept albums before. No one has."

"I am changing that now," I said. "We are a new band, starting today."

"So," John said, "you are going to be the little dictator telling us how to write our songs now?"

"See it my way," I said. "You will still have all the same writing brilliance that you have always had. The only difference is that now each album itself will have an entity. You have given life to individual songs. You will still do that. Except that now we will also all breathe life into each album. Record albums until now have only been collections of songs. Now the new collections will have life in themselves. Each song will have its own layers of meaning, but will collectively suggest something as well." Those words just came to me. They were not premeditated.

"Now you say it's your band?" John asked.

I was not sure how to read his question. I said, "Don't see it as me trying to take your band from you. If you have more to offer, tell us all about it. Tell us about your leadership. It has been your band from the beginning, but what have you done?"

"Haven't you read the papers?" John asked.

"I am asking what you do as a leader," I said.

"Everybody knows what to do," John said. "They don't need a boss. We're a band, not a factory."

"Bands are businesses," I said. "Strong leaders with clear creative vision **bring greater success**. I am the one with the vision **for our new direction**. I am the one to work week after week, day and night, if I have to, in order to get every song just right. I will work a hundred times harder than you do. I will do it all without getting a dime more than you. But if you think I will give up everything instantly to play this role, I had better be free to play it like it has never been played before! I am not taking on this role just to write silly love songs!

NOTE: Teddy Adorno applied his musical genius to his ambition for global consciousness transformation. He fully supported the Stanford Research Center plan to change society through music. Their plan, enlarged upon by others, was to cast a net wide enough for the entire rising generation, and as many others as would come. They would start with silly love songs, since that was popular at that time, and because it would hook the simplest of listeners.

Once hooked, the ever-increasing fanbase would be guided through a maturation process, turning their music against outmoded thinking in favor of a revolution of awakened consciousness. Along with oppressive institutions, individual personalities would be dissolved globally, and rebuilt transformed.

Teddy claimed to despise his own shallow music except as a means to the greater transformative end. William, like Teddy, understood that the early Beatles music was trite in order to capture the youngest generation, and that it was evolving to be much deeper.

"Teddy boy" objected to William's comedic work, which did not teach people to "be good." However, Bill and Ted shared the desire to create philosophically interesting music that would trigger introspection. William joined the band to create meaningful and provocative music that would change how people think. He did not join to write more silly love songs.

"Friday Night Arrives Without a Suitcase."

Working together, we will revolutionize rock, and will take the Beatles to heights never imagined before! That's exactly what **I'll** do if it's my band. All that I have to offer will **lead this band** on into immortal greatness. **When we are all dead**, our songs will continue on **for generations**."

John shook his head and waited for the words. "From the way you are talking, I would swear you are campaigning, or maybe being inaugurated, as our new totalitarian leader. This talk of glory sounds like you are laying the foundation of the Fourth Reich! If your ego is so enormous that you think calling the Beatles your own band matters, then **Paul is** not in you. My friends never sought control **of my band.** Paul's ego did not need it."

"And yours does? Is that the problem? I am offering my all, sacrificing my all, willing to work until everything we do is perfect, offering to take this band far beyond the heights where it plateaued, leading this band as only I can. Is your ego so inflated that you would interfere just to be able to say that it is still your band? Whom would you tell? Why does that matter? Is your ego bigger than the band?"

Alarmed at the sudden tension, seeing where we were taking it, Brian immediately jumped in and made the suggestion that we all sleep on it that night and discuss it further the next day.

Prior to that meeting, upon arriving by train, John and Neil had checked in at our same hotel. At that hour early in the morning, there were no vacancies, but rooms would be ready in a few hours. Until then, their suitcases were placed in a back room along with others waiting to receive rooms later as they became available. John noticed people pointing in recognition, but no fans approached him.

It had been another hard day for John. After our meeting, Brian and John visited the Louvre Museum, taking in the splendor. As they walked about, Brian tried to comfort him. Brian acknowledged that I did not make a fine first impression on John, but that the McCartneys had accepted me fully. They said that already everything that was Paul's is mine. They have chosen me to be Paul for them. That made it a done deal. John had let **Paul** join the band. Paul let in George. George let in Ringo. Ringo, you might think by the pattern, **let me in**; but it was Brian Epstein, as recommended by his brother.

Back at their hotel that night, John's suitcases had all been stolen, presumably by someone there after his own bags, but recognizing John's. John's bags did not have his name on the tags, but were likely noticed when he dropped them off. He was always noticed. Most of what **John** lost, he had bought days before in Hamburg. When he **arrived** at the hotel Friday night, John was **without a suitcase.**

21[(23)]

"Saturday Night's Alright."

The next day, Saturday, I skipped in "Lady Madonna," not having any useful material for it. However, **I choose** to include it in the book, and to borrow **a phrase from** one of Elton John's songs. I always appreciated **Elton**'s piano playing and his writing with Bernie Taupin. Elton and I are really not as close as we probably would have been if he were not already such a close friend of John. Only kidding! Actually, Elton, I've told my people to call your people for another benefit concert. It will be a show to remember. So, Elton, my good friend, let's make it happen again!

Saturday was all right. John was in a startlingly resolved mood. Overnight, he decided that what I asked for was reasonable enough. **He determined** that he did not need to call the shots. It did not make that much difference to him whether **it was his band** or not. He started it. **That meant something to him.**

Under other circumstances, it would have meant more to him to stay at the helm. Yet, now that the

Revolver had come as Paul predicted, he revolved out, and I revolved in. **It was Paul who set it up**. He did it before, **and fully attracted it** according to his expectations. When John finally accepted it, he accepted me. He saw how fate dictated that the band should be mine now, and chose to accept it.

You know John struggled with it for untold hours. However, by the time I saw him on Saturday, he did not show any signs of resentment. I had anxiety about seeing him again. I had really doubted myself. I feared that John would call the whole thing off and end the band. Brian feared that too. However, thank goodness, he agreed, and tried to accept it all as a fait accompli.

Having that change of heart, John did not want to argue or belabor any negotiations. In effect, John told Brian to work out the details and to write it up. Out of love for **Paul**, John determined to do what seemed expedient. I was **surprised** and intimidated by what amounted to spiritual maturity in **John**. He accepted everything in the spirit of love for Paul.

John spent the next hours with Neil and me at the Louvre Museum. As we walked, John talked about Carroll's *Through the Looking-Glass,* and, other than replacing Paul, about most any topic at all. I learned of his creativity beyond music, and that we shared interests in art, and in expressing meanings in layers. I realized that John could be a most fascinating guy to work with. We would learn a lot from each other—and it would be fun.

Hearing John's reasonableness and recognizing his extended friendship, I was glad that I too had told Brian to work out the details and to let us know how everything settled. I had lost the drive for me to win all the chips on the table. I had already gotten more than my fair share. I felt a bit like **a robber**. I could not press for anything else when I **saw that** John would not defend himself. I could not do it. Now, with that out of the way, I felt his **friendship**, which was something I had not before given much thought to, and which was worth more than anything that could be bargained for. For the rest of that day, he seemed completely openhearted to me, even after meeting my unreasonable demands.

As time went on, over challenging years, John and I generally worked very well together. We had tiffs from time to time, mostly from me relentlessly pushing the band forward with my perfectionistic idealism. I admit it. I was a bit of a workaholic. However, that is what I signed up to do. I was doing my side of the deal. For *Sgt. Pepper's,* our first album together, **I also felt** a great need to prove my own worth to **the band**, to the world, and mostly to myself. I **had to show** everyone that I was worth having the role of **Paul, that I deserved** all of the good things I was inheriting from **him**. It was also a way for me to deal with the hard loneliness. I needed to keep busy, and to create Beatles products that were great enough to justify what seemed like an insane level of commitment to do Paul well.

I had to give myself reasons to justify deeply **hidden levels of** self-betrayal. I had to eventually deal with **my** self-loathing that made me willing to drop my **own identity**, giving up who I was, in order **to be someone else**—some dead guy I did not even know. I had to win at all costs.

Our time at the Louvre Museum changed my perceptions of John entirely. Before, I had supposed that we were merely there to pass our time while Brian readied the papers; but it was more important. Having that time with John was healing. He let me into his private world.

Ending the Paul taboo, Neil said, "How does it feel to be one of the beautiful people? You're a rich man now!" Years later, while John and I were each working on the *Yellow Submarine* soundtrack, that question from Neil reverberated in John's brain until it grew into a little song. He sang it to me. I had remembered the same conversation. **I liked** it and sang along, then wrote another song, **this one** around Neil's line about being rich. Although we first wrote and recorded them as separate songs, nesting one into the other made "Baby You're a Rich Man" complete. Earlier, the combined title had touted his side of the song. It was called, "One of the Beautiful People." However, I felt that my own line had stronger emphasis, making it the better title. While still walking around the Louvre, after Neil asked about it, I abruptly realized, "Oh my hell, I'm that famous guy! One of the beautiful people!"

Typical of John's humor with my material, at the end of the song, he added a joke about Brian, messing with the lyrics. Then, with twisted lyrics at the end, he dedicated it all to Brian. Where we had rehearsed singing, "Baby you're a rich man too," John sang, "Baby, you're a rich fag Jew." That slur was received well by Brian in the humor that it was intended. We were close enough to Brian to not let such things divide us. His sexual orientation and Semitism were not John's concerns per se, but by including that reference to both, it acknowledged attributes that **John knew** were significant issues or notions for **Brian's** own mindset. John was neither ridiculing Brian's **wealth** or homosexuality, nor criticizing his **race and religion**, but cleverly used the word pattern to greet our good friend.

One of Rex Makin's associates had a law office in Paris. While the rest of us were walking about the Louvre, Brian was at that office on the phone with Rex Makin and the French attorney, working in each needed detail, bouncing around various concerns. Besides their professional relationship, those lawyers had a long-time friendship and mutual trust—as did also Brian and Rex. They all worked well as one.

Once finished with the phone conference, the French attorney completed the long document and was back on the phone again with Rex, reading the latest version and discussing further concerns.

During our meeting that followed, the solemnity of the legal contract brought what we were doing into sharper focus. Neil's words kept echoing in my

Billy's Back!

brain. Now I am one of the beautiful people. In a day's negotiation, **I'm suddenly** someone else. Now I'm beautiful. I'm **a rich man** too. It was true. Yet, I was still the exact same man I had always been. Now **I was** Paul, "the cute Beatle," and was **obligated to look like him**. The series of treatments would start **almost immediately.** They said it was urgent that I look the part before needing to make any appearances. It was a matter of time before everyone would want proof that Paul was still with them. I had to live that absolute proof.

Now I have no regrets. At the time, however, the sense of loss was staggering beyond words. We all joked about it. Yet, it was worse than any joke could express. Crying could never fully convey it either. Out of my desperation to say, "Look at me! I am suffering," **I created** some of my best material for you all to take **a closer** look. I said in countless ways, "Paul is **dead**. I am not him." My courage to use conspicuous "**Paul** is Dead" clues increased

NOTE: The media promoted the idea of Paul as "the cute Beatle." Without that manipulation, the others of the group may have each seemed cuter to more fans. However, for the globalists to use a band to change the world, they sought for a face that could symbolically feature the all-seeing-eye. Paul's high eyebrow (inherited from his father) made him their best contender.

A few others of that inner circle, also impressed by Paul's resemblance to William, considered the possibility and implications of Paul eventually being replaced by the magician's son. For four years, they pushed for that prospect.

For the eye symbolism intended by all, and for added significance if they were to choose to replace Paul with William (as pushed for by a few), the elite demanded that the media not only make the Beatles the brightest stars in the heavens, but that they single out Paul for his looks, making his symbolic right eye a subconscious point of adoration when fans gazed at their idol's face.

To help elevate the Beatles, the elite ordered George Martin to not only contract with the Beatles and to produce their work, but to use his own musical skills (as if performed by them) to present the Beatles' music as perfectly as possible. All other bands would be as they are. The Beatles would be perfect.

when John and non-Beatles did it. When I first heard the Rolling Stones and Donovan work Paul into their songs, after John (at my suggestion) had enmeshed Paul into "Strawberry Fields," I thought, "If they can do it, so can I!" All of my albums from *Pepper's* on have clues or references to Paul. It is a rule that **I made** for myself. For any album, if you listen for **them**, they are not hard to find. You just need to **pay attention.**

As many years and decades have come and gone, my thoughts of Neil's question have still evolved. Years do that. It was an exciting thought; but I also sensed some resentment. As an outsider, he was not including himself in that class of people. **I** was a working class stiff like him; but now, with a **deal**, had finally arrived. I went from being a nobody like **him** to being a somebody. I was such a nowhere man that I was not recognized in my new role. If Paul had taken my place, people would have noticed.

At least that is what I thought. I was mistaken about that as well. Proving my wrong thinking, I made many public appearances, and was hardly ever recognized. **Some** of my appearances were in front of large **audiences**. People usually see what they expect to **see.** Until someone with an authentically new view can point an honest finger and say, "The emperor is naked," no one can see it. However, once enough people open their eyes to it, they create a critical mass that reveals the bare-naked truth as it is. One voice ignites others, who then open the eyes of thousands and millions, and on until that awareness fills the world with illumination. My story is only a key to open your mind to that bigger worldview.

This book also benefits me. Creating that critical mass that acknowledges my work gives me peace. I have no intention of relinquishing my name of Sir James Paul McCartney. That iconic stage-name was earned. **I own** it. I have been Paul McCartney since 1966. My children were named McCartney. I have been **Paul** far longer than Paul was Paul. The Paul **McCartney** persona is much more me now than the earlier Paul. Whenever the world thinks of Paul McCartney, they nearly always think of me, not my antecedent. When Paul played this role, he did not have the depth to create his most meaningful music

NOTE: However astonishing it may be that Paul was replaced, the bigger story is that the substitution occurred as part of a global mind-control operation by Tavistock, and that this project (and many others) succeeded (and are succeeding) through access to the Committee of 300's resources. Most notably, it required the cooperation of national governments and the media that are mostly controlled by the same people at the top of the pyramid.

Replacing Paul McCartney—when he was the most adored celebrity on the planet—was only possible by the powerful central global organization that could direct national governments to stay out of the way while the world's largest newspapers, television channels, radio stations, and the most influential players in the entertainment industry, perpetuated the myth first of all that Paul's public persona was real, and secondly, that his part is still being played by the same man.

As brazen as it was to create such a fictional superstar in the first place, and then to switch him out for another actor, it was neither the beginning, nor the pinnacle, nor the end of their global mind-control. By controlling public perception and opinion through the media's presentation of false flags and other fake news, and by creating (or taking control of) media platforms (such as YouTube and Facebook) that repress alternate perspectives, the Committee of 300 still controls public perception. When the Committee of 300 seeks to frighten the world into war, totalitarianism, gun control, vaccines, or any viewpoint, opposing views are blocked and labeled as subversive unsafe misinformation that violates community standards.

To fully comprehend Paul's replacement is to know that we are still being manipulated by governments, and by the media, who act under the direction of globalists with their own agenda. William says, "My story is only a key to open your mind to that bigger worldview." If this book is ever discredited for damage control, it will be because William began to reach that goal too soon.

until he began dreaming of me. **In a cosmic way,** that I do not fully understand, **I influenced him** then. We are all connected to each **other**. Whether we do it intentionally or not, all **energy fields** influence other fields, that then **influence others.**

Think of your favorite Paul songs. Most are usually from me—or from Paul when he was obsessing about me coming to take his place.

Until I realized how we are all connected as one on the same universal grid of intelligence—the vast, loving, and glorious stuff of which we are made—I could not comprehend how I could have influenced Paul. Now I see that the universe, or God, or fate, or this infinite grid, or whatever **you want** to call it, or envision it as, by giving **Paul** all of those dreams of me, it raised his **consciousness**, deepened his depth of feeling, and broadened his musical abilities.

Waking up with the tune of "Yesterday," and plugging in his concerns about me replacing him, changed him. **He was** never again quite the same. It led him to **more** instrumental quality mixed in with his **concealed** fears of death, such as are found in his "Eleanor Rigby." The universe, or the Divine, or whatever you call it, transformed him into me at the same time it was grooming me to become him. Then, when **Paul** did cross over, a core part of him **continued through me**, furthering our cosmic connection. We have been merging since before his exit. **I was** a session musician. Upon dreaming of me, **Paul** began writing far beyond Beatles talent, **needing** session musicians. Paul's awareness of **my coming** began his transition to me.

Years of reflecting on Neil's question supported my belief that "**Love is all you need.**" That original idea of **Paul's love gave us** our view of the universal energy field as **God's** love. We were under the influence of **divine love.** I could not have become Paul if I had not loved him first. Fate always acts according to love. You can say divine love emanating from the universe set me up to replace Paul for the world's greater good.

There is no meaningful difference between us. Each of us has a part to play. If I can be one of the beautiful people, then so can you. Hear what **I am** telling you. You do not need Paul to be **greater.** This position makes me no greater now **than any** other. As I play my roles, or you play yours, all that matters is **how we love**. That is the only objective that **makes people beautiful.** So, how do *you* feel being one of the beautiful people?

22⁽²⁴⁾

"Sunday Morning Creeping Like a Nun."

I left with Brian for the North of France after dinner Saturday evening. After a quiet contemplative six-hour drive, we reached the Grosse Horloge, where Mal Evans stood waiting below the clock, at one in the morning. From there, the three of us left in Mal's car. Heading to the nearest tavern, Mal went out of the way to show us some Rouen sights. One was the Church of St. Ouen. Mal explained that it was built as the abbey church of Saint Ouen for the Benedictine Order. We sat in the car a half minute looking at the outside of the building as Mal described how it looked inside. Brian also related a story about tunnels below the church. Mal interrupted, "Wait a minute! **Look there!**"

Even through the dark, **we could see** three nuns by a bush on the side of **the church**. It was not light enough to see what they **were doing**, but Brian said that they were breaking **their curfew.** One of the nuns had a flashlight. The others held shovels. It gave us cause to wonder, but nothing for any of us to be sure of. It was a memorable moment, an amusement to remember about the trip.

Billy's Back!

Next, we went to the tavern. Mal had received Paul's checkbook and various other belongings that seemed irrelevant until Brian and the lawyers created my contract. As per the lengthy Beatle agreement, I was required to sign many checks, most of which were postdated. Brian carefully filled in the details. I signed check after check.

Before doing so, they gave me the time I needed to practice Paul's signature. His left-handedness made signing his name awkward at first; but I soon had it down and got the work done. Paul intended to use each of those checks as inheritances, and to buy silence. Mostly, Brian used a list of names and amounts that Paul had written on a bus in America. Having written that will appendage by hand, and having signed it before a witness, it was uncontested.

Ordinarily, Paul would have formalized it with legal assistance. This time, however, between all the venues on their American tour, practically every hour of **Paul's** time for personal matters was either **on a bus** or on a train. With Rex Makin not being **with them** to give legal help, Paul wrote his list of whom to pay on his own. It was conditional. Each recipient would receive an inheritance based on specific helps to the replacement. Paul intended each check to help me to perpetuate his own reputation.

NOTE: At that time, William used his right hand to practice Paul's signature, and then signed those documents with his right hand. Soon after, he began practicing Paul's signature with his left hand in order to give autographs. However, even left handed, he never did get the slant right. Soon, he let Paul's autograph evolve to a left-handed version of his own natural handwriting. Over the years, it evolved to his current autograph, in which fans have recognized his obelisk.

"Sunday Morning Creeping Like a Nun."

I saw the list at the time, but did not know most of the people. Later, when I did get to know them, seeing that list again could have been useful. Most of the checks were modest. As **Paul explained it**, I had to have the bulk of it **in order to carry on as** though I were **he. Paul thought it out** carefully. Giving too much, or **giving it** away to heirs all at once, would have blown the **cover.**

Nearly everyone whom Paul paid would have remained silent anyway out of respect for him. Everyone who was close to him had already talked to him about it. Those who were most privy to his death dreams were generally also asked what they would do to help make his plan a reality. "What could you do to make it work?" he had asked more than a few of them. He wrote their answers, and had them compiled on the payment list. Those who would do more got more.

Ending our visit, a large American in the tavern shouted, "Look at the time!" Brian stood abruptly. Counting hours, he said it would be 7:00 before he made it back to Paris. He rushed us to Mal's car, keeping the remaining business for another day. After dropping Brian off at his car, Mal and I went straight to the Bordeaux Airport. That morning, 18 September, one week after Paul's demise, Mal and I flew back to London.

NOTE: William is probably correct that loved ones remained silent out of respect for Paul. Additionally, insiders understood that blowing the whistle would make them outsiders, or worse. In light of who was required to pull off such a switch, interfering could be dangerous. Well before advancing to illuminated levels, initiates swear, on penalty of death, to use their means to support the organization, and to never speak against them. *The Memoirs* endeavor to objectively reveal what they do without judging or condemning.

I can scarcely imagine such a pivotal weekend. I left London as Bill, hoping John Lennon would give me a good deal. **I returned as Paul,** now over everyone in the band. **It was so surreal that** I could hardly comprehend it. **The Beatles were my band!** What a dream come true that shift was! I not only took over Paul's roles as co-lead songwriter and as a bass player, but also took over John's position as the band's leader. The pressure was on to deliver the acclaim that I had promised.

Thrilled to work with George Martin, my first concern was to meet with him to discuss my plans. I wanted to go over it with him first in order to use his kind influence with the others. He would also help set reasonable schedules and expectations. We met at Abbey Road studio.

I did not have time scheduled there, which was necessary to use their facility. Nevertheless, I was a high priority for George. He voluntarily arranged to do a favor for another band in exchange for an hour of their timeslot.

Very soon, George and I were together in a mixing room trying multi-tracking experiments. I told him what **I** had in mind with our first album, and was **delighted** by his valuable insights and suggestions. **George** and I hit it off right away. As it turned out, he and I had more in common than I had with my Beatles bandmates. **He** became a close friend. As we **worked on our albums**, the time I spent with George Martin **in the studio** was far greater than my time with the others. He was an

"Sunday Morning Creeping Like a Nun."

extremely important talent for the band from the start; but it was not until we teamed together that he did his most extraordinary work, which mostly went unrecognized. He and I understood each other.

There we were, creeping about that Abbey Road studio, on the same day that I had been in France, having amusement from the nuns creeping about their abbey. "Sunday morning creeping like a nun" evokes Abbey memories of both locations that day, Sunday, 18 September. I had not yet begun the actual work that **I signed to** do, but did make an important **connect**ion **with** George Martin, which benefited **the band** to no end. I could not have reached my Paul excellence without him.

NOTE: Although *Sgt. Pepper's* was William's baby, John and George each provided excellent material. Their talents, along with that of Ringo and many session musicians, contributed immeasurably to the whole. William's work in writing, singing, playing various instruments, and directing much of the project was helped immeasurably by the extraordinary work of Producer George Martin, and of Engineer Geoff Emerick.

In *the Memoirs,* William refers to George Martin's brilliant contributions, but not to Geoff Emerick's. When questioned about that glaring omission, William indicated that the material given to the Encoder had references to Geoff and others that the Encoder excluded at his own discretion. "When counting lines and letters," William said, "a lot gets left out."

Like William, Geoff was a prodigious talent from a highly connected family. EMI hired him at 15 years old to help create the Beatles sound. He would also work with other artists whenever no Beatles work was in progress. His EMI employment began the day before the Beatles recorded their first hits. From the band's start, Geoff's training began as Norman Smith's assistant engineer, and then became the Beatles' chief engineer as of their Revolver album—already pioneering innovative recording techniques before taking the band to the *Sgt. Pepper's* level.

With the creation of Apple Corps in 1969, William persuaded Geoff to leave EMI to direct the building of Apple Studio, and then to continue as their engineer. When William dissolved the Beatles the following year, Geoff continued to work as William's engineer. Handlers had groomed Geoff to be "Paul's guy" from the start.

Geoff's exceptional work was recognized with a Technical Grammy Award (2003), and with three Grammy Awards for Best Engineered Recording (Non-Classical) for the Beatles albums, *Sgt. Pepper's Lonely Hearts Club Band*, and *Abbey Road,* and for the Paul McCartney and Wings album, *Band on the Run.* He has also received four other Grammy nominations.

Before going back to their small roles in *How I Won the War*, John and Neil were both trying to put everything into perspective, but could not. It was all too much. We were all dazed and overwhelmed; yet, John knew he would have quiet downtime ahead of him in Spain to sort through it all.

John and Neil flew to Spain the day I returned to London. The *How I Won the War* movie set before our visit was in a NATO tank range in Celle, a small town near Hanover. However, by Sunday, they both had to be in Carboneras in southern Spain, across the Mediterranean from Algeria. That site simulated a North African desert. That was the main movie set.

I was eager to start writing and recording songs. For John's peace of mind, however, my work on our next record was not to begin until he returned to London. He was emphatic about it. **He did not want** it to start without him there, with **me running the** entire show. He said, "It is, after all, **Beatles music** we're making." Yet, although a part of me seriously wanted to get right to work, and another part of me needed to slow down and ease into this new role. The pressure on me was intense. For me, the first task was to be my transformation. I wanted to work on music, but had to set my primary focus on being **Paul**. My goal **was to** become Paul McCartney by October's end. John would **return** from Spain on 7 November. By then, Paul would work **through me**.

At sunset Sunday evening, 18 September, Brian brought bandmates, George Harrison and Ringo Starr (Richard Starkey) over to meet me. Brian had informed them both days before, but did not have them meet me before John. We followed my uncle's strategic plan. First Jim McCartney's family would

"Sunday Morning Creeping Like a Nun."

have to approve of me. That way John would not have to make such a difficult decision. He would go along with what the family had already decided. Then, having signed the agreement, I was ready to be presented to George and Ringo, not to discuss and approve of me, or maybe vote against their new band member, but to learn of what has already occurred with John's consent.

I was delighted to meet them. They were both curious about me, to be certain, but were completely gentle, not wanting to make me feel as though they were interrogating me. Brian agreed that it was not his place to deal with informing them of the band's new direction and leadership. He had wisely decided to save that for John. I agreed. There was no reason to drop that on them so soon in the game. We all wanted the first visit to be as pleasant as possible—and it really was very enjoyable for all of us. We entertained each other with conversation for about an hour. Soon after Brian left, the fun began. The night turned jovial as I sat down at the piano, and George picked up a guitar. We all sang some of their hits and other popular songs.

They taught me a song of **Paul's** they had played on nights when their **amplifiers broke down** in the Cavern Club or Hamburg, usually **from blown fuses.** Needing minor improvements **here and there**, I touched it up, and sang the song with a different style.

NOTE: Some fans believe that the Beatles were so democratic that they made decisions by the unanimous vote of all four bandmembers. Such idealistic equality brings to mind the romanticized Knights of the Round Table. William and others have supported this narrative because of its appeal.

In reality, until William joined and could lighten George Martin's work directly with the remaining members, Martin called the shots for the big decisions. John and Paul were next in line for decision-making. William decided most significant issues by 1967.

We had such a good time with it, we all looked forward to sharing my new version with John.

Eleven weeks later, on 6 December, it became the first song that my new band recorded with me singing lead as **Paul** McCartney. The song, "When I'm Sixty-Four," **had a melancholy** overtone, being about Paul wondering what his **life** would be like at that far distant age, nearing retirement, which he never reached. Paul died forty years too soon. In Paul's memory, we were all glad to include that good old song of Paul's on our *Sgt. Pepper's* album. It was not about his death, but recalled his life.

George marveled at my ability to step into, and so readily improve upon, the role of Paul. He had entertained the idea of going to India in search of further enlightenment. Now that idea became his obsession. He realized that **Paul had received** many accurate messages of **his own demise** through repeated dreams and other ongoing **omens**, and that he prepared my own smooth transition to cover him. George wanted to commune with Paul, spirit to spirit. He quickly sensed it in me—and sought to enter that numinous state himself—the presence of Paul. It became an obsession for him and John.

Feeling that the answers he sought were in India, **George** flew there as soon as he could arrange it. He **let us know** Sunday that we would not see him again until he returned from India. Since I prepared to infuse **ethereal dimensions of his beloved** Paul into the **Beatle beast**, George also prepared to receive Paul's whisperings into our new music.

23[(25)]

"Monday's Child Has Learned to Tie His Bootlace."

"Monday's child is fair of face." That line is where I found the phrase, "Monday's Child." The old Mother Goose rhyme describes children born on each day of the week. My allusion to the rhyme is not about when the child is born, but that this child has the fair face. By the time my song came out, I donned the fair face of Paul, "the cute Beatle." I am "Monday's Child" in "Lady Madonna."

Although I brought great musical talent to the band, it was not what John really wanted from me. Yes, **I was gifted**; but all he wanted was Paul's fair face. **The Beatles** was such a great name brand that song **quality mattered** less than the band name. Big brands sell inferior products easier than small brands can sell quality. In "I've Got a Feeling," I sing, "All these years I've been wandering around wondering how come nobody told me. All that I was looking for was somebody who looked like you." Being as if Paul and I were one, but talking to each other, Paul was looking for someone who looked like him, or like me, depending on which aspect of me is doing the singing.

During much of the last year of his life, he had wandered, looking for me. Then **I** wandered around in the mistaken idea that they **wanted** my raised musical quality. While everyone was **more** than satisfied with my musical abilities, **for** which I labored far more than anyone to get it **all** right, I felt frustrated by the realization that **the others** only wanted me to look the part.

As most people would guess if they stopped to think about it, the song that those lines came from, "I've Got a Feeling," began as two songs. We each sang the part we wrote. John wrote his song in response to mine. It is like a conversation. We had not developed either song well enough to stand on its own; but they worked well together—as did John and **I generally**. My part got the song title because it **felt stronger**, more dynamic, and more likely to be remembered. **By the time** we wrote the song, a few days into 1969, **I had** had almost twenty-eight months of **that frustration.** I was complaining about that in my song, but particularly about that past year. We all knew how our frustrations were compromising the band's coherence. By 1969, it was tearing us apart.

Even though my almost screamed part explicitly explains the feelings I was singing about, most fans never gave it much thought, never connected it to the rest of the song. I interrupt the music to interject an outburst of emotion, to express my feelings. I sing that "**I've got a feeling**, a feeling deep inside." What did **you think** the feeling was? Most fans thought **it was a love song** because that is all they expected to hear. I sang that it is "a feeling I can't hide." I suppose **I hid** it a bit better than I had planned. **The ongoing feeling of frustration** grew. I wanted un**paralleled** Beatles quality, but always had to deal **with the apathy of the others.** They complained that my standards were too high. That feeling that "everybody knows," or at least that everyone in **Paul's** old circle knew, kept me on my **toes**. My quality remained; but I complained that their **lack** of support made it a hard year.

As **one** would expect from John, he agreed that it was a hard year, but also a good one. **It was** the kind of year that had it all. It was not just **hard** for me. It was hard for all of us, and good **for all of us.** It was good and hard. "Everybody had **a hard year**. Everybody had a good time." I felt **that I absolutely** needed to put my foot down **with some issues**. Yet, "Everybody put their foot down." It **was hard**, but a good dream for all of us. That was the brilliantly musical way that John answered my complaint about my feelings of frustration; and **he was** right. It was like a round where I kept **going on** singing my way, yet he kept answering **in his same way.** As with the song, we went on without ever settling the matter, forever stuck in our own perspectives. Both sides were right, but without empathy.

Each of us had our own challenges. Although John was right about that, generally dismissing my emotions that way did not settle anything. It did not reduce their apathy, instill greater cooperation, or lighten the inequality between us. On the one hand, it was my band now, and up to me to drive it into our new direction. On the other hand, John treated me as an upstart even though I was clearly no novice to the industry. I did most of the work and got great global acclaim for it; but the gratitude I got from the band did not motivate cooperation. They talked of love, but withheld it. While I was sacrificing everything, they were more prone to scoff than to show loving appreciative support.

Perhaps some of you remember the old song, "One-sided Love Affair." **That song about** unequal love sometimes played in **my brain** back then as I felt that frustration. It **was written back in 1955** by a young aspiring artist. When it was recorded the next year by the king, Elvis Presley, that success ignited the writer with a determination to make a life-long career of writing popular music, and not only writing it, but also of recording it. It gave him modest but encouraging royalties, and set the course for his life. At that young age, he did not know how to make a record himself, but started life at the top by sending it to the top recording artist at that time. What became of this talented writing artist? Who was this aspiring musically-minded boy? **It** was Willi**am** "**Bill**" Campbell. I liked the name.

Rightly, the song was of an unrequited childhood infatuation; but you can apply to any type of love. "If you want to be loved, Baby, you've got to love me, too." That was the main message of the song. Feeling as if it is all giving without getting is vexing, but **only** to the immature mind. We can learn that it is not **great** love only to love those who love us. If my **love is** conditional, then it is not really love **enough** to call it love. If I condition love on getting **love** or something else out of it, it is plain and simply a bargaining chip. Still, that is where I was in the sixties with my unfulfilled expectations from my three bandmates. I felt that **I was** giving my all, and not getting enough respect **for** it.

Having discussed the "**fair** of face" bit, and the ongoing frustrations that **play**ed out with seemingly everybody merely wanting my fair face—which, by the way, is about Paul's grave face when I later sing, "My Brave, My Brave, My Brave Face" ("My Brave Face")—we are almost ready to discuss the outcome of what that fair-faced child has learned to do. However, first consider what a brave face I needed and acquired for this Paul role. Consider how brave it was of me to have my face permanently gone for this role without any guarantees that it would work out, and to live Paul's lifestyle to which I was entirely unaccustomed. It took courage.

"Monday's child has learned to tie his bootlace." The boots bit of this line refers to "Beatle boots." After John and Paul's stint in Hamburg, they saw Chelsea boots on display in Anello & Davide, a London footwear company, and thought they would add it to their new attire. John already wore boots, which sometimes came in handy as weapons in night brawls in Hamburg. He also used them to kick intruders off the nightclub stage. Now with their new suits and a cleaned-up image, Chelsea boots would add a touch of class. **This** was all back in October 1961, before they **made it big.** With the addition of Cuban heels to make them look a little taller, they ordered these boots for the band.

When the group made it big, still wearing these boots, their Beatle Boots became the fab fashion in America, Great Britain, and throughout Western

Europe. Beatle Boots are tight-fitting ankle-high boots, with a sharp pointed toe. Holding them tight to the ankle, Beatle Boots have zipped or elastic sides. I amused Paul's family by trying on his Beatle Boots. They were humorously small. He was not a big man.

Every detail of the transition had its own special challenges. The hardest of all, as far as my natural skills were concerned, was the switch to Paul's left-handedness. Some of it, like smoking, was mostly a matter of habit. Other talents, such as with Paul's backward strung bass guitar, took colossal effort to master. Representing me handling those backward strings, **I sing that** I learned to tie Paul's bootlace, emphasizing **the difficulty of** his strings over all else included in **my journey** of walking a mile in Beatle Boots. **Like tying shoes, it required new dexterity.**

Sunday, after the studio, I went over to Paul's estate home and tried tirelessly to play his backward bass. I called George Martin for some timely tips. Among other things that I also tried, he suggested that I make chords with my right hand rather than trying to finger everything with both hands as I had done before right-handed. That helped a lot; but the left-handed playing, I could see, was much harder than I had imagined. I tried it up until late into the evening, and then put it down for the night, feeling discouraged and fearful. Almost boastfully, I had sounded as if it would not be a problem for me to play left-handed. Now it seemed hopeless.

Bass guitars have their own souls. On Monday morning, 19 September 1966, I held the bass and envisioned myself as Paul playing in front of a large packed stadium. I put on the Beatles' new *Revolver* album that was released the month before, less than a week before their last tour. **It was the first time** that I heard it. I plugged the bass into Paul's amp, and closed my eyes. **I imagined myself as Paul.** Letting the music move me, I played along as though I were on tour with it **romping across America.**

"Eleanor Rigby" came on right after "Taxman," and affected me profoundly. For "Taxman," all the bass playing, on my part, was very clumsy. It was like using a new foreign instrument while doing orchestration for strangers. The backward bass was awkward for me, and so was the music. I found no oneness with the music at all. It was much worse than my worst day ever as a session musician.

Then "Eleanor Rigby" began. **Even before I** learned the background story, I **was so moved by** the song that I ceased being aware of **my own playing**. When the song ended, I pulled the needle back to hear it again, and then again. Somehow, **I knew** in my heart what **Paul McCartney was singing to me** about. I put down the bass, played the song again, and wept on the floor. Immobilized, I left the needle down and finished that side of the album. I did not get back up for another hour.

That afternoon, **I played** that entire album while playing along with **the bass**, again imagining. I had some high points. **It** was not great bass, but was much better than it **had been** before. It was not the exact same bass notes that **Paul** was playing, but was becoming close enough, **in** my awkward way, that I felt very encouraged by **it**. I practiced that way with that album quite a lot **back then.**

Realizing the crucial importance of playing Paul's bass well, I practiced heavily night and day. Monday by Monday, marking week after week, I was aware of significant improvements, but was still obviously far from playing it naturally. Then, after six weeks, I had a very strange encounter, one that needs more explanation than belongs here. It was on 31 October. One week later, on the 7th Monday, during what began as an ordinary practice session, I received the talent as a miraculous gift from Paul.

After tea, I picked up Paul's bass and played perfectly as him. That was on 7 November in the year of 1966, only a few hours before John returned from Spain. The 31 October event is in "Hey Jude." Since that first Monday of November, I have played not merely like Paul, but as Paul.

The line, "Monday's child has learned to tie his bootlace," refers to those great breakthroughs that I experienced on Mondays, 19 September and 7 November, learning to play Paul's bass strings. "Monday's child," as **I said**, is also about Paul's fair face alluding to the **old Mother Goose** rhyme.

Extending the **meaning,** consider the Native American proverb, "**Don't judge** a man until you have walked two moons in his moccasins." It had been practically two moons that I had walked as Paul before he attached himself to me—or before he integrated enough that I could play as him. That saying has been modernized. Two years after I recorded "Lady Madonna," Elvis recorded the Joe South song, "Walk a Mile in My Shoes." It says, "If I could be you and you could be me for just one

"Monday's Child Has Learned to Tie His Bootlace."

hour . . . you'd be surprised to see that you'd been blind." Having been Paul, I know his inner and outer workings. I am Paul. I can tell you what is in Paul. However, since no one else on earth can fully walk a mile in his shoes, or in his Beatle Boots, since you cannot fully be him, or me, I ask that you do not judge either of us for this Paul role I am playing. As that songs says, "Before you abuse, criticize and accuse, walk a mile in my shoes." I had nothing to do with that song, but do like the message. I hope letting that message take root as you read this book of secrets will help keep you from developing too low of an opinion of me. **I am telling you** that I am a real person, and showing you **how it happened.**

The things **I am sharing** have been hidden for generations. I share them **with you** now in hopes of having greater peace **before I die.** Do not get me wrong. I have more peace than most people that I know. Fans deceive themselves by putting people on pedestals, making them bigger than life idols. Now that you can know **I am a mere mortal**, just another guy like everyone else, many fans are going to think of me differently. **However,** it is not just me. As all of **your celebrity idol**s, I am the same as everyone else. **Please do not judge us**, or be in awe of us. It is just my job. **We are all one.**

Notice that I, "Monday's child," follow Sunday. **Paul died Sunday.** From a purely daily perspective of Monday's child, Sunday is "Yesterday." Then, following Sunday, Monday is "just another day." With the "Yesterday" representation of Paul, I wrote representing myself as "Another Day."

As his death day, we represent Paul as Sunday. Recalling the day John learned of the death and had gone mad over it, Paul is also Tuesday, as in "Stupid bloody Tuesday." Three days (Yesterday, Sunday, and Tuesday) represent Paul in Paulism. In the song that references Jane Asher's ladder use, "She Came in Through the Bathroom Window," I sing parallel lines with the identical meaning that Paul McCartney now talks to me: **"Sunday's on** the phone to Monday; Tuesday's on **the phone to me."**

I might as well explain more of that song. The silver spoon was not, as some people claim, intended to be a drug reference. It was about Jane having been born into affluence. "She said she'd always been [an entertainer] a dancer." I called her a dancer to take listeners off her trail. **Jane Asher had always been**, let us set it right, **an actress. She was** born in 1946, and had **her first** movie appearance in 1952. Letting her career take **priority** over relationships, she was always off somewhere filming. I describe it as "She worked at fifteen clubs a day." I imagined her as an exotic dancer going from club to club until late every night. Jane was not like that; but it was how I felt. I found Jane attractive, but could not let her completely take me over, as she had Paul, because I did not feel important enough to her.

As I connected with Linda, one reason I never forgot her was that she never left my side. Linda's beauty attracted me first; but her persistent loving presence made the most powerful of all impressions on me. I do not mean that Linda attached to me in a way that would interfere with my work, but that she understood my heart enough that she put nothing above our relationship. Still, Paul in me wanted Jane.

This line had a word reversal: "I quit [joined] the police department /And got myself a steady job" means I joined the Beatles (becoming its Sergeant), which was a steady job, as opposed to all the session work I had done. **Jane** "could steal" Paul's things that she **said** were hers, "but she could not rob." She felt **I had robbed John** by taking his band **when he was the most vulnerable.** Still, even though she did not go along with all of it, "she tried her best to help me."

As she went off without me to be a successful star, "by the banks of her own lagoon," so to speak, I added sarcasm. **I explained** it in an earlier song: "You became **a legend of** the silver screen" ("Honey Pie"). It is not all **Jane.** She just inspired it. Paul and I found her attractive; **but** she was too much effort for me. "I'm **in love** but **I'm lazy.**" That song was of the old music hall, or vaudeville, style. I recorded it with the Beatles; but it was actually more of a Bonzo style song. I tried to blend the bands.

24[(26)]

Tuesday, 20 September 1966

I awoke Tuesday morning realizing that this new Paul role did not require me to stop doing what I **could** already do as William, but that I could **continue on with** it as Paul McCartney, or as any **other personas.** Weeks before, I had agreed to write the feature-film score for *The Family Way*. I meant to be finished with it by then, but had forgotten all about it. I called Brian and offered to pay him a fee if he could arrange to have that work transferred from me as William to me as Paul. He objected since everyone knew that Paul knew nothing of music theory, and could not even read or write sheet music. Nevertheless, when I said I would pay him to book it for me, he agreed to set it up.

Each scene would have its own unique emotion captured with a musical mood that led to another, as I did later on some albums. The challenge was to have each part independently interesting, yet connected to the whole. Going back and forth between the piano and the screenplay, I wrote the score's first draft by hand in one day. I added in each instrument later.

Tuesday, 20 September 1966

"Paul McCartney" is credited with writing that entire movie score even though he could not read sheet music. I, however, having spent years as a first class session musician, was not only able to read music, but could also write scores well. I had entertained countless live audiences, filling in for various orchestras in London, and have done an ample amount of studio work, requiring sheet music.

Some bands that I sat in for in recording sessions told me the key they were in, or what chords they were playing. In some cases, I would improvise with utterly nothing at all to read. However, the more serious music, **I** mean all of the classical music, required me to **read** sheet music. Paul could not read or write sheet **music.** To downplay that stark evidence of a personnel change, we said that Paul had already agreed to write the score months before.

For a few minutes that evening when Brian came by, I showed him my rapid progress. I expected to impress him with the quality and quantity of my work, but alarmed him by the clear contrast of Paul's lack of formal musical training. With dismay, he said, "You are a better Paul than Paul ever was."

Making matters more alarming to Brian, he learned that Cheri Ann had a birthday party that Paul should have shown up for, or excused himself from, the day before. Paul's absence was conspicuous. Cheri Ann was a woman whom Paul had met on one of Jane Asher's movie sets.

Our gathering in my home Sunday had convinced George to go to India, his center of mysticism. The religion of his youth had failed him. He wanted much more. **Paul's** premonitions—followed by me entering the **scene** and taking Paul's place as he foretold—**demonstrated that** there were spiritual forces at play. **We needed to** understand them.

George, wanting to **tap the cosmic network** of enlightenment, hoped **that** studying yoga and Indian philosophy **would help**. He hoped to retreat from **the world** unnoticed. George quietly checked in at the Taj Mahal Hotel in Bombay under the pseudonym, Sam [after the reporter] Wells, but was recognized in the lobby before he could reach his room. Brian was told all about this second hand, and related it to me in our Tuesday visit.

Enough of a fan-frenzied disturbance ensued that George could see that his only chance for peace was for him to hold a press conference, satisfy curiosities by answering all the questions, and then to escape to another hotel. They held the press conference at the Taj Mahal hours before my visit with Brian. He was miserable thinking of what George might say that could accidentally tip off the public about Paul.

I asked him if George were careless when he spoke in public.

Leaning forward as if to keep others from hearing, even though we were all alone in my home, he said, "You got to be careful about George. He just says what is on his mind. He is too honest."

Well, as it turned out, George did okay. He told the press that he was there to learn their old culture

Tuesday, 20 September 1966

and philosophy, and to learn to play the sitar—which was all true and completely safe enough information. Yet, he wisely did not explain how the year of Paul's prophecies groomed him for it.

Before leaving India, George visited among other locations, the Digambara Jain temple for the yogis of Kolkata, in West Bengal. On one stone wall, he saw a carved swastika above an open palm. In Hindu divinity, the swastika (seen throughout India) symbolizes Brahma, their god of creation. The hand added to the meaning. George was told that the hand is a symbol of blessing that also suggests a continual need for coexistence and sarva dharma sambhava. In palmistry, the hand, or palm, is a symbol of mystic determinism. **In Paulism, the palm is** a mystical coexistence with **the deceased Paul-M.**

Shiva is a four-armed god of destruction whom George learned about while there. Hindis say Shiva had a child made from her dirt. She asked the boy to keep guard while she left to go bathe. However, in cleaning herself, she became unrecognizable to the boy who blocked her return passage. Shiva took vengeance on the young boy by chopping off his head. When Parvati pled for the boy's life, Shiva affixed an elephant's head to the boy's torso, thus creating Ganesha the mystical elephant-headed god.

Centered on the bottom of the *Sgt. Pepper's* cover, see a statue of Shiva, the Destroyer, with two hands pointed down to Paul's grave: one pointing to the wax Paul, and one to me, to whom **Paul's head is affixed** figuratively, for Paul **to continue through** me. Beheading **the mystical boy, who bestows that new head** on another, confers the rule of that **head** that I wear like a crown, **to the replacement**. Going with Shaivism for this imagery, we credit Shiva, the Destroyer, with taking Paul's life, and with enhancing me, magically giving me Paul's head. It transforms me into a mystery idol.

During his trip to India, George learned legends, philosophies, and symbols that I applied to Paulism, mixing that Hindi branch of spirituality with the mysticism that I have participated in throughout my entire life. Although religions do not attract me, I have always respected spirituality.

25[(27)]

Impersonators

When I stepped from my St. John's Wood home Monday morning, 3 October 1966, and saw a crowd encircling the fence, I thought something was wrong. One man called out, "**Where is Paul?**" Although I had begun my physical transformation, it was not yet progressed enough for me to meet the public. I was about to shout, "**I am here**," but knew better. Saying that **Paul was** somewhere else could mess things up **down the road** as my transformation increased in Paul's resemblance without completely diminishing all of my own looks that they might remember. Any in-between versions could be problematic.

Saying nothing, I rushed back into the house. **I** telephoned Brian. He said that he too had **heard** intimations of Paul's death. There were **rumors** buzzing rapidly about the streets. John was still gone filming *How I Won the War*. Brian worried that I might blow my cover before John returned. The crowd needed answers. Brian arrived with Peter Brown. They chatted with the crowd before coming in.

Every injection and surgery made me look more like Paul; but I was not ready for the public. It was a drawn out process. It took time. Brian, Neil, Peter, and I discussed the urgent need for an appearance to create the assurance of Paul's continuance, to stop all suspicions about the collision.

Obviously, I topped the others based on talent, voice, and linage, but not on looks. We knew that my new talent would help the band more than a closer Paul face, and that the appearance would improve in time. The better look-alikes were shorter. Some had Paul's round head. Others looked more like me. A round head would be simulated by check injections. Camera tricks would adjust my height. We would accomplish most of the changes within a few months. Until then, others made appearances, and a couple of them helped in the recording studio. One of them, as if me, working as if Paul, had a hit. For this transition phase, **I fooled around with** disguises to be Paul McCartney **looking like** someone else.

The other Pauls after **Paul** had their purposes, but none of them had a permanent contract as only I have. I am the true messenger of Paul—to borrow another fitting image from Carroll. The king enters a game with Alice by telling her that the Messenger "lives on the Hill." Here I am, living high up on the hill proclaiming the message that Paul is down below it. Above or below, who is the fool?

I, before and after taking on the Paul role, enjoyed dressing up either for comedic effect or to act out certain parts. My Bonzo friends and I did impersonations and such to entertain each other, and mostly ourselves. **I would** be William dressed as Paul who would **perform** as Vivian Stanshall who puts on a gorilla suit. We **layered** personas for greater hilarity. Just Billy **in** a gorilla suit was not as amusing as **Bill or Phil as Paul as Viv** as a gorilla. **In disguise**, I could still go out and play under **these alter egos**, and make fun music, and **could be my silliest** Bonzo self, and make everyone laugh at **me**, even though I had become a big Beatle. As Paul, **I still played the fool.**

The most amusing thing about it all was that no one seemed to notice who I was. I sang, but no one heard my voice. No one heard that it was the same voice as Billy Pepper, or that it is now that of Paul. Everyone could see that I was just a fool—far from any Beatles superstar. I felt like shouting that the fool they were laughing at was their favorite Beatle idol. I could have changed everything with a word. Of course, I never give that answer. Even when I did sound too much like the current Paul, the audience only perceived as another imitation. I am the man of a thousand voices, singing like Elvis Presley, then Little Richard, and sometimes like Paul McCartney. I knew they who mistook me for Paul were the fools.

Once, while playing as Vivian, when the audience started heckling me, I thought, "They do not like me as the fool; but these same people love me as Paul McCartney. If they only knew that the same singer they are disrespecting was their prized Paul, they would gladly pay a small fortune to have admission to this show." The world always loves to see **the Fab Four** act foolish, but only if everyone **knows** it is them. Otherwise, when they act like **fools without** the Beatles stamp, it is hardly worth **respect** at all. This role I play has taught me a great deal about biases.

I never showed my feelings in those challenging times of rejection. It is the way of clowns. If people laugh, that is enough. What hurt the most was that I knew that I was more myself as Viv than as Paul. The loneliness was intense. Up on the stage, day after day, I was the fool, alone on a hill.

Emphasizing the implication of my false identity or disguise on *Sgt. Pepper's*, the album included a nifty insert of Sgt. Pepper's costume cutouts. It had a picture of me dressed up, disguised as Sgt. Pepper, only, not in my band suit, but in a military sergeant's uniform. The cutouts had stripes for sergeant's uniforms, a badge of the *Sgt. Pepper's* drum skin, another badge of me disguised in the sergeant garb, and a fake mustache. The fake mustaches for our fans resembled the mustaches that all four of us had on that album. My mustache covered a plastic surgery scar. The others wore mustaches to fool everyone into seeing us all as being equally altered. The band's new look was to promote our new band with a new leader (Sgt. Billy Pepper) and its new sound.

Our mustaches—and the rest of the new look—were a cover-up. When you hear, "Sgt. Pepper's lonely," played at the end of the Reprise in the normal direction, it covers my backmasked message: "It was a fake moustache." That message ties the cutout disguises to our own facades. Here is how the new message was added backward. After recording the vocals in the forward direction, we would get it set up backward to hear how that sounded. Hearing that a backwards "Sgt. Pepper's lonely" already has a compatible sound, I sang along with it, overdubbing it. My headphones played the first recording backward, as I sang along, "It was a fake moustache." That method was how we did a lot of our backmasking. **We would** play our vocal tracks backward and **listen for any sounds** that resembled utterances that **we wanted.** If the sounds were close enough, **we could add all the words** we wanted and not mess up the forward track. Singing along with the track played **backward**, we shaped the sound as desired, giving the forward track a richer sound. Our hidden messages were always about Paul.

Having multi-layered tracks going forward also provided another way to conceal our Paul messages. Everything is still there for an effective subliminal message, but can easily be buried far below our rational awareness. In that closing Sgt. Pepper's line, after "hearts," I shout, "PAUL IS DEAD!" It is there, even though it is hard to hear. After "club," I shout, "REALLY DEAD!" You hear it subconsciously.

NOTE: Awareness occurs in levels. Successful societal programmers provide material on a cognitive level to construct a framework for what is received subconsciously or unconsciously. The deeper the program is embedded, the less it can be filtered by the individual receiving it. Unconscious beliefs and behaviors prevail over what can be thought out and thereby dismissed. The way to change any unconscious belief is to bring the light of consciousness to it. We do so in levels.

Just as each re-reading of this material brings more consciousness to these subjects, so too can we deprogram ourselves on any subject by bringing light to it, increasing consciousness layer by layer, such as through meditation. To reach the deepest levels of Paulism embedded in our own psyche, it helps to know that it exists, and how it got there. The example above of shouting a message, but burying it under other sounds is one of many methods.

William effectively spread Paulism without being detected. Whether by accident or by design, the public frequently sensed William on a subconscious level while being completely oblivious to him consciously. For example, he often sang back-up, or played an instrument, anonymously for other artists. He gave those songs the McCartney sound, energetically pointing fans to him. When listeners subconsciously hear him, he is elevated that much more. Usually, he is unidentifiable. For example, most people do not know it is him crunching on celery in the Beach Boys song, "Vegetables."

After a little bit more, I shout, "We're the band, the greatest band of all time." Then I add this last line finishing on the final chord, "Sergeant Pepper's Band!" That last line is so faint that **I suppose you** would need special equipment to **hear it** at all. However, on the *Sgt. Pepper's* cutout, we say it again. In the largest letters on the cutout, it says, "Sgt. Pepper's Band." Again, **the point for all** of you is that it is my band now. **I am Billy Pepper.** These, and other messages **buried deep** in layered sound, are all to tell you that **Paul died**, and that John gave me the band to keep it going.

With the Sgt. Pepper's costume cutout inserts, I did not expect to see a wave of our fans suddenly impersonating me dressed up as the sergeant. It was to make the interactive point that I was dressed up as the fictitious character. I was not claiming to be a sergeant, but was suggesting that now the Beatles had a new leader. I was the new authority.

My "OPD" ("Officially Pronounced Dead") patch is visible on the album's gatefold picture. When I told the questioners that the patch I wore had been made for the "Ontario Police Department," that was as honest as I could be without revealing what the patch's initials really were. When investigators discovered that there is no such department, it encouraged those in the **"Paul is** Dead" circle while simultaneously **fortifying critics** who could then rightly see that I was correct **generally.** Officially, I explained it away saying that my patch does not suggest "Officially Pronounced Dead," and that it is simply from *a* Canadian police department.

On the gatefold picture, however, we twisted the sleeve forward to see most of the patch that fell naturally to the side. We conspicuously displayed it exactly that way. The police explanation was also a good answer because the police, just like the military, have Sergeants. I am Sgt. Pepper.

The lines "And so I quit the police department, And got myself a steady job," had been written originally, "And so I *joined* the police department," referring to my new OPD *Sgt. Pepper's* career. Reversing that word set another context right since the new Beatles band was my steady job replacing session work that always varied. It was never steady. ("She Came In Through the Bathroom Window"). I joined **the Beatles** once Paul was Officially Pronounced Dead, or, **in code,** of the "Ontario Police Department." It **was a steady job** that was far better than any session work I had done before.

I should also mention, as long as I am talking about my session musician work, that in that line of duty, we were all frequently impersonators. Without credits, we would do our work, singing or playing instruments, with the public believing it was done by the talented guys on the album cover. **It is not** as though anyone committed **fraud**. **It is** standard performance illusion. That's **showbiz!**

The OPD patch was **another illusion**, a camera trick. Nothing is real. We bent the OPP patch in order to get the camera angle to make the final "P" look like a "D." Some mechanic from the garage of the Ontario Provincial Police gave that patch to John after their Toronto concert on 17 August.

BILLY'S BACK!

As is understood and exploited by advertisers, perception can create reality. This phenomenon lets people alter reality just by convincing others. Such impressions are especially effective when those led to believe a thing are of an impressionable age. The brain's frontal lobe, which is vitally involved with sound judgment, is not fully developed until our mid-twenties. That is one of the reasons that most all of our greatest fans became devoted to us before reaching their mid-twenties. It is much harder to sell older people on it unless they, in their youth, have already bought into something close to it.

Illusion plays a big role in the success of all bands. Now that I have left EMI, I can tell you a little trick they did to promote the Beatles—long before I joined. This story has been around a long time, but with an incorrect date. On 23 July 1964 (not August of 1963 as is often reported), under the direction of EMI, a trick was played on the public to help promote the Beatles, and to help sell newspapers. The Beatles did a flying ballet sketch for television at the London Palladium. It was great fun, from what Ringo told me. **They were all hoisted up into the air with winches to do one part of that show in which they all pretended to be flying. As they left the show, a few girls gathered** near them and were photographed.

The picture was cropped closely **enough that** there was no way to see **the crowd magnitude**. In reality, there **was** no **significant** crowd around them, only a half dozen or so fans showing support. By morning, newspapers all over had the cropped picture and front-page headline, saying, "Police fought to hold back 1,000 squealing teenagers." Reporting the sensational story of the police trying to hold back the riot was quite a brilliant promotion, outstanding for creating the reality that Tavistock personnel wanted instilled in young consumers.

Making the news that way reinforced the illusion that they had established in the US when hundreds of screaming teenage girls mobbed the Beatles at the Kennedy Airport. Actually, the girls had all been transported from a girl's school in the Bronx, and were each paid for their performance. They showed everyone what to think of these idols, effectively creating one of the largest television audiences ever. The Beatles' performance on the Ed Sullivan Show for over 75 million **Americans**, after showing them how to **respond to** it, set America up, especially those under **their** mid-twenties, to adore their new **English idols.** It launched Beatlemania in a very big way. Then, back in Great Britain, when they made more of the same illusion, they kept the world in motion to feel after them.

NOTE: Perception creates reality. Because the media directed Americans to perceive the Beatles as the ultimate band, that belief made it so. The term, "Beatlemania," first appeared in print in a 1963 review by the *Daily Mirror* (a newspaper owned by Lord Rothermere, a prominent media baron connected to the Rothschilds). Although the mania was entirely manufactured, the belief in such a thing as Beatlemania helped bring it into existence.

While it is fascinating to understand how the media created Beatlemania by presenting it as already accomplished, the greater message is that we can each employ that technique to create our own reality. The more we focus on what we want created, as if it existed already, the more readily we (or the universe) bring it into existence. Believing it makes it real as a matter of consistency. Our reality becomes consistent with our beliefs. To whatever extent we believe that this method does or does not work, we may be right.

26[(28)]

Recording with the Beatles

With both **Pauls**, up until the break-up, the Beatles recorded and **released** ten hours and twenty-eight minutes of music. **I am** still amazed by the great power of ten and a **half** hours of music to lead the world in entirely **new** directions. Years after the break-up, much more Beatles material has left the vaults. In all, in 2003, global Beatles sales passed 1.2 billion (million million) records.

Intermittently throughout Friday and Saturday, 16-17 September 1966, when I first met John at the Eiffel Tower, and when we visited at the Louvre Museum, we spoke of modern music, art, and the new direction **I wanted the** band to take. I said that modern art and **modern** music were, at heart, the very same **avant-gardism**, and that taking the Beatles in that **direction** would be cutting edge, inventive, and most delightfully controversial. I persuaded him in repeated discussions, each with specific unique reasons, why it was time for the Beatles to grow up and to mature into a much more interesting and sophisticated kind of music. I named examples of their songs that were too childish and out-of-date for the time, and contrasted them with others that were attractively progressive.

Not having heard *Revolver*, I took John's word for it when he said he already understood what I was explaining to him, and that they were already doing it with their latest album. Since we both knew about dada and other avant-garde movements, we could speak the same language.

As I discussed these changes in **Beatles music**, in each conversation, he again agreed that there would not be any more love songs, but **would** instead pioneer newer sounds, and subtly **weave Paul into** each of our songs. It was my idea to use **double** entendre to convey a story line on one **level** and to work hidden meanings into that **material** that only the esoteric would understand. All that I said, I believed. However, it was mostly still theoretical.

I was mostly just showing off, trying to impress everyone, especially John. Sometimes he seemed to genuinely like my ideas. Other times he responded as if I were some ignorant pompous twit. It was hard to read him then because I did not know him that well, and since I underestimated his devastation at losing Paul, and his readiness for me to begin my life as Paul. He was patient with me out of deep respect for his lost bandmate. As per our agreement, each of us refrained from writing love songs for the four years that I was in the Beatles, but both quickly set that rule aside as soon as I dissolved the band.

Meanwhile, whenever **I received** the inspiration ordering me to write **love songs**, I did so, but either gave or sold them **for other bands** in order to keep up our new Beatles image. Another explanation I gave John and the others was that the Beatles were now in mourning. They took that reason to heart more than I anticipated, being more true than I had dared to believe. With his prophetic dreams fulfilled, the band venerated Paul as a seer, more than one could imagine. Paul's death was like a kick in the head to them. The news dazed them all. It cost them all of their innocence, and their ability to enjoy the same kind of music as before.

Neil and **John flew off** to Spain on Sunday, 18 September. Something **deep inside** of John said, "Yes, take **the Beatles** deeper into avant-garde music." Another **part of** him resisted it. The make-over, **changing the band**, changes the world. Still, something **felt wrong**. In Carboneras, he wrote what ultimately became the Beatles' first recording of phase three, "Strawberry Fields Forever."

During that time when John flew to Spain, I returned to London. There George, Ringo, and I met for the first time on the night of my return, and had our first jam Session. **I was** at the piano. We got things going with a song **that Paul** had written and enjoyed, "When **I'm** Sixty-Four." It went into our first album, my *Sgt. Pepper's Lonely Hearts Club Band.* It was **the** first Beatles song recorded that ended up on that album, the first song for which I sang lead, and the **second** song of phase three.

Out of my old home to live as **Paul**, I could not tell most of my friends and relations what I was undertaking to do. They could never know what happened to Bill. However, Paul's associates, relatives, friends, and others kept introducing themselves to me, saying that Paul had foretold his new life through me. I realized how one-sided this clandestine deal was. I thoughtfully considered each of my family members and **friends** to determine who could be let in, and who **must** remain out of the way of what I was attempting to **do. The** first people **I confided in** were my closest **music** friends and **some key relatives.** Though it hurt me to not tell **the rest of my relatives**, they love to go over the latest **gossip.** Although I loved them all, I knew they could not stop themselves from talking, undermining my work by reassuring all whom they met that I am fine and am pretending to be a Beatle.

None of the Bonzos were kept out of the loop; and Denny Laine, another long time music friend, did not pose a threat. I knew I could always confide in him. There were others as well, but not nearly as many as Paul had let in on it, giving them all early warning of his goodbye and my hello.

No time was wasted when John returned. He shared his "Strawberry Fields Forever," written in the desert in Spain. I played for him my polished version of "When I'm Sixty-Four." He told me I could also finish writing Paul's "Penny Lane," but said "Sixty-Four" would be the B-side of his more substantial "Strawberry Fields" single.

I decided I'd make "Penny Lane" quaint, with a Fern Hillish (Dylan Thomas) memory Paul may still hold of Liverpool, and to finish it for that single, giving a better balance to John's song—but more importantly, to have one that **I wrote for my** first hit ever. I had made a few of my **own records** that never went anywhere, and had used my voices and chords on other groups' records; but this single would be my own first hit. Every single that they had made before me had reached the top on both sides of the record. Chart topping was expected. Any new single **I would** make, I wanted to be mine. That motivated me to **finish** Paul's "Penny Lane." I need to tell you later about **Paul's work** on "Penny Lane," and about Penny Nickels and Denny Laine.

Going into the EMI studios with John and the others to record his "Strawberry Fields Forever" was extraordinary. I was not new to the studio, but to be there as Paul, helping John record what would no doubt be one of the world's new favorite songs, was surreal beyond measure. Words cannot express it.

Thursday, 24 November, we began recording. John stood before George Martin and played his guitar while singing "Strawberry Fields Forever." George, who sat on a stool in front of John, fully enjoyed the whole song. **I could** see his pleasure in hearing it, and felt his **delight** that John would write such a song without **Paul.** George also gave sincere praise for the new quality of John's work.

Our work on that song went on for a week of days spread out over a month. Between sessions, we rethought the best ways to approach that song. George Martin and I grew in mutual admiration then, laughing together as we worked through John's tracks, experimenting, bouncing around ideas to do it better, all to raise John's work quality. In all of my studio hours before, none was as stimulating. That launch of work with George Martin, engaging his talent and ingenuity, exhilarated me. I learned how to do quite a bit from him that I put to good use when I took on the *Sgt. Pepper* work.

Everyone saw **the Beatles** as a circle of close friends, which we **were**, but **not** as much as their yesteryear had been **with Paul.** I had more in common with George Martin than I did with any of my Beatle bandmates. Although George Martin should never be thought of as a band member, he invariably raised the quality of nearly all of their work all along, which was his special assignment.

Recording us all together on "Strawberry Fields Forever," I played the bass, George played lead, Ringo was on drums, and John again sang along with his own acoustic guitar. I encouraged John over the weekend to add more instruments for a fuller sound. George Martin agreed when we returned to the studio. I offered to write a score for added cellos and trumpets; but George Martin ended up doing it. That additional orchestration enhanced it greatly.

During those years, **I learned** to talk all about Paul's life, making up **Paul's history.** It was needful to pull off the new identity. **I would make** things up about when I, Paul, wrote **Beatles songs** from before having met those guys, or **about how I came** up with certain Paul lyrics that would blow my cover if I ever explained the real contexts. However, now and then my stories created relationship complications. In an interview I did five months after John died, I thought it would be safe by then for me to build my reputation a bit at John's expense while he was no longer around to correct me. However, others were involved then who were offended. Since some of them will see this book of confessions, and because doing this book is about coming clean on everything else, I will set the record straight here too.

On 3 May 1981, I said, "We were always in competition." That part was true. "I wrote 'Penny

Lane,' so he wrote 'Strawberry Fields.' That was how it was." That part was almost true, except that "Strawberry Fields" was written first. Paul had started it long before; but it was given to me to finish his work after **John wrote** "Strawberry Fields." And, he wrote **"Nowhere man" before Paul** died. It was a year after he **died** that I wrote, "The Fool on the Hill." He did not copy me there either. It is entirely possible that I reversed that set once too. I wanted to make it sound like I had been around awhile, for people to think of me as the same Paul that had been working with John from the beginning.

You probably want me to mention the Paul clues that John wrote into "Strawberry Fields." In Paul's tree of his life, I am the branch that he produced. I have tuned myself in, feeling his energy, and channeling it to the world. When John wrote this song in Spain, he had only seen me one weekend in Paris. **I had** made the claim that I would soon become **Paul by** connecting spirit to spirit, attuning myself to **his** energy. John did not yet believe that I could do that, but said it did not matter. I did not **need to connect** that way. I just had to make a good Paul pretense to record the music. "No one I think is in my tree" is enough to say that no one is waiting to take John's place as **I took over for Paul**. "It must be high" like **from heaven "or low" from hell**. The source **did not matter.** Either way, I am now in Paul's tree of life to take over where his tree was cut off. "That is you can't you know tune in but it's all right." It sounded too good to John to be true. That was before John was a believer. John said that it was all right that I would not be able to tune in to connect to Paul spiritually. That is, he thought it would not lessen my work. If I failed to tune in, he says, "I think it's not too bad."

"Let me take you down," reflects back on Paul's song, "I'm Down" when he sang "I'm Down" to suggest his coming burial: "**I'm down,** down in the ground." After John alludes **to Paul's burial**, he explains why: "'cause I'm going to Strawberry Fields." Notice the pronouns. John buries Paul 'cause John, not Paul, is going to Strawberry Fields.

The Salvation Army acquired property and renovated it into an orphanage in Liverpool. It was operational from 1836 to 2005. With Paul being entombed, John has been orphaned, left behind. **John knew of** that orphanage as a child because of **the fund-raisers** he attended there. "Nothing is real, and nothing to get hung about" says I am not as I seem, not really Paul, but that my fears of legal ramifications were unwarranted.

In singing, "Strawberry Fields forever," **John** suggests that since Paul will forever be buried in the strawberry field, and since I **would not "tune in"** enough to spiritually channel him back to John, John is to be forever left behind. Paul is not coming back. John is orphaned forever.

"Strawberry Fields" plainly warns the Beatles' worshipful fans (who in this song receive notice that "nothing is real"), that "Living is easy with eyes closed, misunderstanding all you see." Senses and instincts were not to be trusted. Appearances are deceptive. Referring to my difficulty in being Paul, my challenge is stated, "It's getting hard to be someone but it all works out." With the same emotionless indifference as shown before, whether or not I could succeed at being **Paul was** not a matter for John's concern. We were not **doing it** for John, but for Paul. "It doesn't matter much **to me.**"

On hearing the song without reading along, one cannot know whether John sings "know" or "no." Reading it, we see it is "know," not "no." With the deliberately ambiguous "no," John corrects himself, making it, "Always, no, sometimes." The real words are not far off in meaning, except that the conflict enlisted is not a correction, but an expansion. "Sometimes" does not replace "always," but merely tempers it, adding moderation. "Always know" and "know sometimes" both suggest that our fans can overcome the misunderstanding caused by thinking all is real when nothing is. "Always know sometimes think it's me." By understanding the substitution, you can "always know" it is me or John working every song as Paul. That "always" is firm. The "sometimes think it's me" line was inserted because, losing Paul, **John** was under the assumption that I, the replacement, **would not be** able to do all the labor that had been **done by Paul.** John could not believe that **I could do** it.

All **Paul work that is beyond** me, as John imagined, would fall on **him.** He would do it. As he let us all know his doubts as to whether I would be able to "tune in" to Paul to fully do his work, he lets us know here that he also imagined that much of the work, especially Paul's song writing, which the world would be told is by Paul, would in fact "sometimes" be John. He wanted you to know it has not been Paul since Paul died; and to understand that sometimes what is heard is actually from another, particularly from John himself. But don't always think it's John—just sometimes.

The next phrase, "But you know I know," is John assuring you that he was not deceived. He knows about Paul, and about who is doing what work with each song. It is not as if I am fooling him. Saying next that "it's a dream," has drug overtones that work well with the song, but is mostly about the self-sacrifice in Paul's dreams. We were all playing out our parts according to what Paul had dreamed. When Paul shared his death and substitution dreams, his hearers all had their own interpretations of how each detail would play out. It was far from how John had anticipated it. He had imagined someone recording as a substitute, not taking over the band. We reached an agreement in Paris when John finally surrendered, telling himself it was Paul's will, and saying my demands did not matter that much to him. It did not set well with him. By the time he reached Spain, John wondered what he had done. He sang, "I think I know of thee, ah yes but it's all wrong. That is **I think I** disagree." He knew of me, but objected. I **will explain**, and prove, the "I buried Paul"-"**cranberry sauce**" overlay in the "Paulism" chapter.

Recording of "Strawberry Fields Forever" being done, as we had all supposed, we used our time in EMI Studios on 6 December recording Christmas and New Year greetings for bootleg pirate stations off the coast broadcasting our music from ships. With that work finished, we rehearsed, and then spent the rest of that reserved five-hour session recording "When I'm Sixty-Four." Paul had written that tune at a relatively young age, around sixteen years old, and added the lyrics years later. Some of our historical documentaries (based on my lie) say he added the lyrics for his father's sixty-fourth birthday.

Billy's Back!

Every presentation as fact should be considered suspect. All of our official stories are just that. Do not trust them. **The real truths are** presented in fiction, such as **in this so-called novel.** I learned that back in their early Cavern Club days, Paul added the lyrics to give them more performance material. Eventually, it became their stand-by song to play whenever the electricity went out, or when their amplifier blew a fuse. Paul's father, Jim, born in 1902, was not sixty-four years old until 7 July 1966. That was only sixty-six days before Paul died. Again, this book of "fiction" gives you the straight line rather than the traditional party line. Look to this fiction for fact, and to my fact for fiction.

Entering EMI studios all alone, on 8 December, for my own private three-hour afternoon recording session, I overdubbed my lead vocal. As I listened to it, I became nervous, concerned that my voice was obviously lower than Paul's. I imagined him doing

---

NOTE: William says, "Look to this fiction for fact, and to my fact for fiction." What he is saying specifically about his own disclosure is also true of how the globalist work generally. Since time immemorial, the greatest manipulations have occurred by presenting fiction as nonfiction, and by presenting fact as fantasy. That perceived distinction always fools most people. The most absurd stories are seen as real merely because they are in newspapers, on televised news, or on websites that pretend to be truthful even when those news outlets are controlled by those with incentives to promulgate the most dangerous lies.

The most trusted fact-checking websites or television programs go to great expense to maintain their reputation, and may be useful to check on urban legends or on threats of computer viruses. However, providing many true statements for each deception, along with disproving false rumors, they also claim to "debunk" (a trigger word that makes people believe them) proof of scams perpetrated and upheld by specific treacherous corporations.

The reverse is also true. Fictional formats (such as movies or novels) can condition the public to think in particular ways about events that are actually planned. Sometimes directors or writers are tipped off sufficiently to include specific details in order to add those ideas to the collective consciousness. Whether the purpose is to instill subconscious dread or acceptance, this foreshadowing technique is especially useful. Using fiction to plant ideas in advance allows directors and writers to program how viewers and readers respond to each issue as the programming is activated by real-life events.

the song sounding younger, more rooty-tooty. Mine now sounded much too self-serious, even turgid. That evening we all met together in studio two. In going over it, others felt the same way. It was not at all like Paul. The best way for me to describe it is to say it is like my Vivian Stanshall act at the end of the *Magical Mystery Tour* film. **A tongue-in-cheek**, affected, cabaret **sort of a song, it had a Bonzo** Dog Doo-Dah Band **feeling to it**. That is the way I sang it. However, **the humor did not carry well**. It sounded too sincere **for such absurd lyrics**. All that I could do at that point was to press forward; but we had to do something to fix it.

For the next two sessions, we were back to "Strawberry Fields" for still more overdubbing. It appeared to be finished again with that work we did on 9 and 15 December. On 20 December, we were back to working on **Paul's old "Sixty-Four,"** but all agreed to have that **work interrupted** for each of us to do interviews for **the weekly television** series, *Reporting '66*.

Rumors had been buzzing around London, and beyond, at first that Paul had died, and then that our energy, or cohesiveness, was missing. Revealing internal disharmonies had completely shocked the public. I had been the worst of all. I was too honest, and far less skilled at dealing with the press then. After intense friction with John one night when he was drunk, I believed it was over. In a public pub, I uttered that I **was no longer one of the Fab Four.**

John and George had both expressed doubts of lasting long with me at the helm anyway. With Paul gone, it felt to the others that there already were no more Beatles. Observers picked up on the sudden disharmony. When John returned from Spain, at the casual gatherings where we were expected to be seen together as old chums, onlookers suddenly found a completely different story. The 20 December interviews were to convince our fans that we were all still one big happy Beatles band, that we, being old childhood chums, were still inseparable.

Returning to the studio the next day, three session musicians added clarinet to "Sixty-Four." Then John added more vocals and another piano track to "Strawberry Fields." We were back at it the next day, 22 December, again fixing "Strawberry Fields." Playing what were the two best tracks, one excluding the trumpets and one with them, John decided the song needed a minute to build up to it. Yet, rather than calling those musicians back for another session, **John wanted to splice** the two recordings **together** exactly at the sixty second point. George Martin objected because John had recorded each track in **a different key; and** that one had a **faster tempo than** the other. John went on about favoring **the beginning** of the one track and the end of the other. **We played** them again and listened, letting us all hear **their incompatibility** for splicing.

Then, with the kind of brilliance that made each day of working with George Martin a joy, he suddenly lit up and said, "Yes, I think maybe we can slow one down a little, and speed up the other just enough to match it, it might work." In the track that came of it, having a compromise tempo and tone, John's voice is slightly unnatural, but is better for it. Unless you know to listen for it, the seam is mostly unnoticeable.

Not satisfied with "When I'm Sixty-Four," but not yet knowing what to do about it, I decided to get going with "Penny Lane" for our next Abbey Road studio session. It was on Thursday, 29 December. On my own again, from 7:00 pm until 2:15 am, I recorded the basic track of "Penny Lane," as well as new percussive effects. When I returned the next day, before continuing on with "Penny Lane," I let George Martin know what we needed to do to fix my "When **I'm** Sixty-Four" recording. I told him I would sound **more like Paul** if we sped up the track, picking up the tempo **a bit**, using that same variable-control tape machine that he had used to change the speeds on "Strawberry Fields."

Even though George agreed that it would make me sound younger, more like Paul, he immediately rejected the idea. The change was too substantial. However, I insisted. We had to do it. As George protested, I persisted and prevailed. The master take had been recorded in C major, but was sped up in order to raise the key by one full semitone (half step) to the key of D-flat major (C#). To the delight of all of us, my new Paul-polish made it more Paulish. It sounded a lot more like him.

NOTE: In 2009, *the Memoirs of Billy Shears* made many verifiable facts available that were not known before by "Paul is Dead" investigators. The above is one such example. To verify the story about recording "When I'm Sixty-Four," slow the recording a semitone, from the key of D-flat major back down to C major. If you do so, you will recognize William's natural voice that the world now knows much better.

When William started this new role, he was concerned that his natural voice was too distinct from Paul's to go unnoticed. That concern diminished when *Sgt. Peppers* trained fans to identify his own voice with Paul's.

Billy's Back!

Later, throughout January, **I polished** "Penny Lane" as well. George Martin and **the band** all agreed that it would also be an A-side song. "Strawberry Fields Forever" and "Penny Lane" now became the Beatles' third Double A-side single. Although it is correct that John's song did better in some charts, "Penny Lane" did better in others. There was a big commotion in the press about it being the first Beatles single to reach

NOTE: Although the Beatles are best defined by their albums, they also produced 63 singles. At a time when most artists put great effort into their A-side song, but put a throw-away song on the B-side, the Beatles intended both sides of their singles to be big hits.

John and Paul never took turns being featured on the A-side. Yet, it came out rather evenly between them. George Martin put whichever song on the A-side that he thought would be easier to sell. When John or Paul wrote their own songs, the writer would sing lead. Songs that were brought to them were assigned to the voice that was the best fit for that particular song, but which would also keep John and Paul generally balanced to maintain the appearance of Lennon-McCartney equality.

Normally, John sang lead for one side of the single, and Paul (or William) sang lead for the other side. Following the single featuring "Penny Lane" and "Strawberry Fields Forever," in which both sides were presented as A songs, John was given the A-side with "All You Need is Love." The B-side was a mix of them both in "Baby, You're a Rich Man."

In William's mind, it made him look inferior to John to share the B-side with him while John occupied the single's A-side. Furthermore, in this case, John had written his part of the shared song first. William wrote his part specifically to go with John's. When William considered what he had allowed to happen, he was troubled, feeling more like a helper than a superior.

After the "All You Need is Love" single, William sang lead on a dozen more singles, but never allowed another one of his own songs to be in second position to one of John's—or to anyone else's other than Paul's. Whenever William did not have the best song, deserving the A-side, he put one of George's songs on the single in his place. He gave George the A-side for "Something," and the B-side for "While My Guitar Gently Weeps" and for "Old Brown Shoe."

The only other time William took the B position was for "Helter Skelter," topped only by Paul on the A-side with his old recording, "Got to Get You into My Life," making Paul appear to be on both sides. The next single also combined a new song with an old one, having William's "Back in the U.S.S.R." on the A-side, and John's old "Twist and Shout" cover on the back.

only the number two position in the UK. It entered the top 40 in the US on 4 March 1967, hit number one there, and stayed firm in the top 40 for nine weeks. When recording that song, I froze with insecurity, and received more help with it than **I** now can admit. Though for a Beatles single, it **was** below expectations; for me, it was **fabulous**. Years of wishing for hits made that sudden success feel all the more extraordinary. It also showed a lot of insiders that **I was** a viable Paul, a good fit. The consensus was **that Paul** would have done better, and hit the top in the UK, but that I was a fine stand-in.

Locals scoffed at that song because the street was not picturesque in their reality. While across the pond, fans loved Penny Lane as a faraway fantasy, folks in England knew better. I could not fool them into loving the place. They were too wise for that bliss.

NOTE: With the control held by the super elite over all large radio stations, they had full control over which songs would make the top 20, and how each would rank. They decided against making Penny Lane a number one hit in the UK for the reasons that William explains, but also to show William that he would be more successful without the unacceptable level of assistance that he received with that song. In his later hits, without that level of assistance, the elite directed the stations to spin his records enough times to make them number one hits for the prescribed duration.

No top 20 hit was organically ranked as such by the will of the people. Those in position to control public attitudes always dictated the top songs. Even when listeners would call in to request songs, no major station was permitted to allow those requests to override the pre-determined ranking of the top 20. Protocols also determined what songs could be requested.

Concluding William's Paul service, the elite are now turning the youth's attention to him with extra media coverage, and by having other artists honor him. To further transmit that face of the Illuminati to the next generation, they are helping him complete his life on a high note.

Currently, with personalized music stations, the public has much more control over what they hear. With logarithms based on individual preference, we can now make our own top 20.

27[(29)]

Donovan

Donovan's "Mellow Yellow" is unique in that it features both of us Paul McCartneys. Paul did some of the backup vocals days before the crash, and I did some more after. Since Don was an insider, I did not need to pretend with him. When **fans learned** that Paul sang backup on it, many thought **he was** the one singing "Quite rightly," or **as** some misheard it, "Quite right, Slick." That was **someone else**. It is very hard to recognize either of us in that song. He mostly repeatedly whispers "Mellow Yellow" again and again. I later added party sounds, showing that we were having a good time.

Now, being while John was gone for the film, we were not working on any Beatles songs. You can know it is true if you check the recording dates. **Donovan's "Mellow Yellow,"** I should also note, **is historically significant** as the last song that Paul took part in recording. When his tour ended, he hung out with Donovan at Abbey Road Studios. Paul was mellow, ripened for consumption. Written by Donovan, produced by Mickey Most, and recorded on the Pye label, that last mellow song that Paul took part in recording does not credit him. His participation was as private as his passing.

As for yellow, the color was on Donovan's mind because of a **Paul** song released the month before. **Under Don's influence,** "Yellow Submarine" was **made** as **a children's song.** They knew Paul would leave **when mellow yellow**, when it was his time. Writing a children's song was Donovan's idea.

When Paul wrote of the submarine, predicting his death, the sub, as his car and coffin, was yellow as a symbol of ripeness, like a banana. They began recording "Yellow Submarine" in May. Donovan's song, "Mellow Yellow," extended the idea.

Donovan also wrote the Submarine line, "Sky of blue, sea of green," referring to Paul's burial under grass, as opposed to under the deep blue sea. Don understood the song completely. Notice the burial mound of ground taking the place of water over the submarine on the original *Yellow Submarine* album cover. The casket-like craft is buried down under the dirt hill where the Fab Four stands.

Whereas Paul's burial, as he predicted it, would not be in water, the lyrics referred to "the land of submarines," a cemetery of subs. As it happened, he did not end up in a public cemetery. Substituting

NOTE: Besides the examples provided in this chapter, Donovan also assisted with many other Beatles songs, sharing ideas for lines and for instrumentation, and even singing back-up on some songs—especially on *the White Album,* for which George Martin did not provide the material, direction, and regular session musicians that were standard with the early Beatles albums.

public for private, it was a lot like the cover with earth in a small hill over that solitary container. That album came years after releasing the song.

Really, "Yellow Submarine" is a fine children's song. **It is** for their escape fantasy. Paul made **the song for** them, and intentionally used words simple enough for children to love, including bits to harness **their imaginations.** Besides showing that Paul would be buried, it was mostly made to entertain children—as was John's "The Continuing Story of Bungalow Bill," and Ringo's "Octopus's Garden." My "All Together Now" worked well for them too, but was mostly a big joke.

Rounding out both of these yellow songs, as Paul later sang backup on "Mellow Yellow," Don had, oddly enough, sung backup on Paul's "Yellow Submarine." These two songs mirror one another. Unlocking the secrets of "Yellow Submarine," you see what "Mellow Yellow" turned into merely a few nights after the first tracks were recorded. It became Paul's swan song.

Donovan, one of Paul's friends who expected the replacement, was eager to meet me. When he did, he called me D.O.P. **I did not like the sound of** it. It sounded like dope. I asked what he meant by it. He explained, "D.O.P. **Duplicate of Paul."** I wondered how many other insider friends of Paul would be calling me to see Paul's new replacement. I could not see how we would keep it from leaking out if all of Paul's old friends had already been let in on it.

At first, we were careful of whom I met. I could not live as openly as Paul had. I had to learn how to be Paul before I could pass myself off as him.

Laughing at Don a little, hiding my resentment, I corrected him, "D.I.P." He seemed confused and ensnared. I had caught him at his own game. I said, "Duplicate *IN* Paul."

"Duplicate In Paul," he said. "D.I.P. Dip. So, you're the big dip? Huh? That's wild!" he said.

"Maybe, Don, you should call me Paul," I said, realizing that a dip was worse than a dope.

"Everywhere you go now," he said, "you'll be Paul McCartney. Tell me, what's it like being Paul? Dippy, that's trippy!" The meaning of D.I.P. evolved to "*Dead* In Paul" when it all hit me that I lost my life to obtain his. Don comforted me with his "Epistle to Dippy," I was dead in Paul, the great "Paperback Writer," who made Donovan "Paul's 'Paperback Reader.'" Paul set up this whole hot plot. **Donovan's song was about** me transforming, changing into **an evolved Paul**. "Through all levels you've been **changing**." Here, "all levels" means becoming Paul **on all levels**, and leads into the elevator metaphor. **Paul's head** was broken down, but mine, Don says, **works just as well**. "Through all levels you've been changing. / Elevator in the brain hotel / Broken down, but just as well."

Everyone missed the *Sgt. Pepper's* tie-ins to Donovan. **I pinched some** of his creative imagery very clearly **for our album.** It went both ways. We shared ideas back and forth. In December of 1966, at the time we were working on *Sgt. Pepper's*, Don recorded "Epistle to Dippy," and made up a story to explain it away as if to some friend in the military. He sang that I am "getting a little bit better no doubt." Owing a response, I answer yes, "I admit it's getting better. A little better all the time." His song was not released here in the UK; but he gave me a copy of a US released album. In February, it peaked in the States in their top twenty. I played it here too because it was about Paul and me. It was nice for Don to give me that copy. Stuck in my head, I responded to it by recording "Getting Better" on the next month's schedule.

Where I sing, "it's getting better," John adds his ridicule by his humorous, "It can't get no worse," suggesting that I did not begin very well. Admitting Don was right, I sing, "**I have to admit** it's getting better, a little better all the time." Backwards there, on that spot, I sing, "After all, **Paul is dead.** He lost his hairs, head." Equating hair with head here was not as morbid. Ringo re-used it later, singing, "You were in a car crash and you lost your hair" ("Don't Pass Me By"). In that same Ringo song, he, like Donovan, also points to me. Again, we added in a backward message. Where "Don't pass me by, don't make me cry, don't make me blue" is recorded forward, playing it backwards renders, "Who'd we pay for now? We paid for now? It's that one."

Wanting another verse, John autobiographically inserted the part about him having been cruel to his woman. It had nothing to do with me. **I was never** cruel like that. It fit the song in that it is yet **another** way that the fictional persona may be getting **better.** Until domestic violence is brought out into the open, the shame of it keeps people trapped in that cycle of longing for peace and connecting love, but suffering for the sake of oppressive fear-based control issues.

After receiving Donovan's "Epistle to Dippy," some of our own songs with Dippy influences were recorded for *Sgt. Pepper's,* including our "With a Little Help from **My Friends**" and "A Day in the Life." If you **would play** Donovan's Dippy Epistle, then *Sgt. Pepper's,* **and** then back to Dippy again, you **would** likely **notice that we pinched** quite a bit, not only in **words and content**, but also in tone. **Giving thanks now is overdue**. "With a Little Help from **My Friends**" answers Don's question: "Over dusty years, I ask you / What it's been like being you?" I imagined the world asking that.

Using Ringo's voice (because it is less polished), I answer Donovan as a set of interview questions. Posing as me, Billy "Shears" Shepard, Ringo gives answers to each interview question as I would—or actually as I did in that song. "What do I do when my love is away?" I missed her terribly. **I felt** like I needed her help to do this work. But that does not fit the song. "Does it worry you to be **alone**? How do I feel by the end of the day? Are you sad because you're on your own? No, [I am lying here. I'm in denial.] **I get by** with a little help from my friends. I **get high** with a little help from my friends." Obtaining drugs to ease the pain of loneliness is not to say that people should use them, but that I was hurting. No one else needs to experience my

NOTE: The line, "I get high with a little help from my friends," predictably resulted in the BBC banning the song for its drug reference. With that same concern, the BBC also banned, on that same *Sgt. Peppers* album, "Fixing a Hole," "Lucy in the Sky with Diamonds," and "A Day in the Life."

As premeditated, the cooperating media helped the world contemplate the government attempting to block the Beatles from encouraging drug-use. Naturally, after the fans' initial shock of being told that their idols encourage drug-use, most Beatles fans sided with the band, objecting to those who would prevent Beatles airplay. With that media and government support, many people tried drugs because of that strong celebrity endorsement. Publicity from the ban also boosted album sales.

When choosing sides between a conservative government and the drug-culture, even those with no interest in drugs are generally more inclined to stand with their rock icons than with those who would repress them. Consciously and subconsciously, with the reception of *Sgt. Peppers,* millions of people across the globe suddenly opposed those who opposed drugs.

Banning those four songs placed the Beatles at the top of the drug-favoring counter-culture. Although the Beatles were already bigger than life ever since their first engineered hit, the government's intervention against their music made them unimaginably larger to the world. It also created division between fans and the government. Siding with the Beatles, now against the state, many fans took drugs as their initiation into the Beatles' counter-culture.

William recycled the phrase, "I get high," from "I Want to Hold Your Hand," which was one of the first of many songs written for the Beatles, and credited to Lennon-McCartney. At the start, protecting their wholesome starter-image, and keeping the song from being banned by the BBC, the phrase was muffled by a light overdub of the phrase, "I can't hide." Many who did not know the official lyrics "misheard" the true lyrics. Others received that covert drug reference as subliminal programming that would not be activated until the Beatles overtly repeated that message.

As Billy Pepper and the Pepperpots covered "I Want to Hold Your Hand" on *Merseymania* in 1964, the line is, "It's such a feeling that, my love, I got high, I got high, I got high!"

When confronted with the rumor that Billy Shepherd and Jimmy Fraser wrote "I Want to Hold Your Hand," and that Pepperpots originally recorded it to help George Martin teach it to the Beatles, William said, "That's an early Lennon-McCartney song. George's change in the lyrics from 'I *got* high' to 'I *get* high' made the song more present. He also made other improvements. That's the way with George. Whatever he worked on, he made better."

256

mistakes. The song interview continues, "Do you need anybody?" I admit, "I need somebody to love," et cetera. The interview is to answer Don's epistle.

Another Dippy Don line that appealed to me was his "Over dusty years, I ask you." The line joins the new happening of today with the dusty decades past. That idea fit perfectly into what I was attempting to do. That is part of why **I** wrote, "It was twenty years ago today, **Sgt. Pepper** taught the band to play." Until I **made** that song about *my* band, not merely **the Beatles**, the album had no focused concept.

Playing our new songs for Donovan, and then explaining our album in progress, had him intrigued and delighted. When I sang the line, "The teachers that taught me weren't cool," I was singing about not only my old school days, but more particularly about my recent Beatle-craft schooling. **My** teachers did not fully appreciate all the **sacrifices** I made. John, George, Mick Jagger, and others, **were** overdoing their training. They sought **to teach me**, but were not cool about it. Hence, Don threw in **a bit** on the school teacher idea, combining it with what George told him about all the beautiful women who were getting with me once I became Paul. George saw the harm in my lack of moderation. It made him nervous that I was "crazy" enough to have my hands on so many girls. As Donovan said it, "Made the teacher suspicious about insanity / Fingers always touching girl." The "teacher" idea was Don's.

On the album, after reading Carroll, John has "A girl with kaleidoscope eyes." She's "the girl with the sun in her eyes." Don thought of needing special eyes to see me. It was a trip, but that girl could experience reality. She also paralleled Paul. Look for him, and he's gone. However, it took the special eyes to see it. George also wrote about how blind people are in his "Within You Without You." That song is partly about being without Paul, and how we, and you, can, by our love, connect to him. Maybe **I will** write more on that in another chapter. The **issue** here is how we cannot discern enough with our **programmed vision, or** natural eyes. We need help, or **altered eyes, to see truth**, and to know the difference. John later called it "Looking through a glass onion." Well, Donovan's gaze into reality came not through "kaleidoscope eyes," but by a prism, "Looking through crystal spectacles," and ultimately looking "through all kinds of windows." All kinds. He meant that.

The thing that Donovan found most far out about **my transformations had** to do with my harsh **physical changes.** Although I felt divided

NOTE: Some people have imagined that in a single trip to one doctor, William had all of the surgical work done, and then returned with Paul's face. However, as is chronicled by photographs over the first few years, William's transformation was brought about by a series of less radical surgeries, some as simple as adding blemishes, such as a scar on his chin. Fans have pointed to a scar or other blemishes as proof that William is Paul, but miss the fact that those blemishes came with time. They are missing in William's early Paul pictures. The chin scar had to be done twice.

The injected fillers had originally been intended to occur every six months, but were not that frequent in actual practice. William found reasons to put it off. He also complained that the extra thickness in his cheeks, besides feeling unnatural to him, interfered with his singing. The injections became far less frequent and less substantial starting in the Wings era once the primary people who had enforced the injection agreement passed away.

In the Wings years, William increased his Latex use, experimenting with several facial variations. Sometimes, in the same music video, he uses subtle adjustments that almost make him seem like different people. Although his ability to alter his appearance may be a PID clue, it was more about William's pleasure of dressing up, his interpretation of a song, or to set a song's mood. When watching his music videos, consider how his altered appearance for a specific song reinforces the lyrics, music, or mood of that song.

about the alterations, I pushed ahead, motivated by all of Paul's stuff I would receive. I gave up what I had and loved, **in exchange for everything** from Paul. Mick Jagger and others resented it. Exchanging all for **all seemed fair to me. Paul had become a millionaire** by then. In the sixties, that was a lot more money than it is now.

As I weighed it all out, I considered how hard I would work for that much money. I also saw it as an unparalleled opportunity for my own music success. Although I knew I had more talent than Paul, I lacked the ability to promote myself. Considering how swiftly this would change all of that, I willingly accepted the surgeries. Doctors gave me Paul's appearance. We used photographs to show what they needed to do. I already looked a little like Paul, but more so after the surgeries and injections.

Donovan was intrigued by the way fate dictated everything. Paul's fatal collision, followed by my process, pointed to a greater power in charge. That otherworldly aspect playing out inspired Don's yearning for his own greater spiritual connection. He depicts that desire by having a monk meditate as the song begins. That is how he ties the monk to his repeated line, "The doctor bit was so far out." It was enough of a spiritual drive that **Don joined us in** our retreat to India. He sought **that higher power** of love and enlightenment that we all sought after. Our group of friends added to the positive energy: Mia Farrow, Mike Love, Donovan, the four of us Beatles, and others including, of course, the Maharishi.

Back to "Mellow Yellow." After Paul died, the song became more set on him. Before then, it was really about sex. Donovan sang the phrase "mellow yellow" to describe a ripe banana. As he had originally intended it, they (his lovers) called him "Mellow Yellow" suggesting it were his reputation to be ripe and ready. When Paul died a little later, the unintended double meaning emerged by the historical context. Back to the sexual intent, Don compares himself to an "electric banana," which, as he explained, is a kind of vibrator that he saw it in a sex shop. He claimed to be ready at the press of a button. Realizing the historical Paul significance, and then bringing it to our attention, out of respect for Paul, Donovan played down the sexual meaning, and called it his "Farewell to Paul" song.

Owing the yellowness of Donovan's song to the "Yellow Submarine," let me emphasize that Paul no longer dwells under the "sea of green," as Don put it. Actually, he never did. No grass is growing over his gravesite; and that is not where his enduring essence is anyway. As foretold in the song, his spirit ventured upward. "So we sailed up to the sun till we found the sea of green." That is to say that the spirit ascends to the sky, "to the sun," as his rotting corpse pushes up daises, or, in his case, rhododendrons.

Now, **I will tell you about** another Donovan hit. The main lines of **the philosophical song**, "There is a Mountain," stem **from Zen Buddhism.** Donovan became interested in, and rather enamored with,

Eastern thinking at around the same time that we Beatles all did. The good old saying, "First there is a mountain, then there is no mountain, then there is" is a Zen proverb of impermanence. All that comes, naturally goes. We are to accept whatever is when it is. Mountains come and go. You can move them, says Jesus, if you have enough faith.

What are we up against? The big mountains that we might face today may vanish by our faithful acceptance. Our mountains disappear, but reappear every time we need them. Our mountains are things we perceive as too big for us. **We think we** do not like them sometimes; but they **are the realities** that we each create to fill our subconscious needs. Loving or hating the circumstances is not ever the issue. Our true selves, or our non-selves, always create our own reality to match whatever we need, or whatever we subconsciously think we need.

Another way to look at it is that "first there is a mountain" of stress and anxiety within each of us. Next, we may accept that whatever mountain exists, it is perfect in that it is what we have created for ourselves, or is a gift from heaven. Without resistance, **the mountain of stress vanishes** from awareness **until we resist it again.** If we have not fully settled the issue within ourselves, that mountain reappears as the returning anxiety for us to try again.

When we have **full acceptance** of it, realizing that it **is our own creation,** an extension of **our infinite selves**, we have peace.

Each recurrence of that mountainous issue calls us back to accept that **we created** it to serves us as part of **our perfect world.** It is what is. However, reaching that point, it is no more, yet is.

Lastly, about that song, **I do not believe** Don had Paul and me in mind when **he wrote it**. However, I still remember the time he sang **to me first**, in EMI Studio Two, "First there's Paul McCartney, then there's no McCartney, then there is." Then he said, "The second mountain and the butterfly are both you, Dippy. They are both you." Don went on singing, "The caterpillar sheds his skin to find a butterfly within." He was suggesting that the biological Paul had to cease in order to allow the emergence of the butterfly, the more evolved Paul. That is I, the new Paul with Wings.

Considering its relevance to this book of Paul, I wanted to add that clip to this book's contest CD. I offered to buy that rare Donovan recording, but was told that it no longer exists. **If it does** still exist, then, maybe this attention will **help someone find it**. If so, I think the world would **be amused by it.** If it ever ends up on some rarity collection, just remember that you read about it here first. It is also possible that it was taped over and lost the day that it was recorded. I had always said, "Track it and save everything!" However, Don was not that way. He could redo it.

I still have respect and kind feelings for Don over these dusty years. We became friends because he wanted to stay close to Paul. **Donovan had** a lot more in common with him than with me. **His** McCartney-Mountain song inspired my **"Butterfly."**

NOTE: The butterfly, especially the Monarch, also symbolizes the trauma-based mind control system used to break and re-program William, whose worst trauma occurred at three years old. To those who invested in him, his disassociation assured life-long compliance. The sadistic occult ritual, adapted from a German method, guaranteed unwavering dedication to his work.

William's childhood traumas put his life and work into perspective. It explains why he has been so extraordinarily driven since his program was fully activated to be Paul McCartney, "the world's greatest superstar." It is natural for readers to be put off by William's obsessive compulsion to prove that he was not only the best Paul McCartney, but also, "the greatest superstar of all time." However, that was his specific trauma-based programming.

By identifying with that role that was so sadistically programmed into him, William's very existence desperately requires that program to be true. It is not as though he would receive external punishment for failing to fulfill that role. The tormenting punisher is entirely internal as an integral part of his program. Failing would trigger severe depression. He must be the best, and prove it.

In *the Memoirs,* William often laments the heavy burden of living as Paul. From an outsider's view, it is inconceivable that the poor billionaire super-celebrity has any cause to whine. After all, most of his relatives and his closest friends were fully aware of his new role, and were supportive. For William, however, the life that he lost was not one of their associations. It was his life before his internal trauma-based program became fully activated.

Once it was switched on, his life beyond his work largely ended. Although he worked to maintain that playful element, such as while playing his Viv Stanshall role, he could never fully return to his authentic peaceful nature. However he plays, his work program always runs in the background.

By understanding William's position, we also better understand countless others. William is not alone. For the elite to carry out their global agenda, they have many children traumatically programmed to eventually step into key positions. The entertainment industry's power to shape opinion makes its celebrity control especially important. Replacing them with programmed workers may be the most effective way to govern the masses.

Understanding how replacements qualify for celebrity roles should stir compassion for all whose lives are set that way. They are not robots or clones. They are individuals with their own personal struggles. Just as we would not judge soldiers with PTSD, it is unfair to be overly critical of those who act according to their ritualistic trauma-based programming. By breakthroughs developed through extensive experimentation, mind-control programming is scientifically designed to be extremely difficult to break.

Billy's Back!

Even though Don and I were good friends, and were both singers, song-writers, musicians, and heroes of the pop scene; and even though we had some good times together, his interests in me extended from Paul's friendship, and what **Paul had** foretold. Donovan Leitch was one of **Paul's friends** who were expecting me to show up after Paul's demise. Donovan and I had very little in common, actually. He was lazy; **I was** a workaholic. It was Don's laziness that prompted a closer friend, Paul Simon, to write of him in "**Faking It.**" Identifying him by name, a woman says, "Good morning, Mr. Leitch. Have you had a busy day?" She is addressing Don Leitch, whom **Paul** Simon **is** singing as. Don is "**a dubious soul.** And a walk in the garden wears [him] down" as if by looking upon a snail there. *Zzzzzz* (Don snoring). That fine 1967 Simon & Garfunkel song has Mr. Leitch "Takin' time to treat your friendly neighbors honestly." But he has "just been fakin' it, . . . not really makin' it."

By saying he was lazy, I do not mean that Don was not a good friend. However, like Paul, and unlike Paul Simon and me, **Donovan** liked to take it easy. Don would say he **was** not lazy, but that I was a workaholic. He made **a** valid point. People who work too much lack **good** times with family and friends. He was a good **friend**, but my idea of play looked like work to him. I worked hard until, in Japan, they forced me to stop for a while. Then, with Linda's help, I saw that my Paul work needed a breather while I spent more time with my family. I needed my children more in my life.

28[(30)]

Penny Nickels, Denny Laine, and Penny Lane

Penny Nickels was one of Paul's many friends who came to meet me after the big switch. She and Emily Little had met and become close friends at a two-week dance workshop in Los Angeles. Penny Nickels' name struck me as a fantastic stage name. I was sure she had made it up—as I had also made names for myself from time to time. **We were** very open and honest with each other, **sharing secrets**, yet I never could get her to tell me her birth name. I called her Penny Laine, named after "Penny Lane," and joked that it would be her name if she and my friend, Denny Laine, ever married.

Now, before I go on about Penny, Emily, and others girls, I should write about Denny. The name Denny Laine was also self-invented. He was born Brian Frederick Arthur Hines. His first alias, Johnny Dean, was a persona he used for his first band, Johnny Dean & the Dominators. "Johnny" was eleven years old when he started that band back in

Billy's Back!

Birmingham, England. The band had considerable natural musical talent that developed as he did. The Senators, another Birmingham group of kids, needed a lead vocal, but already had an interesting sound. Brian, then "Johnny Dean," convinced that young band to be his new backing group. It was for that band that he adopted the persona Denny Laine. Now, the Senators became the Diplomats. That was back in September 1962.

Everyone in that band had considerable talent, and some **made it big.** They felt they were on the verge of stardom when they were promised a recording contract; but no record ever materialized. Even though they had a good sound, they lacked stage presence. Then came Nicky James, who, after a realistic Elvis impersonation, joined the Diplomats, performing as "Nicky James with Denny Laine and the Diplomats." That impersonator completely changed the band, and several years later inspired me, as Paul, to do an Elvis-type voice with "Lady Madonna." I was not imitating Elvis, but was originally inspired by Nicky's Elvis imitation—or the idea of an impersonator changing a band.

NOTE: William is being coy about his involvement with Denny Laine and the Diplomats, wanting readers to figure it out for themselves. He speaks of that band as if detached from it, but then explains how the addition of Nicky James changed things, and how it inspired him to use an "Elvis-type" voice for "Lady Madonna." For those who miss that clue, he becomes more obvious. However, he sees his work with the Diplomats, and the band before it, as training exercises, not as any great accomplishments. They were part of his adolescent education, not something to list on a resume.

Ultimately, the high point for Denny Laine and the Diplomats was when they opened a concert one night for the Beatles at the Plaza Ballroom in Old Hill. Some "Paul is Dead" investigators will likely tell you **I played then**, not **as** the Beatles' Paul McCartney, but as The Diplomats' **Phil Ackrill.** Everyone ought to consider this question, "If I were Phil, why wouldn't I admit it now?" **He was a** dandy singer and guitar player, and a **fine person.** Who would this Bill rather have been than Phil?

Their band was big in Birmingham, but did not have a distinct sound that could sweep the world. Obviously, the band needed a change. Although it made many recordings—intentionally enough for an album—none were released. As I write this memo for the book, **I am** thinking about buying them now and releasing **them** with a vintage collection when this book stirs the interest. Denny, what do you think, Denny? **Let's reminisce about** the days of our "Silly Willy with **Phil**ly Band." Could be!

The Diplomats went on without Denny in 1964 when Michael Pinder and Ray Thomas recruited him to start The Moody Blues with them. They got a good thing started there; but Denny moved on to invent his Electric String Band, which laid the foundation for what band-mates and others would nearly resurrect as ELO (Electric Light Orchestra).

NOTE: The Diplomats opening for the Beatles at the Plaza Ballroom in 1963 was significant because it was their first meeting. They went on to open for them at various venues. To help William know Paul better, on one occasion, to the envy of other bands, handlers had the Diplomats and Beatles share a dressing room. To avoid the appearance of prior knowledge, it has been important to conceal William's grooming for Paul's position.

Billy's Back!

By that time, I think Denny joined Balls. I now go on and on about Denny because he introduced me to Paul, and also connected me to Brian Epstein. As Linda and I finished our *Ram* album and were ready to take it on tour, I called on my old friend. I said, "Denny, how'd you like to go on tour to sing backup for me for a change? I want you to come along and play your guitar." It felt good playing with him again after all these years. Linda and I considered the advantages of making Denny a permanent part of our family business. The three of us formed Wings. Linda was never the super star that **I was meant to** be, but did have quite a good **understand**ing of the work, and was an equal. The band's name was in reference to Paul's death. I had **Paul's broken wings** and learned to fly. **With** the new band, all three of us were flying with **his Wings**. Leaving the Beatles and growing Wings, **the three-**winged beast began where the four-**headed beast** ended. I will identify the seven **heads on** that four-headed beast in another chapter.

Having left the Moody Blues **on good terms**, Denny remained **in the same circle of influence.** Early on, as their band took off, Brian Epstein, the Beatles' manager, signed The Moody Blues. They got to be close friends with the Beatles, touring together, frequenting the same clubs, and going regularly to the same parties. Although Denny left the Moody Blues weeks before Paul died, he still ended up at many of the same parties. I had gone with Denny to some of those parties back in 1965 where **I saw the Beatles**, Rolling Stones, Jane, and several other **big** celebrities; but I never did feel welcome in their **circles**. One night, at a spring celebration in 1965, Paul, Keith Moon, and two interesting women were laughing about something when one of the girls leaned back and tripped right next to me. **When I helped** the pretty girl up, Denny introduced me to **Paul** and Keith. Paul's face turned ghostly pale. Horrified, **he rushed away.** Later that same night, Keith apologetically said that Paul had seen my face in a dream, and that the dream must have been after seeing me at another party.

On 6 November 1966, in Los Angeles, Emily Little had a dream of two musicians who looked very much alike. The first one died; and the second one there said that the death was his own new birth. Emily recognized Paul, whom she had met at a party in Los Angeles while they were on tour. Paul remarked, "If you don't believe I'm dead, call John. He's already got my replacement."

It was 9 November when she reached John at my home by telephone. John picked it up it, but did not say much before shaking his head, astonished, and saying as he handed me the phone receiver,

"This is Penny Nickels' friend in California. She wants to talk to the new Paul."

"How could that be?" I said. "Who is that?" I was confused.

NOTE: Although William acknowledges Denny for introducing him to Paul, he understands that if the introduction had not been made by Denny, it would have been made by another.

"Emily," he said. "Paul's giraffe friend that we met on tour in L.A."

"She's tall?" I asked, holding my hand over the mouthpiece.

Though John shook his head, he said nothing. I answered the phone. "Yeah?"

"Are you him?" she asked. "This is Emily Little. Are you him?"

"That depends. Who are you talking about?" I knew, but did not appreciate her assuming that I did.

Emily answered, "You're Paul's replacement. I can tell. He told me they found you. You even sound a little like him. Not a whole lot, but a little. Enough, I guess. Keep talking."

"Paul told you about me?" I asked. I did not see how that was possible.

"And Parker," she said. "Parker knows about it too. We've been dreaming of Paul, but none of us understood what it meant until he told me in a dream that you took his place."

"Look," I said, "if you care anything for Paul, and it sounds **like** you do, you'll never breathe a word of this to **anyone**."

"It's just horrible **that** it really happened, but in a way, exciting too. When he was here, he said it would happen. We **thought he was** joking. It is sad that it happened, but **amazing** too."

She went on to say that she wanted to come meet me, but that she could not take off work then. She would come stay at Penny's flat in London from the afternoon of February 15th until the 17th.

She was surprisingly pleasant. Although Emily's kindness was nothing romantic, as she had a blue-eyed love in California, we had a great time. Penny introduced her to Denny that Friday. **We had** lunch. Emily said she would be back **that spring, but** never returned. She promised to help me garden. Until Linda ended my gallivanting, **I hoped Emily would** get back here someday and maybe **turn** in that direction. What was the most amazing **to me** about her was her psychic power. She could **telepathically** call a specific cat to her lap **from another** room. I did not believe it until I saw it. At Penny's flat, sitting on her bed, I whispered to Emily which cat should come. Without saying a word, she would think it; and that specific cat came right to her.

Right then, I knew I could connect to Emily in a psychic way. Up until that time, it was the most outstanding display of telepathy I had seen. I could convey some simple thoughts to her. It worked well until she left. Then we quickly lost our magical link. I tried sending her a few messages later, but could never restore the physic connection. She ceased listening to me, preferring to tune in to her love down in the States, I am sure. Nonetheless, it was all right with me. Once I filled Paul's position, the girls stood in line to see me. I never had trouble getting any dates. I just missed Emily's friendship.

About six girls called that October/November, each of them thinking that they were something special to Paul, and likely were. When Emily flew back to the States, never again to return, Penny and I remained friends. I will always remember that time with Emily. On 17 February, after a full fun day with Em, Denny, and Penny, **I worked** at Apple Studios, until 3:00 in the morning, **on** what John and I both recognized as a filler for ***Sgt. Pepper's***: "Being for the Benefit of Mr. Kite!" That poster-inspired song showed the shallowness of that lonely-hearted life. I played bass and lead guitar.

Cutting back to Em's call now, on 9 November, I told John that she said she and Penny would come over to meet me in February. Before that call, John had played "Strawberry Fields" for me, and had very strongly encouraged me to prepare to record "When I'm Sixty-Four." Until then, John and Paul each always sang lead on one of the two songs they released on each single. To fill the B-side, I would record Paul's "When I'm Sixty-Four" as soon as John finished his "Strawberry Fields." I said we could each record our own new song for the single.

After Emily's call and mention of Penny, John dealt me an offer. He told me that I should record a song tying me to **Paul**'s past, and that Paul, more than a year before, **had mentioned** in an interview that he might write **a song called "Penny Lane."** He had said he liked the poetic sound of those words. That interview occurred on 1 November 1965 during a break from taping *The Music of Lennon & McCartney*, a program that aired 17 December 1965.

Trying to make good on his word, **Paul started** working on the song, but never got far with **it** before deciding to scrap it. John told me **I could finish** writing the song, sing lead on **it**, **and call it mine** enough. John had helped Paul with what little had been put together, and sang that much. They wrote about a fifth of the lyrics that ended up in the finished song. Much of that fifth, it appeared to me, did not actually come from Paul. John seemed to recall the gist of it, but adlibbed his own words.

"Penny Lane," as Paul first knew it, was a bus roundabout in Liverpool. As I wrote "Penny Lane," after hearing the parts John recalled or invented, I imagined how Paul would then remember it. For us to get the right effect, it would be from the dead man's perspective. Since Paul said it was poetic, I looked over "Fern Hill," a poem by Dylan Thomas. I appreciated his quaint picturesque descriptions of childhood under the apple boughs and starry sky, his charming trails with daises and barley, his singing on his farm, and so on. Having become Paul, **I** adopted Liverpool as my own heritage. **I sought** to collect every bit of it much like Dylan **Thomas** had recalled Fern Hill. I wanted nostalgic memories of the place captured in my head for Paul, and **to show the world** that I, as though I were Paul, treasure **all of these** kinds of memories of Liverpool. All of these **things** in the song would give me Liverpudlian roots.

Each part of "Penny Lane" was based on what we saw when John showed me the place. I naturally did embellishments, but based it on our experience. We saw a barbershop, but would not stop there to use it. John's hair was already too short by then. Although, if we allowed it, we bet the barber would post our pictures on the wall and advertise for all to

Billy's Back!

see that he was the big champion barber who had cut off a Beatle mop-top! We laughed over that would-be barber hero. I imagined the barber taking pictures next of every haircut he ever did, "of every head he's had the pleasure to have known," and then proudly going around showing off his fine handiwork. There is a bank on the corner. **I imagined that** banker in Paul's motorcar. **Paul's wealth was safe in my** bank account. That banker never wore a **Mac**. I was really wearing a Mac since it was raining, but was also wearing Mac, meaning McCartney. I was both literally and figuratively doing what Paul's own banker would never do. That is why the children are secretly laughing at him. He handles the money, and thinks he is important; but the banker is just another hard working stiff. Because I wear this Mac, I get much more money than his bank would ever know.

NOTE: In retrospect, it is difficult to remember, or even comprehend, the prevailing narrow-minded intolerance of 1964 when the Beatles were launched on the unsuspecting American public. The fact that we can scarcely imagine it now is a testament to that social engineering success.

The Beatles "mop-top" haircuts, along with other marks of rebellion, were intended to offend the older generation. It worked. The elders rejected the new idols, driving the youth to reject their would-be stabilizing elders. By dividing the generations, freeing the world of their own nourishing roots, those targeted were free to discover and embrace the artificially generated pro-drug youth movement that was taught to not trust anyone over thirty—even though those who set up the scheme were all considerably older.

The Beatles were conservative enough for wide acceptance by all except the squares who were seen as too old to know anything. Bands immediately followed with more blatant rebellion, and with so much longer hair that the Beatles original mop-tops were quickly seen as conservative.

In the text, William, tongue in cheek, laughs at the idea of the Penny Lane barber cutting Beatles hair. Actually, their original mop-tops were kept neatly trimmed. Their meticulously controlled image required regular hair-cuts. For the sake of the song, they did each receive a haircut by that barber who did indeed display their photographs. However, the barber did not, as William's joke suggested, violate their intended image.

Everywhere I went with John, he filled me in on the local humor. I do not know how much of it had to do with Liverpool, and how much was a mere reflection of John and Paul's own language from a while back when they were juvenile delinquents. However, two of John's "Liverpool obscenities" did make it into the song. One was "finger pie." John joked that the Beatles were "Four of fish and finger pie," having our fingers in the women. We also refer to male anatomy with the "fireman" who "likes to keep his fire engine clean." **I thought** this Liverpool smut would convince **the local lads** that I was one of them. It did not–and no one else **got it.** That Liverpool connection failed.

Really, the entire song flaunted a fully false vision of Liverpool to all the locals who knew the place. I had been there several times, but still fancified Merseyside as a magical Beatles land. Everyone else knew better. The song was a flop here: the Beatles' first single in four years that did not hit the top of the British charts. It did, as I said, hit the top in the United States, but not here where they knew the place. It worked in America because they knew even less of Liverpool than I.

I also remember girls calling about Paul from Wales, Germany, Spain, California, Alberta, and Tarsus. (Just kidding about Tarsus. It is an old Paul joke.) For us, it was a big secret; but **Paul had** to have his fun. Fortunately, none of **his friends** betrayed him. Those who did talk were not friends.

It occurred to me some time after locals, who disliked the place, scoffed at "Penny Lane" that maybe it would have sold better in England if I had made up a street name instead of borrowing one. If **I had called it** "Donna Lane," it would have been as **magically ethereal** here as in the States—and the girl slain and "lain" to rest could have been mentioned.

After I fell for Linda, I considered that if I had sung, "Melinda Lane," those with ears could have broken the simple code that Melinda means "My Linda" just as I sang Madonna to represent "Macca's Donna." It would have worked. My Linda Lane is in my ears and in my eyes. It suggests that **all I see and hear is** Li**n**d**a**, or her la**n**e. It would have a nice meaning with various overtones depending on what people **c**an bring to it. Penn**y**, the girl, never did mean anything to me. It was just a girl I met who had a name like Denny. On the other hand, in all my life, no one has ever filled my heart, mind, soul, and imagination as did my lovely Linda.

29⁽³¹⁾

"High Brow"

Paul's right eyebrow was a real pain in the forehead for me. When I started this act, it was **a**n absurdly big deal to John. He insisted that I not sing without raising my right eyebrow. When lifting **u**p my left eyebrow, he would hassle me about it. Naturally, I **was** obliging, in light of who **I am**, and learned to do it right. Yet, activating the Eye of **Ra** or of **Horus** motivated him less than the chance to irritate me. He claimed it mattered to him because it mattered to those who gave me that role. I must never sing as Paul without raising my right eyebrow.

Raising both was okay; but the right had to be included. It could not be outdone by the left, just as the sun cannot outshine the moon. I could never neglect the highbrow mark of Paul in my forehead even though it made my forehead stiff and sore for

---

NOTE: Aleister Crowley's, *The Book of the Law*, channeled from Aiwass, is a primary religious text for many in the Illuminati. According to Crowley, that book marks the beginning of a spiritual age called the "Æon of Horus."

With some design variation, the Eye of Horus, or of Ra, is the Eye of Providence, or All-Seeing Eye. In Masonry, it usually has semi-circular glory below it, or is enclosed by a triangle or pyramid. In Paul, we see both. The semi-circular glory below the eye is formed by his semi-circular lower eyelashes, complete with rays. The pyramid's upper lines are formed by his high bending eyebrow, combining to create the modern Eye of Illumination.

277

months. I had to pay my dues with repetitions of right eyebrow lifting. If **you know** that's easy, you should try it sometime. **Sit** there for an hour at a time doing nothing else, **just** repetitions of working forehead muscles. It **ain't easy.** I would go back and forth: raising my right eyebrow over and over again, then raising and dropping both of them again and again. If you do this exercise right, repeatedly pushing yourself, you will understand.

I welcomed the awareness that comes with the eternal Eye of Paul activation, and its associated mystical benefits; but my upper-face hurt for the first horrendous months. If you try it for just one hour, you will have empathetic pain for days. It builds enormously strong muscles, or, at least strong for facial muscles. The standard "Paul is Dead" legend about it was that I had surgery to look like Paul. Well, I had facial surgery too, but not as fully as is described. The eyebrow muscles took work. I have to pay my dues if I want to sing Paul clues.

NOTE: The All-Seeing Eye comforts some, but unnerves others. It reminds Freemasons that the Great Architect of the Universe observes humanity's thoughts and deeds. On the other hand, the global elite network, ruled by Illuminati families, uses intelligence gathered through nearly all national governments, and other major corporations. Many Americans understand that phone calls, text messages, and other electronic communications are recorded and analyzed by NSA computers, and by others; but might not realize how much of that data is also available to the elite who are connected to the NSA.

Likewise, satellite imaging, cameras in street intersections, and elsewhere, have staggering information-gathering capacity when facial recognition software is applied. Search engines and social media sites compile user profiles based on searches, clicks, likes, comments, and purchases, dictating what information and products to market to whom, and informing various corporations how to manipulate each human specifically. Micro devices are learning to communicate with each other, sending personal data that may potentially be exploited. Most of us are being tracked via our cellphones. Before long, if some globalists have their way, everyone will be tracked and controlled by chips embedded in our bodies.

The all-seeing eye reminds us of the cute Beatle. Yet, in light of how each human's file is gathered and beamed around the planet for control and for commercial purposes, let the great eye in the sky also remind us that our illuminated Big Brother is watching us.

Whenever **we wrote**, we always wanted double or triple **layers of** meanings in our lyrics. Once I had **lines** about John's insistence that I keep my eyebrow up. John hated that song because its double entendre suggested some sexual inadequacy, which was contrary to the intended Beatle image. Having never had to worry about falling short in that way, I just thought it was funny. I still do, which is precisely why I don't mind sharing it here. The lines were, "Well, she said I'd let her down now if I didn't keep it up. So I gave her my new number, saying, I think you're in luck." That "she" was John. He and I both enjoyed adding material about each other to our songs that we made sound as though we were singing to lost or new loves. That was a common Beatles practice. Some of the lyrics of our best songs we wrote or gathered that way. I still have rough tracks of those "High Brow" lyrics. Once I considered making it a Bonzos song; but with John singing backup, I decided to save it and work it into a future Beatles release. If I do, I will re-work it. I get off on revisions.

Actually, I have quite a bit of material with John, and some tracks of Paul before me. I will keep releasing more songs now and again, whenever I feel the time is right. I have become the guardian of the treasure house. **I am the** core of the apple. Seeds of fresh new **Beatle life** can spring from me at any moment, and often do.

Every time I sing now, I raise a high brow to Paul just as you might raise a glass to him. Now, doing it feels natural. I learned **to** automatically lower them to sing as Vivian, and **raise them** to sing as Paul. Originally, though, it **was an effort** and a frustration to me, and also to John. **At first**, John bothered me about it to no end. It did not matter if we were singing to learn a new song, or if we were recording, or whatever we were doing. If he ever caught me singing with a relaxed forehead, he ordered me to "sing right." He later complained that I was ordering him around too much; but he truly was ridiculous about this whole eyebrow of Paul mark in my forehead. No one ever knew how terribly irritating John could be to me. It was not something we shared publicly. **He was** far more open about me being **much too bossy** even though he was at the same time being **a pain in my head.**

Here's to Paul: "I always lift my eyebrow to you." It has become so much a part of me that I probably could not sing with a relaxed forehead now even if I wanted to. Besides, it would be a mockery to cut Paul out now, might just jinx my whole musical career.

Notice how different my eyebrows look when I sing as Paul from when I sang as Vivian Stanshall. I only sing with my eyebrows pushed up for Paul, and only sing with them pushed firmly down for Vivian. That distinction gives each their own look. More than Viv's fake teeth and latex, eyebrows changed the appearances, making each distinct. However, both are unnatural to me. When I am interviewed or on stage as **Paul**, I still keep it up. It is my disguise.

Brian Epstein **had** received training in such things. Very subtle mannerism **differences** make a persona seem entirely unique. The subconscious mind is impressed by such details that most of us are not aware of consciously. An eyebrow pencil made Vivian's brows look thicker also, making them seem heavier on his face—the exact opposite of Paul's.

30[(32)]

"The Parting on the Left Is Now . . . on the Right."

Lefties stand out all right. Not only did I have to learn to play all of Paul's guitars left-handed, but everyone tried to get me to part my hair on the left side as **Paul had done his** whole life. The problem for my **hair** is that it **naturally** parts on the right.

Unless I paste it down, my hair naturally falls to the other direction. That is why all of the pictures of Paul from his early childhood up until his death in September 1966, has his hair parted on his left, and why from that date until now my hair is always seen parted on the right. Even **when** it is not combed at all, it naturally goes **that** way.

Right off, my biggest **challenge was** to learn to play the bass backward, it **being** Paul's instrument. I also had to learn to play **Paul**'s other instruments that way. Once I could play it **like that, I still had** to get it to my lap backward. I had **to get into the habit** of picking it up backward. You would understand if you have played for any length of time. You pick up a guitar and play. After a while, you no longer have to think about it. It is automatic.

Billy's Back!

With that automacy, I have sometimes forgotten. Memory is in the muscles. **The body** unites with it. Imagine how unnatural it **would** be to all of a sudden have to pick up a guitar and **hold it** wholly backward, and then to play it entirely **backward**. It is kind of like playing the piano while facing away from the keys. It is possible for you to learn **to play** it with your hands behind your back, or maybe not. Either way, even if you could do it, it would not feel normal to you. If you simply wanted to play a song, it is not the way you would approach the piano or guitar—unless you deliberately switched it.

Sometimes when I am talking, or when anything is on my mind other than remembering how to pick it up, **I reach for** it forgetting to pick it up backward. Then there is **the** awkward moment of switching the guitar to the **other hand.** Imagine how ridiculous I have felt, looking as though I did not know how to pick up my own instrument!

At first, whenever **I** composed, I played right-handed. I also always **played** right-handed when I recorded alone. With **Paul's bass** rewired for the lefty, I would **sometimes** go back and forth, doing each part to mastery right-handed before learning it left-handed. Still, right-handed feels right.

Even in the music video for "Penny Lane," my first single, I reach to pick up my guitar to play it right-handed, then quickly correct myself to hold it in the backward position. I have been caught playing the guitar right-handed from time to time. I would already be playing it when someone would stop in on me, but not usually while they held cameras.

"The Parting on the Left Is Now . . . on the Right."

Usually when I knew I was being filmed, I remembered, but not always. 50 minutes into *the Beatles Anthology 7: June '67 to July '68,* for example, I am playing guitar right-handed. I could have edited it out, but do not care anymore. It is a mistake I still make now and then. When I am alone, especially when **I am** composing a song, it is still easier to play **right-handed.** That has never changed. For my public performances, I still make myself learn to play them left-handed. However, after all these decades, it is still extra work.

By filling in for someone who is left-handed, there are handedness issues that could surface endlessly. For example, from photographs, many people have become aware of my cigarettes in my right hand, and of **Paul's** always in his left. The smoking hand **switch was** conscious on *Abbey Road,* especially since **my** cigarette, the cancer stick, or coughin' nail, is a **coffin** nail **too**. I became more vocal about cancer sticks as coffin nails since Linda and George both died of cancer. For Linda, natural

---

NOTE: William, above all others, yearned to reveal the switch, but also had strong incentives to maintain plausible deniability. He frequently participated in elaborate disclosure measures, as well as in self-protective counter-measures. Like writing a mystery novel, the strategy is to present several bits of solid information, along with one bit that can be discredited, maintaining the uncertainty that guides readers to flip-flop opinions.

For example, after William was filmed playing the guitar left-handed, he had the negative flipped to make it appear that someone caught him playing right-handed. He then drew attention to it to have PID fans take notice. When enough people use the footage to prove that he is right-handed, others will discover that the film had been flipped, thus discrediting the PID camp, maintaining balance with PIA fans, to whom he pretends that he had no knowledge of the deception in the first place.

Making clues and counter-clues has the added benefit of keeping this important story alive. If Paul's replacement had been announced in 1966, the world would have moved on. All would have mourned, but welcomed "Billy Shears" as more than a fantasy. Until the matter is settled once and for all, the energy surrounding it cannot rest. This is yet one more way that Paul lives.

Billy's Back!

estrogen in her breasts, not cigarettes, got the cancer going. However, **smoking is** what killed George.

Now with cancer being **a plague** on the world, I am sorry to have held cigarettes at all, particularly when photographers have been present. That is not an image **I want to promote** to **the** world any more. Having seen what cancer can do, even to a strong, healthy, and **beautiful woman**, I realize there is not enough good that can come of cigarettes to make

NOTE: All poisons are addictive. All addictions require an element of harm. Since the smoke of organic non-GMO tobacco is noncarcinogenic, and not otherwise harmful enough to be highly addictive, most commercially successful tobacco cigarette companies intentionally lace their products with poisons.

Consumers may buy the single ingredient of tobacco, roll their own cigars or cigarettes, and smoke them with much less harm than would come from most pre-prepared cigarettes. Some smokers mix tobacco with healthful herbs such as cannabis. Blunts from organic plants should always be preferred over carcinogenic cigarettes. Where lawful, you may wish to honor George with either an organic Non-GMO blunt, or pure herb, when you reach this page.

According to the American Lung Association, most commercial cigarettes contain approximately 600 ingredients. When burned, cigarettes create more than 7,000 chemicals. 69 of these chemicals are known to cause cancer.

Many of these chemicals also are found in consumer products that have warning labels—such as rat poison packaging. While the public is warned about the danger of the poisons in such products, there is no such warning for the carcinogens and other toxins in tobacco smoke.

For increased profits, big corporations bribe politicians to make laws that are against the common good. For that reason, while unprofitable healing herbs are often illegal, many cigarettes legally contain these poisons:

Acetone—found in nail polish remover
Acetic acid—an ingredient in hair dye
Ammonia—a common household cleaner
Arsenic—used in rat poison
Benzene—found in rubber cement and gasoline
Butane—used in lighter fluid
Cadmium—active component in battery acid
Carbon monoxide—released in car exhaust fumes
Formaldehyde—embalming fluid
Hexamine—found in barbecue lighter fluid
Lead—used in batteries
Naphthalene—an ingredient in mothballs
Methanol—a main component in rocket fuel
Toluene—used to manufacture paint

them okay. Nevertheless, as the photos show, **Paul** never smoked with his right hand; I never **smoked** with my left. I did try left-handed smoking, **but** it was uncomfortably awkward. Later, when my identity was not questioned, it occurred to me **that** my right-handedness was a fine Paul clue. I **was** glad to see my smoking pictures back **then** when I was not yet concerned about promoting cancer and heart disease. I enjoyed giving that clue.

Right-handedness became an issue in the press just two years ago when someone first said, based on my signature, I seemed to be right-handed. Their claim was that since Paul was left-handed, I could not really be him. It mattered because of a legal document I had signed regarding a paternity suit in Germany. The story was in the *Bild* (formerly *Bild-Zeitung*) which is still the best-selling newspaper in Europe, and has the sixth-largest circulation in the world. Many people read about it.

Making a further deal of my handwriting, some people compared my signature (which they say looks right-handed) in the eighties with Paul's on display in the Hamburger Beatles-Museum from the sixties. I, they say, do not have a comparable signature. While it is true that **I practiced his signature**, going over it repeatedly **before signing checks** and documents for Paul **in September 1966**, I have since then drifted to a more creative signature. My left-handed writing is not natural enough for it to look right. Nevertheless even "if I'm wrong [left], I'm right where I belong" ("Fixing a Hole").

With the line breaks where I put them in that part of the song, I hid what I was saying. **I will tell you** how to read it: "It really doesn't matter **if I'm wrong**," meaning, if I'm the wrong guy, or **if I'm wrong** to entertain as though I were Paul. "**I'm right where** I belong. I'm right where I belong." Do **you see** how the right punctuation unlocks the message? **I am** saying, "Even if I'm the wrong guy, **this is where I belong.**"

Even after **I joined** the Beatles, I still enjoyed joining in **the fun comedy** of The Bonzo Dog Band. I wore such distinctive disguises that when a conflict kept me from performing with them, it was easy to be away providing that I loaned them a gorilla suit. I did not have to loan out my latex noses and ears. Even after Vivian "died" to give me more time with Linda, others wore my Vivian costume now and then.

Like those of many bands, members of the Who were all close friends of the Beatles, especially two of them: Pete Townshend and Keith Moon. Through that connection, the Who all became the Bonzos' new friends when I joined the Beatles. So much so, we decided to tour together. The Bonzo Dog Band got each audience warmed up with musical laughter; then the Who put on the main show.

In the years before I became friends with the Who, **Linda had already gotten to know** them, and **many other celebrities,** through her photography. **They were all good friends.** Like Donovan and the Rolling Stones, the Who also made a few fine Paul songs. My favorite one ties into this chapter by including a line about our differing hair: "The parting on the left / Is now the parting on the right."

Going on, still about hair, the next line refers to the instant moustaches on *Sgt. Pepper's,* and to the beard hiding my face later. "And the beards [moustaches] have all grown longer overnight."

That song, "Won't Get Fooled Again," recognizes our "Revolution," revolving Pauls, as leading to the worldwide political upheaval. Pete calls it a "new revolution." John tried to depict the same chaos of having that revolution in his "Revolution 9." Pete refers to it saying, "**We'll be fighting** in the streets." Everyone is all up in arms **about** it, all alarmed. That is the way with revolutions. **Paul** is the *Revolver*.

Recognizing *Sgt. Pepper's* role in changing the world, setting a new drug-friendly moral code, Pete explains that part of the globalists' agenda. "And the morals that they worship will be gone." The same institutions that supported the Beatles and opened media doors for us furthered their NWO agendas by publicly denouncing us—turning the good boys bad. "And the men who spurred us on [those with EMI connections to Tavistock] Sit in judgment of all wrong / They decide and the shotgun sings the song." Letting them call the shots, **they privately supported** us while publicly villainizing us for **further division** of generations, **breaking down the family** in order to unravel society's **fabric in preparation for the** new order with the **NWO** constitution—and my deal.

With a double **meaning**, Pete refers to both the government change and to **the new constitution** of the Beatles who revolved Pauls to make that change. With respect for it, he says, "I'll tip my hat to the new constitution / Take a bow for the new revolution."

Insiders, including Pete, just "Smile and grin at the change all around me." They don't say anything. They just quietly enjoy being aware of it. The next lines are of me ("another day") from my perspective having to play Paul's ("Yesterday's") bass guitar. I "Pick up my guitar and play / Just like yesterday." That bit is of me learning to play Paul's left-handed bass just like Paul, but can be generalized, as John had put it, "Nothing has changed it's still the same." Then I, or Pete, pray that we, the whole world, are not ever fooled that way again. "And I'll get on my knees and pray / We don't get fooled again."

Being around when **Paul** was having his death dreams, dying all the time, trying desperately to work everything out before he **died**, Pete also had early warning. "Change it had to come / We knew it all along." The world's values, toppled by *Sgt. Pepper's,* were liberating to our generation, and would not have taken place if not for a look-alike. "We were liberated from the fall [Paul's death] that's all / But the world looks just the same /And history ain't changed / 'Cause the banners, they all flown in the last war." Everything looks the same as before our revolution. As a dual meaning, it says the Vietnam War was the same as the Korean War that went before it. Both had the banners of Communist and Anti-Communist.

"I'll move myself and my family aside" was of me giving up my life and loved ones to take this role. **My connection to Paul**, having two Pauls in one flesh now, **makes my combined self** only half-alive. Reaching toward Paul **in the sky**, I thankfully hold up my contract. "If we happen to be left **half alive** / I'll get all my papers and smile at the sky" knowing

"The Parting on the Left Is Now . . . on the Right."

that fans, having been hypnotized by our music, will go on as if I'm Paul. "For I know that the hypnotized never lie / Do ya?" Hypnotized, they swear I am Paul.

Here again, with the Paul revolution, there does not appear to be any change. "There's nothing in the street / Looks any different to me." Our slogans have changed even though we use the same Beatles banner. **The love songs** have been replaced by Paul's goodbye. "The **slogans are replaced**, by-the-bye." Under our old slogans, **it was "She loves you, yeah, yeah, yeah." Now he screams, "Yeaaaaaaaaaah!"**

The song's last lines use one of our double audio track tricks. They sing, "Meet the new boss / Same as the old boss." On one level, it is saying once again that everything is still the same. Subconsciously you may have also picked up on another meaning.

"Won't Get Fooled Again" was originally much longer than the heavily edited single version. The Who recorded it in the Rolling Stones Mobile Studio early in the spring of 1971. They overdubbed the last line at a lower volume with the same words except for the last one that says "Paul." When you hear "Meet the new boss / Same as the old boss," listen to it carefully to hear, "Meet **the** new boss / Same as the old Paul." Since the **brain can** only process one thing at a time, it **subconsciously** selects the most reasonable message, **favor**ing expected lines over unexpected overdubbed **messages.** That is one of the advantages of overdubbing.

The "Paul is Dead" revelation of 1969, which failed to reach general acceptance, followed by me ending the band in 1970, made it time for Pete to tell the story in 1971. In his song's final couplet, he lets the world in on two of our secrets. The first was that Paul died. **The second** was that I, looking like Paul, **became the new Beatle boss.** "Meet the new boss / Same as the old Paul." If you listen intending to hear "Paul," you will likely hear it, but will also hear the final "s" sound of "boss," making the word unintentionally sound like "Pauls." Listen for "Meet the new boss / Same as the old Pauls."

Replacing Paul was seen as **a revolution**. He was the revolver. By **replacing Paul**, I inherited him, which **further empowered** the social engineers to put **their revolution** of global consciousness into force **to prepare for** their new age with **the new world order.** Having the Beatles evolve helped **the world** to evolve with us. The world **was prepared for the new constitution**. "You say you want a revolution. . . . We all want to change the world."

Since you are going to run to the Internet now to see that Paul's hair parting on the left is switched in every picture past his death on 11 September 1966 to my hair parting on the right, here is some even harder evidence for you to find while you are at it. Once you know what to look for, the switch is obvious.

My facial injections and other alterations gave me a Paulish look. Still, one change that I did not make, you did not seem to notice. Human earlobes come in two basic styles. Based on one's genetic dominance, earlobes are either both detached, hanging free from the head, like you can see mine are; or they are both attached, joined to the head, like Paul's.

"The Parting on the Left Is Now . . . on the Right."

With the ease of Internet image searches, you really do not have to look very long or hard to find profile pictures of myself and of Paul. You may see that in September 1966, Paul suddenly switches from attached to detached earlobes.

Here is yet another ear clue. Besides the fact that his are attached, and mine are not, while you are at it, also notice that our ears are of entirely different shapes. Paul's ears were more rounded than mine, and popped out. Mine are more interestingly shaped. Again, if you consult **Paul McCartney** images, it is easy to see that he **does not have the same ears**. Notice, too, **that I have** less space between my eyes.

31⁽³³⁾

"Hey Jude"

In a séance one night in mid-November 1966, speaking with Paul's own voice, John and others heard me utter, "Take this, brother. May it serve you well." John quoted those lines in "Revolution 9." Again, in "Cry Baby Cry," I sing, "Brother can you take me back?" It ties into "Hey Jude" and others.

Doing the Paul role right was going to take time, partly because **I was** driven to be certain that I would always do it **better than he** would have. He and the others would go record a few takes of songs, and go home, leaving the rest up to George Martin and others. That was never how I did things. It still is not. In October 1966, Brian Epstein told me that it was time to record an album, or a song as a single, for the Christmas market. I told him that my first Beatles record would surely be of far greater quality than that. It would take some time. We released our first single in February.

For two weeks, Brian tried repeatedly to persuade me, telling me that it is how all of their records had been done. I said, "That was John's band. This is my band. We do things differently."

On 31 October, in the morning, he met with EMI and broke the news that there would be no new material for Christmas. This report was entirely unacceptable to EMI who stood to lose significant potential profit. As a compromise, they decided to release a Beatles' greatest hits album that was called, *A Collection of Beatles Oldies.* I am the tall blond man on the front cover. New mix sessions were set up to turn previous released mono recordings into stereo mixes. Although we were urged to be a large part of it, I **was not** interested. "Hey Jude" looks back at what happened that night.

All of the song, "Hey Jude," is clearer when you grasp how Paul's entity became attached to me. Séances, I want you to recognize, are practically always **a bad** idea. Don't do them. For direction, kinesiology is much safer because it communicates with your own muscle cells rather than trusting just any **lying** spirit. Séances open the doors to any **demon** or evil spirit who chooses to mess with you. Now, I was lucky that it was Paul who showed up and not some imposter. Too often, when people divine with the help of familiar spirits, those who come to them are not the people they pretend to be. You can mess yourself up that way. When trying to communicate with the dead, most people tend to overlook their lack of positively identifying the spirit.

NOTE: Besides brazenly positioning William on the front cover of *A Collection of Beatles Oldies,* we find him dressed very modernly, far less conservatively than the Beatles had been with their matching suits. It showed that even the Beatles were now out of date. Their "oldies" (recorded from 1963 to 1966) included hits released only four months earlier on *Revolver.* The world was braced for the new Beatles direction.

BILLY'S BACK!

It takes very positive energy to discern entities. Unless one's own energy blocks them, spirits reached by séances, or by Ouija boards can attach to those who sit in on such things, causing many illnesses of mind, body, and spirit. **Paul McCartney is not** what I have usually thought of as **an evil spirit**; but even he has brought me considerable pain. He still has an awful lot of stuff to work through that is now attached to me. **I must deal** with his burdens.

Letting **this information** out disquiets me. Even though I do not want any of my readers to think I lived any of my life conservatively, and wanting full disclosure of my poor choices along with my many really good ones, I care about all living things–including my readers whom I do not want hurt by emulating my mistakes.

The Beatles were not as happy as our image could portray. We were **all extremely miserable. This Paul bit took a terrible toll on us all.** Although everything may seem wonderful to outsiders, there was more pain than you would ever want to imagine. I decided it was time to tell all in this new revealing book, including our involvement with the occult, and various other things that you can know about on some level, but not ever do without also receiving every pain that naturally comes with it—which I cannot describe.

The Beatles' biggest hit was "Hey Jude," which was our debut release for our own new Apple label. One day, during John and Cynthia's break-up, **I was** listening to the radio in the car, and mostly **singing** along, as I drove out to Weybridge to visit with Cyn and Jules. The Drifters were doing their popular Pomus/Shuman song, "Save the Last Dance for Me." In that song, another guy holds his date's hand in the pale moonlight, and dances every song with her. The singer urges her to remember who is giving her a ride home at the end of that dance. I imagined myself on a stage singing, hoping my date would end up with me when it was all over, but watching her dancing with, and being romanced by guys I could play for, but not interrupt. It could be a troublesome position.

I compared the song to what was going on with John and Cyn. Cynthia helplessly watched as John and Yoko grew in their mutual obsession, but could not interrupt it. As a soda commercial came on, I turned off the radio, thinking about what I could say to Julian that might give him some comfort and encouragement. **I sang,** "Hey Jules, don't take it bad," which became, "**don't make it** bad." I have said that "Hey Jude" was **about Julian**; but that line is about as far as his connection goes with it. I wanted him to envision John and Yoko more positively.

Though I was ordered not to interfere with the work Yoko was sent to do on John, I never encouraged it. John fancied me singing for him to go after her: "Hey John, don't let me down. / You have found her, now go and get her." However, I never made a secret of my utmost disregard for her, and for her absence of musical talent. By then, the band was already disintegrating. Clearly, Yoko's intolerable recording interference did not help. John knew I would never endorse their union. I hated Yoko then. Yet, since John was unstable, Yoko was sent to be his handler.

Some call it a drug song. **I sang, "Let** it out and let it in," reminding them of **shots of heroine** entering the blood stream: "let her **under your skin**" . . . "let her into your heart." **The useful drug slant** entirely misdirects what the song **is** about. It is a slight of hand causing all **to look away from** its real meaning, distracted by **that** which they think are hidden messages in another **direction.**

The name "Jude" is the first missed clue. Who is Jude? That question leads us to whom the song is about. The **Jude** most of us know of is the Jude dude in the Bible. Who **is** he? The first verse of his book says, "Jude, **the . . . brother of James**" (Jude 1:1). In plainer words, **I am Jude, the brother** of James. I assume the name Jude **symbolically** as the brother **of James Paul McCartney.** In this song, I am singing about what has to do with the way Paul and I became one. It gets a bit mystical here; but hear me out. You will see that it is true as you find the bigger picture woven through this mystery book. I would not have believed it myself if it had not happened to me. I do not ask you to **believe** me right off, but to gather it in along with **everything** else **in this book of** secrets to see what realizations come to **light.** Just wait a while to decide if it is true or not. **That is all** I ask from you.

Here it is. Not at first with our initial visits in Paris and London, but about two months later, we invited Paul to create a better connection by joining us in a midnight séance around a table. We set a chair for Paul across the table from me. I just sat and stared into empty darkness above the chair. We held the séance for over an hour before I spoke to the group with Paul's voice. Later, they all denied that Paul had spoken to them, even though only Paul had known things I said. John called it a lark. They argued that I did it on my own since my own voice is somewhat similar to **Paul**'s. There were six of us counting Paul. George **sat at my** right. John sat between George and Paul's **empty chair.** On my left were Brian Jones and Mick Jagger. Paul spoke of his brother, Mike McCartney, and of Jane Asher, wanting me to befriend them both in his place. He said, "I will love them both through you."

Ringo, who only had my word for it, having missed that midnight séance, said, "How convenient! Only you know if it came from yourself or from Paul; but it gives you access to his girl!" Mick told him that Paul "supposedly" also told me that I was welcome to all of Paul's royalties–a point everyone questioned, especially Mick. However, I already had Jane and the money by then.

As Paul's words came from me, in a voice that only I could be positive was not my own, I felt a burning sensation in my left shoulder. **That is** when and where Paul permanently attached **himself** as an out-of-body spirit. Since his death, **he has** continued here as an earthbound entity **attached to me**. He is under my skin, and has been **since that encounter.** As one of the spirits comprising my own soul at this time, **I always feel his** influence and sometimes think his **thoughts.** From this oneness, and from my dreams of him, my transition and transformation was surprisingly simple. There is now a genuine encompassing part of me that is James Paul McCartney. **I am literally part Paul**. I have always let him work **through** me because he is me.

I embody **Paul's own spirit** as completely as I **embody** my own. I truly do not know, and do not **fully** care, which notes, or which lyrics, come from **the Paul part, and** whatever music comes from **the Billy part of me.** It no longer matters. In the beginning, **I wanted** everything to be my own, but was also thrilled **to channel some** of Paul's music into my own **creative process**. My pride wanted to say it was all me, **that** I **was** the **brilliant** one. Really, none of it is all me, or all you. In our most creative moments, we connect to the universal mind that is given to all of us. Nonetheless, I am more connected to Paul because he, or his spirit, is attached to me.

Having fully integrated with the **Paul** part of myself, it has all become me. He **will not go** until I go to the light with him. **He is mine for life.** He lives through me, combining our interests and our musical talents. "Hey Jude" is about me, the brother of James Paul, fully letting him into my heart. It is about me forsaking my reluctance to be totally one with him. It is for me to perceive him as myself, not as a sub-personality, but as an integral part of the whole, just as my William past is of the whole. I was told, "Whom virtue unites, death will not separate."

While joining with Paul was partly positive, his overwhelming emotional pain devastated me. Not knowing how to distance myself from it, I was martyring myself every day. With that background, consider me, as Jude (James' brother) being told to yield to the discarnate spirit of the late James Paul McCartney. I will enlarge the song for clarification:

Hey Jude, do not make being one with Paul a bad thing. / Take this sad song of Paul's death that ended his life in his body, and make it better through you–who are getting better, better, a little better all the time. / It is not enough to merely have Paul whisper to you as **the angel** on your shoulder. Remember to let this **entity** into your heart. / Then you **can start to make** it better. / Don't be afraid of **this transformation**. / You were made, predestined, to go out and get that entity. / The minute you let **P**aul under your skin / was when you began to make this situation better. / Hey Jude, whenever you **a**ctually feel Paul's emotional pains, / just hold off a bit, back away from that connection. Refrain a bit **u**ntil he **can** let go of his pains for another season. / Don't carry his heavy world upon your shoulders. **L**et this **be** a good thing. Don't make it bad. Be happy with Paul. / For well you know that it's **a fool** who plays it cool /By making his world a little colder. You do not have to suffer to be cool. That much you know by now. You don't have to feel all of his pains merely because he does. /

That would disappoint me if you suffered all this pain, Jude. Don't let me down like that. / You must affirm your oneness with all but Paul's pain. Now that you have found Paul's soul, go and make him completely you, as he makes you completely him. / Remember to let him into your heart. / Then you will have the best of Paul connected to the best of you. Together, you will start to make it better.

BILLY'S BACK!

Enough of his pains. **Let the** hard feelings out; and let Paul's great love and **creative energy in**. By doing that, all the best of **your union** will begin. / Jude, you're waiting **for someone to perform** with. However, the power is already **within you.** You're the leader of the band. / And don't you know that it's just you? You think you are not enough, but you'll do just fine. / Don't wait for the others to move you to action. The only movement you need is by the angel on your shoulder. Paul will move you.

Seeing now what the song is really about, if you go and re-read the genuine lyrics, you will see everything in a very different way. You will also begin to understand why it became easy to channel love and talent from Paul. The insiders thought it was weird that I instantly became so close to Jane. For me, however, it was as though I had loved her for as long as **Paul had**, except that I also had all those **other interests** from the William part of me as well. **He was** in me like a multiple personality, **overly devoted to Jane** with part of my mind, and sabotaging it with another. It was not until I mutilated **that relationship** that I was free to love another. It **was at a perfect time** for lovely Linda Eastman **to enter my life**. Still, the Paul part of me continued to long for Jane, as I expressed in songs.

NOTE: In the seventies, William was often asked how Linda Eastman was related to George Eastman, founder the Eastman Kodak camera and film company. Some people thought that she had inherited the Eastman Kodak fortune. William always answered that they were not related. A better question, one rarely asked, was how she was related to Brian Epstein. She and Brian were both descended from Epsteins in the old Russian Empire.

Linda's father, Leopold Vail Epstein, as named by his Jewish Russian immigrant parents, changed his name to Lee Eastman without any connection to George Eastman.

Coming from that Jewish heritage, Linda naturally also desired to raise their children to be Jewish. Although William did not convert, he was always supportive of raising their children in that heritage, participating positively.

William's current wife, Nancy Shevell, is also Jewish.

"Hey Jude"

I like to play with words, sometimes massaging the same line to take on several meanings, with all of them fitting the same song. Besides the

NOTE: William does indeed like to play with words! He says here that he enjoys massaging the same line to take on several meanings within a song. It should also be understood that he is extremely skillful in his word selection in writings prose and in speaking.

Even in interviews, where he does not have the luxury of re-working his lines, he engages in an uncommonly clever level of masterful speaking. He bounces back and forth between levels of meaning so that the take-away message will be one thing for those who believe he is the biological Paul, and (in those same few words) will mean something entirely different to those who can tell when he is speaking as himself, and when he is speaking for the PAUL MCCARTNEY corporate fiction. To understand the method, imagine being an actor playing the role of James Bond. When an interviewer asks if you enjoyed your lunch, you answer as yourself. But when asked how you overcame the global enemy, you answer as if you were that character.

A footnote in the next chapter has an example of William saying things to validate conflicting positions. His ridiculous excuses for "Paul is Dead" clues assure those who cannot bear to know that Paul is gone, giving them a way out of that dreaded thought, while also making the story so absurd that insiders laugh with him at their gullibility—allowing each side to laugh at the other.

The same principle is embedded throughout this book. By masterfully writing in layered meaning, William conveys one message to one group of readers, and other messages to other groups, while winking to insiders who have enough background information to comprehend all of the levels.

This book is primarily written for six audiences:

First, there are those who are open to raising their consciousness. This **gro**up is benefitted by straight information about how the world is run by the **glo**bal elite. They are given this PID context as a gateway to that broader **glo**bal awareness. This group is small, but have a great impact on the world. To them, William says, "**Go! Go! Go!**"

Second, this book is for those who are interested in details about how Paul was replaced. With love for the Beatles, or for Paul, they want to understand the secret messages that the Beatles spent hundreds of hours creating.

Third, this book is for those who do not want to believe that Paul was replaced, but who enjoy letting this magical mystery smash against their fixed paradigms for what some have called "the ultimate mind-f*ck."

Fourth, this book is for insiders who enjoy seeing their secret truths spread out before the world, but in protective layers.

Fifth, this book is also written for specific interest groups, saying enough to acknowledge or inform them, usually without saying enough for them to throw the book across the room—as some readers have done.

Sixth, this book is worded specifically for those who would create legal entanglements if this book were to say either too much or too little.

Based on the awareness, opinions, or interests that one brings to this book, one sees what others miss. We each have our own reasons and rewards.

quickly popular drug meaning of letting her under my skin to make it better, and **besides the** romantic interpretations, and the **spiritual meaning** of Paul attaching himself to me, **it also referenced** the injectable fillers that I received in **my face to** add roundness in order to better **resemble Paul.** It is a particularly strange feeling to have this highly unnatural substance in my face. I keep catching myself rubbing at it. I try not to. I also see that it looks unnatural, especially when I push on it with my fingers. It does not move like flesh.

Having Paul as a writing partner has made my music much better. It is as though I were instantly endowed with greater talent. I already had greater talent than Paul; but we manifested it in our own ways. Since I was infused with Paul's talent as well, that gift broadened my abilities. I still had to learn, obviously, but it came very easily to me in all the areas that he had mastered. People have asked relentlessly how **I** learned to play bass left-handed like Paul. I **tried to imitate** his playing until that kind gift from **Paul** made me one with it. Since that transforming November night, it has been much simpler—not preferred, but natural. The breakthrough was to play *as* Paul rather than *like* Paul. The idea of being Paul, or of working and living as him, rather than just like him, has been powerful. It has caused internal shifting that changed how I see myself and the universe.

Realizing, I suppose, that I am able to channel their music for them, that I am open to receiving it, others have also come to me with their work. It happens now and again. For example, I am still unsure how to understand the song, "Friends to Go."

Who waits for whom? Although I am credited with it, George wrote and channeled the words and the music to me a little more than three years after he crossed over. While writing it, **I suddenly** felt that I was George. First, I **felt his presence**, then my brain and hands became his own. **He was in** control. It was comforting to **me to receive it** so easily from him. **I was George then**. It was a gift of his love to me and **to the world.**

Sensing the presence of the departed is often all it takes to connect with them. They tend to stay around to support us. Donovan told us that all we need to do is to call out individuals' names three times to invite them to us. He sang, "Paul McCartney, Paul McCartney, Paul McCartney, **I call** your name." That line was part of his, "First there's **Paul** McCartney, then there's no McCartney, then there is" song. His lyrics reminded us that we do not need séances. We simply call the people to us, and sense their presence.

In all of the comparisons between the earlier Paul and myself, the most recognizable differences for anyone who knows us is in our personalities, and in how we interact with other people. Height differences made the switch rather obvious too. We had several bodily differences, and distinctions in our voices, just as in the distinct ways we each sing.

However, those with more spiritual sensitivity can understand a deeper difference. On YouTube, watch videos of Paul singing Beatles songs, and then of me doing it. When Paul sings, feel his presence. Feel his spirit. When I sing, feel mine. Feel the difference. His energy is not like mine. Feel who we are. **I possess** some of his energy, but am mostly myself, not **Paul.**

32⁽³⁴⁾

Do You Hear Voices?

In 1962, someone coined the word *voiceprint* from *voice* and *fingerprint*. Like **all fingerprints**, all voiceprints are **by unique genetic design**. In recent decades, **with significant** advancements made in computer **technologies**, voice differentiation has been used to **positively identify people.**

With voiceprints, each is unique—just like the data from hand geometry readers and iris scanners. I have been called the "man with a thousand voices," but all of my voices have only one voiceprint. I lack the ability to change my voiceprint. It is created by the shape of my mouth and my throat. Do not let my many voices fool you. As my voiceprint proves, they are all distinctively my own.

It is for that reason that the technology is not outwitted by a disguised voice, an illness, or by a voice that is emotionally charged. Those changes are not what spectrographs show. All those things make the voice sound different to the human ear, but always show the same distinctive pattern of voice characteristics that is produced spectrographically. I cannot vocally alter a spectrograph.

At establishments requiring the highest security in government, and in the private sector, it is now common to require the scrutiny of multiple identification methods. **Institutions may use** any of the several combinations of **voiceprint**s, keycards, iris scans, hand geometry **readers**, PINs, or keys. Having more than one method can increase the statistical probability **for correct identification**; but each of them, particularly of the biometric methods, is rather foolproof.

When the "Paul is Dead" frenzy broke out in the US in 1969, Dr. Henry M. Truby of the University of Miami used samples from Beatles songs to make **sonogram**s. He apparently hoped to prove with replicable **testing** that I am Paul McCartney. Yet, what he found **proved that** I am not. He showed at length that **Paul's voice** recorded on "Yesterday" **could not be my voice** on "Hey Jude." They were of different throat shapes. Others repeated that same experiment. When that came out, I thought it would decide it once and for all. Dr. Truby proved by that method that the singer of "Yesterday" is not the individual who sings "Hey Jude." *Life* magazine published **it all** 7 November 1969. That issue also gave clues; but it **seems like** any reason sufficed. For example, I explained that the only reason I have a black **carnation** in the grand ballroom

---

NOTE: William saying that he wore a black carnation because no one could not find another red one in all of London's many florist shops—like saying that he crossed Abbey Road barefoot because it was too hot to wear shoes on the hot pavement—shows the role of confirmation bias. Most people cannot stand to be wrong about long-held beliefs. When beliefs are threatened by fact or reasoning, one is tempted to accept any excuse to keep believing. Hence, this fine work to finally un-fool the fooled requires far more effort than was made to fool the whole world in the first place. Fear of being a fool makes us more foolish. Regarding relationships, religion, or rock and roll, it is far easier to fool folks than to finally convince them that they have been fooled.

Billy's Back!

finale scene of the *Magical Mystery Tour*, while all of the others wore red, is that we ran out of red ones. Being hard to find red flowers, **I have** a black one.

Here are some more clues if you can hear them. On 13 November 2000, **the** 30th anniversary of the end of the band, we released a compilation of 27 of our #1 hits. All of the songs had been digitally remastered for a **better, fuller sound.** The CD, titled *1,* was quickly the biggest selling album of the entire decade. Back in the sixties, my *Sgt. Pepper's Lonely Hearts Club Band* album was the biggest seller. No other band has had the best-selling album of more than one decade. We did well. If you own one of the 31 million copies of *1* sold worldwide, try this observation.

Notice, while skipping through the first several #1 Beatles hits, that practically all of their material emphasized falling in love, or needing the girlfriend. The Paul years were of one love song after more and more love songs. That infatuation niche defined them

---

NOTE: Digitally remastering top hits not only improved song quality, but also made the new releases more fully William's, making him largely responsible for all remastered Beatles hits recorded from 11 September 1962 (exactly four fab years before Paul died), and 1 April 1970 (April Fools' Day). Digitally remastering has greatly strengthened William's portfolio.

Some videos at www.JamesPaulMcCartney.com impressed William, but one troubled him when a guest said William "hates Crowley." Although William felt that Aleister lacked love for family and others who should have mattered more, William harbors no hate for the man. William responded, "There seems to be much misunderstanding about my Memoirs. Let's digitally remaster it and re-release it on 9-9-18. We'll call it the 'Nine After 9-09 Edition.'"

The first edition gave William nine years to prepare for this next level of openness. Now, in his final stretch of life, courageously favoring truth over diplomacy, he less cautiously buffers his Crowley connection, Illuminati affiliation, anti-religion perspective, drug use, and sexual liberation. He believes in personal freedom, and intends to use his songs, these Memoirs, and his interviews to encourage people to get over their inhibitions.

until Paul's death dreams. **Then came the best** of his material. It was at that **time that he wrote** "Paperback Writer," which was **distinctively not** romantic. It was not about girls or **about dying**, and is another one of his better songs. Donovan emphasized that he was referring to Paul, the "Paperback Writer," in the "Epistle to Dippy," by singing, "Doing us paperback reader." Two songs later on *1* is **Paul's last #1 hit.** Listen to him sing **"Eleanor Rigby."** That song, the last one on that CD that Paul sang, **is his most sophisticated.** What the song does not have is my own **singing quality.** I understand that most of you love the song. I do too. Only, someone with formal training in singing would have sung it better. **I do not mean** to fault him. He sang it great according to his own background and singing s**kills**.

Consider doing this simple listening inspection. Play "Eleanor Rig**by**" and listen to it. I mean, really listen to be**c**ome aware of his singing ability (or lack thereof) on th**a**t, his last g**r**eat masterpiece. **Hear his** untrained voice. Notice how out of **breath** Paul sounds at the end of each little line. **Pay attention to** every aspect. Listen to the way **his shallowness of** airflow causes his weakness of **voice.**

Saying all of this does not diminish the fact that it is an exceptional song. Just listen to hear how he falters in singing it. Hear how weakly he ends each line. Hear **his voice** and voice quality. Then skip to our "Penny Lane." It **is** the next song on the CD. Notice how **distinctly** it is not the same voice. It is ridiculously **obvious.** If not to you, go back and forth between songs until you recognize each voice. You will soon realize that each are one of the five Beatle voices that you have known very well, only that you stopped hearing Paul's voice once you started hearing mine. By switching back and forth until you know them both, you will train yourself to be able to distinguish between Paul and me as easily as between John and George. You can hear that it is not the same voice.

Lastly, **once you** can distinguish between our two voices, **listen** to my voice quality. Hear how it lasts fully **to the end** of each line with more voice to spare. **Hear the difference** in enunciation. Notice that I do not have a Liverpool accent, that I sound much more educated, and that I clearly had my share of voice training. Comparing his "Eleanor Rigby" with my "Penny Lane" gives you two consecutive hits: his last one, and my first. I do not write of the contrast to boast of my superior voice, or about the effortlessness in my singing. My point is to help you to **hear the variance.** I felt frantic for my first single as Paul **to sound** a lot like him. I needed help with it.

It was **close enough.** That voice, with John's right behind **it** in the harmony, told our fans that it **could only be Paul** singing lead. They could all tell that it was not George or Ringo. Thus, clearly, it could only be Paul. An outsider there was never imagined. It must be Paul singing lead with John doing backup on the Beatles' single. They always did it with either John or Paul singing lead, and with the other one singing backup. They did not ever let George do a single. That only happened later when he wrote "Something."

Only by listening to these songs back and forth, contrasting us as I describe, can you appreciate the very **distinct differences.** He is more nasally, less clear. His Liverpool **sound**, especially as in words ending with an "R,' are **not like mine**; and I play with the notes, adding far more sophistication.

Hearing how well I sing "Penny Lane" is significant because it is right after Paul recorded "Eleanor Rigby." However, the differences are even more clear with us both singing the same song. For an undeniable contrast, pull up Paul's version of "Eleanor Rigby," as well as my own version that I recorded for *Give My Regards to Broad Street.* On YouTube, compare them back and forth, line by line.

Having heard that profound difference, you will understand why John, aware of the difference, feared everyone else would notice too. It made him insecure with his singing. His new insecurity first became apparent while recording "Strawberry Fields." I laughed about him singing in different keys, and realized that he, who had been the leader of the world's biggest band, could not hear the difference. It became worse as he learned what my voice could do, compared to his or **Paul**'s. For the rest of our time together, he favored **singing** harder rock that better hid his voice. Still, **his best** songs were slow.

Next, as John began to **contrast my** music theory background with his, and my **musical skills** with his own, he had Yoko, not me, give him piano lessons. Although Paul had begun to play it before I joined, it was George Martin who had done almost all of their piano work before I took over.

33[39]

"Hey Bulldog"

I am explaining some of the less spectacular songs, such as "Hey Bulldog," along with the many truly great ones. I want to show our frame of mind in writing them, and how Paul was always part of it. We all wanted to create great works of music (or, at least I did), but also wanted to have fun now and again. I got along best with the others when I was playful. **My perfectionist** work ethic, being such a sharp **contrast to Paul's**, wearied my mates who had not been **pushed** so hard. Nevertheless, I not only worked **harder**, but played with greater gusto too. I had learned the arts of fun with the Bonzos.

Recorded 11 February 1968, "Hey Bulldog," was the last song that we taped before we all went to India. We had all gathered at Abbey Road to make a promotional film for "Lady Madonna" when I, the group's bulldog, decided to use that opportunity to make a new song, and to have some amusement. I was not the group's bulldog in a bossy sense of barking out orders, but as the leader. We would play now, and see what we might create while we were at it. It would be a product of playful invention.

As we had reached the studio, George criticized the lot of us for pretending to be recording the song, "Lady Madonna," without considering the irony of our commercial priority. He called our hypocrisy ludicrous. Although it was my song, he took it more seriously, and found it a bit distasteful. He said, "You are mocking Donna who couldn't make ends meet in the first place, and yet, here all of us are, deliberately intending to be false. For what? **For money**! At least she was real. Faking it may boost record sales and profit; but we did not need it. **We are all** wasting our time. Donna lost her life **over the financial** desperation we sing of; but for us it is just a **game**."

"Unless any of you have a more fantastic idea," I said, "as long as we have reserved this studio time, let's record something new." John soon came up with some lyrics he had started before. It was a song that saw me as a bullfrog. **I am** the lowly frog kissed by fate to make me **a prince.** John had become annoyed that I so easily excelled in the role of Paul without having heart, but with such unimaginable talent. **John felt** insecure about it. He wondered when **he too would be replaced.** The line, "What makes you think you're something special when you smile?" was about my new looks. Other lines were about my loneliness.

As magical as was the transformation of this mere frog to become the Beatles' crown prince, it had a down side for me. It isolated me from friends and relations. I became the lonely Sgt. Billy Pepper wanting to get back home, a nowhere man fool on the hill, one of all the lost and miserably lonely people that we described in our songs. As a group, we finished writing the piece. We each put in our own threepence, each shaping the song in our own directions. It has other elements too, but if you look at it as **I explain** it, you will surely admit that it is mostly **about me** replacing Paul—as was common **with our songs.**

Meanings were usually layered so that most of any song's lyrics would seem to be about one thing on one layer while about something else at the same time. We added other words that had a good sound. This song says, "Wigwam frightened of the dark." A wigwam, you know, is a domed hut used by certain Native American tribes. Obviously, huts are not frightened. I added the word because it sounds good, especially with "Big man." **I am** the big man there, being a lot bigger and **taller than Paul** and the others. If you do not believe me, you can contrast pictures of John standing next to me with older pictures of John standing next to Paul.

Notice how John and Paul were equally short in pictures of them standing together. That is why we ended the Beatles tours when Paul died. They had enjoyed sharing a microphone. It was not the same look to have me standing there so much taller. I got my own mic a few feet away.

"You can talk to me," was a point of reassurance that John was kindly extending to me. We were friends now. He says, "If you're lonely, you can talk to me." Saying that I am "standing in the rain" refers to me, the stand-in for Paul who died in the rain, feeling alone. I am the bulldog left alone out in the rain, but John is reaching out to me.

My solitude can be measured out in news of the group's actions. Wherever we go, the press writes stories, and snaps pictures, showing all to the world. I was in the news as if they knew me, but nobody did. **They thought** they knew me; but no one had a clue **that I was someone else.** We sang from my own point of view, "You think you know me, but you haven't got a clue." John had originally penned it, "Some kind of solitude is measured out in news," but did not write it clearly. I misread it as "measured out in you." It sounded good. Since none of us thought the word "news" was any better there, we kept it as I misread it.

The line, "Some kind of happiness is measured out in miles," was John's own way of telling me that happiness would come down the road. He was right. I am happier now. My new life became my own eventually as threats of consequences diminished. At that time, **I had terrible anxiety** about someone detecting and imprisoning me **for** what we now call identity theft. I wrote of **having** that fear earlier on when I **revealed some dark secrets** about the Rolling Stones. From the start, they knew the great Beatles secrets and did not seem quiet enough. It was about my intense fear that the Rolling Stones howled in some of their songs, and for which we sang here, "Some kind of innocence is measured out in years. You don't know what it's like to listen to your fears." **Time will** tell my innocence. Usually, I would **affirm** that I had nothing to do with the death, **that I rightly work as Paul** had said he wanted done **with his name and estate.** I fulfilled his will.

Essentially, this song, which started as "Hey Bullfrog," was about me, the kissed toad, hopping in as the new Prince Paul, but feeling lonely and isolated. I needed to talk to someone.

Going back in time a bit, **John had joked about** Paul croaking out a song like a bullfrog. **Paul** had a better voice than John, but would quickly become hoarse, sounding like a bullfrog. When I took over, I sometimes intentionally made myself hoarse to sound like Paul, the "Bullfrog, doing it again."

Near the end, being in a jovial mood, I barked, growled, and howled like a dog. We liked that new ending, and added on "Hey, Bulldog. Hey, Bulldog," justifying my idea to make "Hey, Bulldog" our new title.

Not only did **I,** as Paul, create clues to show the world that I am **William,** but as Vivian Stanshall, I gave clues to **show that I**, the musical comedian in the gorilla suit, **am Paul McCartney.** With this song in mind, I, as Viv, said, "Gentlemen, I am a bulldog, and you will find my bark is worse!"

Who else claimed to be the bulldog? **It was** me all along, the frog who could croak out **a song** and smile as special as Paul could. I played the part of Vivian as well as I played Paul's part, but neither role was whom **I am**. Now you finally know who I am. **The Paul role** was something that I stepped into and **reinvented** as time went on. The roles of Vivian Stanshall and Phil Ackrill (rhymes with Bill or Will), I invented from the start. I am the Bulldog.

NOTE: William used the role of Phil Ackrill before giving it (attempting to lease it) to Phillip Ralston—while reserving the option to do performances occasionally, and to give recording assistance. Ralston, the new Phil Ackrill, enthusiastically received the role in hopes of a recording contract. When that contract failed to materialize, William lost interest in the band, leaving the role entirely to Ralston who later likewise became discouraged, quit the band, and pursued a career outside of the music industry.

Although William says he "invented" the Phil Ackrill role, the name appears to have been suggested to William by an associate of Ralston's mother. She anticipated Phil's eventual switch, which she believed would be interesting.

William's role as Vivian Stanshall likewise involved another performer, and was likewise less profitable than William intended. Unlike the Ackrill role, William never completely left the Stanshall role to another. As Willian originally set it up, he would collect a modest fraction of each Vivian engagement that was done in William's place. He imagined that the replacement would be a big star, earning enough to live comfortably while also paying William his cut. However, although the new Vivian made some stellar performances, they did not pay well enough to justify the position. Throughout the rest of his life, he was on William's payroll. Although keeping that position going was not financially advantageous, it gave William great pleasure in doing the shows that he wanted, and in passing the rest onto the man whom he paid to live as "Vivian Stanshall."

34⁽⁴¹⁾

Seven in Three

There were seven Beatles total in the three Beatles phases. The first phase, from 1960 to 1962, had several people come and go, joining in for an audition here or a tour there. Still, **not one of them was** ever **a permanent part of** the band except for John Lennon, **Paul McCartney**, Stuart Sutcliffe (who got the name "Beetles" from a motorcycle gang in *The Wild One*), George Harrison, and Peter Best. Pete had considerably more on-stage drum-performance hours than the total of all the other Beatle drummers, Ringo included, but did not look the part.

Others were connected to the group, but these entertainers were the only **Beatle members** of the first phase. Phase One Beatles **was a club** band that endured with these five under-paid performers who never cut records. They built up a following, but not beyond those few areas where they performed. That grueling grunt work prepared the way for a much easier ride in the two phases that followed. Most of Phase One was in clubs in Liverpool and Hamburg.

As they got their first recording deal, not too long after Stuart Sutcliffe's fatal brain hemorrhage, the group, as ordered by George Martin, ousted Pete

Best in favor of Ringo Starr (mostly because Ringo looked more the part). A new drummer and the advent of their recording career marked the band's entrance to Phase Two (1962-1966), which rocketed when they toured North America in 1964.

Paul's death, two years later, revolved them to Phase Three (1966-1970). That is when I stepped in for him. Paul's death put an abrupt end to touring since **I did not look like**, sound, or act like the authentic **Paul enough to pass for him** in live performances. **Being a few inches taller** was no serious problem **in photographs** we could crop, but would look different in relation to the others with each of us in their old stage positions. Paul was several years too old to undergo a sudden growth spurt, as I have discussed in some other chapters. Phase Three never did tours or sold concert tickets.

Having to learn Paul's peculiarities was another reason we did not tour at first. Of all of the adjustments, the hardest for me to learn were Paul's left-handedness, especially with his bass, and his deceptively difficult high eyebrow habit. The raised

---

NOTE: The problem with Pete Best was not his drumming. As William says, Ringo was chosen over Pete "mostly because Ringo looked more the part." That part was for an underdog, not an equal or superior. Following the formula, John and Paul would be the stars of every concert and album, and the ultimate legendary writing team. Paul's part was to be "the cute Beatle" who would become the Christ figure. However, Pete, not Paul, was becoming the most beloved Beatle. Some fans were saying, "Pete's the Best!" His popularity, good looks, and strong stage-presence undermined the roles of John and Paul.

Ringo, who was well-connected, looked like a shy beatnik. Likewise, they kept George, not for any expert guitar playing, but for his timid demeanor. His friendship and history with the band also added realism to the myth. Since their early albums were performed mostly by session musicians, skills mattered less than image. The band only had to play well enough for live performances—which were, by design, overpowered by throngs of screaming fans.

singing brow mattered while we had hope of live sessions; but the closest we got to it was our rooftop performance and the *Our World* broadcast. For these engagements, we each had our own mic, and stood apart, making the height difference less obvious. Our version of the Beatles in Phase Three was primarily that of a studio band, which **I** had done before. As each of us needed help, we **would** either get it from the bandmates or hire others to **do it.** It really did not matter if the other Beatles were in each song.

Each of the three Phases is marked by distinct band members with their own distinct work. Phase One did clubs; Phase Two did albums and tours in every commercially attractive country; and Phase Three did studio albums. Each phase paved every avenue for the work to come. My Paul success in Phase Three was possible largely due to all who did the work before. Thank you, John, Paul, Stu, George, Pete, and Ringo. I, Bill, am the seventh Beatle, the last, but not the least, of all Beatles. Those Six set the world stage for me. Without them going ahead, everything I do and am would be Paulless. I would most likely still be a nameless session musician. My soul would be lacking without Paul. This gig of a lifetime has become my all.

Remember the seven stars, not merely four or five. These seven distinct spirits comprise the single entity, the single band, though divided over three phases. Though divided in time, each one nonetheless made a contribution to the whole. Our successes in Phase Three, and beyond, justify the hard sacrifices each member made before. **The work of those** I never knew in Phases One and Two **help me still.**

Mentioning that we were seven in all, rather than merely a well-known four, is important for what will be following in beast references. It is interesting to note that although there were a total of seven, everyone thinks of the Beatles as only four. Hence, although the Beatles are a band of Fab Four, we are rightly of seven heads, speaking collectively.

This beast with seven heads is the same beast that has four. Although some of us outshine the others, we are the "Seven Stars." Before you scream that I have committed some blasphemy in so saying, let me say that although it coincidentally lines up, I emphatically call it a joke in the chapter of "The Beast." **I am** merely taking this opportunity to mention **the paradox** that the four are seven. And we are all stars. The seventh is the greatest.

All right, having made that point, I also wish to make the point that **I, Bill,** am the seventh son in this line of sons. I **am the seventh star,** seventh spirit, seventh angel, **or seventh whatever** we were, in this line of whatever **I am in, or of whatever** we all are. Yet, however 7th, **I am** all 6's to McCartney's 9's.

Now here is another point to count. **We sang**, "1, 2, 3, 4, 5, 6, 7. All good children go **to heaven**. One, two, three, four, five, six, seven. **All good** children go to heaven." It was not just Paul **who went**. We would all go where Paul and Stu **had gone**, all seven of us.

35⁽⁴⁶⁾

I Am the Grey Seal.

You must realize by now that after Paul died, he was always on our minds. In addition to all of our songs that **can** be easily recognized as pointing to his death, you can **tell** that all of us were always under his influence even when our writing had nothing to do with him. **Everybody** intended to create more than Paul tributes. However, he was so entrenched in our thinking **that** even when we all wanted to write about something else, we would each think of great lines that put **Paul** in it. It was not that we sat down to write about Paul, but no matter where we go with a lyric, Paul **is** there. Even though we worked on other ideas, double-meaning lines would emerge to say that Paul is **dead**.

Elton John's album, *Goodbye Yellow Brick Road*, was written that way. It was not intended to focus on losing Paul, but was written soon after John told Elton and Bernie told about it. It was in their heads.

Let It Be was released soon after I announced our break-up. Five months later was the first pop hit by Elton John. Beatle-John called Elton's song "the first new thing that's happened since we happened."

I Am the Grey Seal.

Virtually every critic praised it. *Rolling Stone* called it a "pretty McCartneyesque ballad." This big hit was Elton's "Your Song." When I first heard it on the radio, I imagined a boy singing it to a girl, telling her, "Remember, this song's for you. It's your song." The lyrics, by Bernie Taupin, sounded like that.

"Your Song," however, was actually about Bernie's feelings toward Elton, who could tell everybody it's his song. **It's Elton**'s song. Bernie hopes he does not mind **singing about himself** instead of about an imaginary girl.

Being impressed with Elton's song, Beatle-John decided to meet him. They met, but were not close friends right away. The friendship grew a couple of years before John and Yoko confided in Bernie and Elton about Paul's death, and about working with me. Those remarks were unfavorable, being when John and I were not as close as we had been, or as we have been since. **The** talk of lyrical clues, telling Elton why the **walrus** was Paul, and pointing to evidence, would have sufficed. He did not need to tell them that I **was** not as great in the Paul role as was the earlier **Paul.** It prejudiced them.

Soon after John and Yoko revealed all to Elton and Bernie, Bernie began working on lyrics for their *Goodbye Yellow Brick Road* album. With Bernie's lyrics, Elton wrote the music. The album begins with a haunting "Funeral for a Friend." It was not for a real one, or for **Paul** necessarily, but was inspired by John losing Paul who **whispers to** me from the grave. Until you see it that way, **you** cannot understand the double-meanings that surface in the album.

321

Since only one of the songs was specifically written about Paul, I will not provide the other lines with Paul allusions. However, if you go through the album looking for them, you will be surprised. Still, all such allusions are only secondary to the primary message of each song. Most of them are not actually songs about Paul. That is an important distinction. When the Stones, Donovan, and the Who did their Paul songs, they were among their greatest hits. Not so with Elton's Paul song; but it is worth mentioning.

Adding to John's walrus metaphor, **I** am not the true walrus, but a "Grey Seal." I **am** allegedly undeserving of the praise fitting **the** real Paul. Bernie's view of me was a **grey seal** that is too little for such a large walrus role. His view has long since improved, but was at that time based on John's insults about me. As John and I became close again over time, I also became closer to Elton, Bernie, and others to whom John had ranted. They all came around eventually.

Making references to our songs about rain and to "Good Day Sunshine," Bernie then calls Paul a sun to say that the one on the screen (that's me in the image of Paul) is not as bright as the real one (Paul). He says that if anyone can **cry for Paul,** then so can he (or Elton). He means, **since he really is dead**, everyone should mourn for him.

John had given me the band out of obligation and guilt. Paul's fears of being sacrificed and replaced now rang true. Since the McCartneys chose me to replace Paul, John knew that there could be no more Beatles without me. Since **I required** the band to enter into the agreement, it was **all John could do.**

I Am the Grey Seal.

John told Elton and Bernie of the McCartney yearnings to have me fill Paul's role. By making me their Paul, they did not so completely lose their own son. They grafted me into their family tree, giving me new family roots. That is why, in "Grey Seal," Elton sings that my roots were twisted.

Also in that song, he sings of something enduring at the core of Paul, his spiritual essence that continued in me, keeping life going. "I was re-born before all life could die." He compares Paul's continuance to the great phoenix that goes in blazes, but returns again to carry on anew. I am flying high with the wings of the phoenix. If Paul, inside of me, can fly, now so can I. "The Phoenix bird will leave this world to fly / If the Phoenix bird can fly then so can I."

Dying in a car fire made that image particularly apropos for Paul. Bernie and Elton also suggest that if Paul flies by what **I** do in his name, then they should fly as well. I **am** less than Paul (they had supposed), but **the** two of them playing themselves without a **phoenix** required to exist through another gave them an advantage, or so they wrongly reasoned. **Or**, to put it another way, Paul is the sun; I am merely the image of the sun. The real sun is brighter. **Paul** flies by me, carried high by the bird, which **is** harder to do well. Since they are the real stars, or suns, and not mere images of the stars, as they saw it, if I can fly, they can too.

NOTE: Paul's death in the blazing car, and return as William, reminded Bernie Taupin of the Phoenix. That divine bird is based on the Bennu, an Egyptian bird embodiment of Ra. It represents the sun god. Bernie and Elton, both high in the Masonic brotherhood, understood the Phoenix's ancient significance. Occultists commonly see the Phoenix as a symbol of Lucifer, the light bearer, who was cast down to the earth only to rise again.

Billy's Back!

I do not appreciate the suggestion that I am not equal to Paul. I excelled him musically, physically, financially, as a humanitarian, and in family life. Do not tell me that I do not measure up to Paul. I was a better Paul McCartney than he ever was. I am not inferior to him in any way. I do not mean to sound ungrateful for this opportunity, but you can simply X out any notions of him being brighter. I gave him credit for my hits, which fans thought were his best.

NOTE: William offended many readers at this point of boasting, "I was a better Paul McCartney than he ever was." Although he does seem boastful, in all fairness, we can have a clearer picture of the situation if we understand his perspective. From the very start, there were critical insiders who argued that William could not measure up to the greatness of Paul McCartney. Although William would prefer to be too enlightened to ever become defensive, the feeling was there, and so expressed. However, elsewhere, he explains that no one is replaceable. Everyone is the best at being himself or herself.

For example, in "Lovely Linda" (chapter 60 of *the Memoirs*), William writes, "No one can replace Linda. Why would anyone suppose that she could be replaced? Linda will always be the only one of her. It is not as though I held a Linda-Look-Alike contest and declared another the winner. Only Linda is Linda. You get it? Jane is Jane. . . . Nancy is Nancy. . . . You are you. Each one has her own enchantments. One cannot replace another."

When referring to Paul McCartney as a particular human, there can be no greater Paul McCartney than the actual authentic human who really is Paul McCartney. However, William is not referring to Paul McCartney as the man, but as the fictional role. William is saying that he played that fictional role better than Paul had played it.

It would have been clearer and more accurate if William had said that he held a closer resemblance to the public façade of an amazing song-writer and great musician than Paul did. With the false persona that was created for Paul, and with the media manipulating the public to buy it, and with all of the assistance that Paul had received in his song-writing, and with so much work of session musicians being passed off as Paul's own on Beatles albums, it is fair to say that William (who, to the contrary, did more on albums than is credited) is better at playing that musical genius role than Paul ever was.

In the difficult position of being compared to Paul at a time when the world could not know how far Paul was from that fictional persona, William could see that he was much closer to it. He was better at that role, or at least better at playing "Paul's" post-innocence role. All things considered, even with the false identification, William, especially as a writer and musician, was arguably more real—much less of a pretender—than Paul.

36⁽⁵⁰⁾

"While My Guitar Gently Weeps"

George randomly opened a book and saw the words, "gently weeps." Looking within himself, he examined, "What is weeping? And why?" In his heart, he always wept for Paul. **George** sought out more of his feelings. He also **wept** for me. Sounding like the same "lonely **for Paul**" bit retold again and again, but with an added layer of judgment about my own lost soul, I was less than genuinely interested. The others also lacked interest. Without our support, he called on another friend

Eric Clapton showed up to record with George the next day. He played lead guitar. I played piano. Some acoustic guitar and organ was added by John.

NOTE: In 1968, on 25 July, 16 August, and 3, 5, 6 September, George and others recorded "While My Guitar Gently Weeps." Joining them on that last recording day, Eric Clapton played the red Gibson Les Paul guitar, that he had given to George the month before. George named her Lucy after Lucille Ball.

Les Paul (Lester William Polsfuss (1915 – 2009)), one of the top electric guitarists of all time, was a great innovator in the music industry. Through experimentation based on ideas of others, he was one of the pioneers of the solid-body electric guitar (such as George's Lucy), multitrack recording, overdubbing, delay effects, and phasing effects. All of these techniques developed by Les Paul were used heavily in Beatles songs before and after the band had "Less Paul" and more William.

George Harrison's "*Lucy*"

It all sounded pretty good. By **Eric** playing lead, it gave George a break, **making it easier** for him to focus on his lead vocal while playing rhythm. Until Eric joined in, it **seemed taboo** for such a great guitar talent to lend us a hand. However, I had hired session musicians, as had the Paul before me. For example, we used a good-sized orchestra for the *Sgt. Pepper's* album. That was obvious to anyone who thought about it.

As I hear George's lovely song now, **I feel** more empathy for his sorrow. Now I can see **that he was** right about me to a point. However, **complaining** that my Paul role had perverted me had more merit when I was new to that role than it was by that time. When I first became Paul, I went a bit crazy with everybody thinking I was someone. Women threw themselves at me. I liked it. Until **Linda helped me** put my life back together, I was far out of **balance.**

I met Linda Eastman in London 15 May 1967, and then saw her again four days later at a launch party celebrating *Sgt. Pepper's Lonely Hearts Club Band.* Going steady with Jane at the time, I was not free to hook up with Linda then, but fully wanted her. At Epstein's house, while celebrating the album release, with all the attention that I was getting for it, it was not the time or place to get to know Linda.

I saw her next a year later when John and I flew to New York to announce the formation of Apple Corps, Ltd. I telephoned Linda a long four months later, telling her that it was her turn to fly to London. She did. We were at last married on 12 March 1969. Yes, George had cause for concern of perversions at that time; but by the time Linda and I were married, I had calmed down quite a bit. Although he says I was perverted; that was back in 1968 before I entered that monogamous relationship. Once I married Linda, that was it. George would not have called me perverted then. But yes, **I can admit** that I was a little bit messed up before **that point.**

Right off, George sings of Paul's death. He uses the same words, "you all," in two sentences, saying, "I look at you all see the love there that's sleeping / While my guitar gently weeps." Here, George is evaluating us, looking at us all. We all see Paul's death and that his love is missing. Then George does what turned me off to the song from the start. Talking directing to me—but remember, this is from before Linda—he says, "I don't know why nobody told you / How to unfold your love." For only twenty-two months by the time he wrote this song, I had been playing the Paul role. I had not really learned to manage my sex life by then, and, as they all said, I had not been good at loving the band.

Paul's powerful bond of brotherly love had held them all together, and was sorely missed. I was all business. That is how I came across. It was the same complaint by George from when I first joined until several years after the break-up. It is the same concerns for me that he expressed in other songs. Love was missing. In "Within You Without You," it was "the love that's gone so cold." This time, he calls it **"the love there** that's sleeping." It died with Paul and **awaited a resurrection**.

Emphasizing how I was coerced into getting the injections and surgeries, he says, "I don't know how someone controlled you. / They bought and sold you." Although all of us must be learning from all of our many mistakes, still his guitar gently weeps. He still misses Paul. About me again, "I don't know how you were diverted [sidetracked from being me]. / You were perverted too. I don't know how you were inverted [turning my life upside down to be Paul]./No one alerted you."

Pounding in the sense that we are all to blame for the massive mess that I had made of my life, he again says, "I look at you all see the love there that's sleeping...Look at you all." It is true. He was right. Unless none of us was to blame, we all were. We all hurt each other. For the lack of Paul's love, we were all short of love for each other.

Just as George had complained the year before, **Paul's love was** missing from the band; but it did not have to be **that way**. The love the band had always felt before was **still missing.** After all that time, "Still my guitar gently weeps" and it would until we all loved each other as they had loved one another before. **We never got** it. That rare kind of love never warmed **the band again.** We all carried mutual feelings of both appreciation and resentment, partly because we all benefited from each other, and partly because we all felt that the others' appreciation was lacking. At the end of the song, sounding like he is weeping in pain, George utters, "Paul, Paul, Paul, Paul, Paul, Paul, Paul." Then, after his guitar seems to echo that same languish, **George** says again, "Paul, Paul, Paul, Paul, Paul, Paul." He **wept for Paul.**

37[(51)]

Apple Corps Ltd.

Apple Corps (pronounced "apple core") is a double pun. Most obviously, the sound refers to the part of the apple that one tosses out. One may burn the core, or bury it to sprout new life as another tree. **Paul teaches us** to see the core as both—something **to be removed** from the present apple, but also of lasting value as containing the seed of what lies ahead. Still, there is much more to it. Apple Corps evokes multiple meanings by its sight as well as its sound. Corps sounds like core; but it looks more like corpse. It is often mispronounced "Apple Corpse." It signifies "A Paul Corpse."

Out of this corporation named for Paul's bodily remains, many business divisions sprang up for tax relief and for our creative outlets. **We invested** our profits as tax shelters, but did it all **in the name** of Paul. It all came together over him, or **surrounding** his corpse, his body or organization. Our **Apple** Studio was "A Paul Studio" in the Apple Building, which was thus "A Paul Building." Right off, we launched Apple Records for us all to make records honoring "A Paul." We also made retail attempts in the name of Paul. Apple Corps, Ltd. owned **Apple**

Retail, which owned our Apple Boutique. Slices, or divisions, of "A Paul" were diversely spread with Apple Films, Apple Publishing, and Apple Electronics. Apple Corps enveloped it all in Paul. All was in and of "A Paul."

Now that **you know** that the core of our Apple is **Paul, or his corpse,** making it personal, imagine how very distressed we all were each time we found that Apple Computer infringed on our trademark. It is bad enough from a business perspective, but also struck at the Beatles' core issue. They infringed without a love for Paul, and without any understanding that our Apple is "A Paul" reference to his own corpse. Out of a purely legal and commercial standpoint, we would have actively pursued our own trademark protection anyway; but the core Paul issue also made it personally meaningful.

Established in 1968, Apple Corps Ltd. began before we launched the public awareness of Paul's death, but well after we had begun releasing albums and such to point to it. Ten years later, we found it necessary to file suit against Apple Computer for trademark infringement. Naturally, we won.

That should have taken care of it, so we thought. It did not. Apple Computer paid us US$80,000 with an agreement, in 1981, at least not to dilute our mark by using the Apple name for any music. Still, it was not long before we all ended up in court again. We had set our bounds by compromise, split fairly and logically. Apple Corps said we would not enter the computer business; and Apple Computer would not infringe by entering the music business. Then they reneged, adding MIDI and audio recording as their next big feature, turning their best computers into synthesizers. **They logically lost** that legal battle too, paid us **a big bundle of cash**, and agreed to stop adding musical hardware to their computers.

Apple Computer programmer, Jim Reekes, was well aware of all their Beatles litigation, but also understood Apple's profit potential with music. There was a beep in his program noticed by their lawyers. It was called "noteCmd." They suggested he change it to "frequencyCmd" to avoid anything sounding like a musical term. Reekes sarcastically suggested calling it "Let it Beep." He resented the Apple Corps limitations. While most co-workers laughed at his joke, one, taking it seriously, said, "You could never get away with that!" Reekes bitterly answered, "So sue me!" That is when he got the beep's name, "**sosumi**" (which he pronounced "So sue me"), which **Reekes** claimed was some old Japanese word without musical meaning. I respected that humorous creativity.

Our final litigation occurred when they put our logo on their iTunes Music Store. We said no. They did it anyway after we ardently turned down their US million dollar offer. When our ironclad case came before the so-named Mr. Justice Mann, he absurdly ruled against us. Imagine my astonishment. I was understandably shocked. An appeal would have been awful for our opponents. They won the first round; yet knew it was a fluke that would not continue to the next round when real justice would prevail.

Now, with the threat of that approaching appeal, people speculated that perhaps Apple Corps was in line to become a major shareholder in Apple Computer, making them another division of our corps. However, in the final settlement, we merged with a peace-assuring compromise. Rather than everything related to our trademark depending on our approval, requiring more of our legal hassles, we just decided to sell them the mark and let them license it to us. Although it was said that we sold out for a mere US half billion dollars, it was more about making peace. Steven **Paul** Jobs said, "We love the Beatles, and it **has been painful** being at odds with them over these trademarks." We love **Apple Inc.** and Steve. He too, at the core, **has united in "A Paul."** Biting that forbidden Apple made him wise.

NOTE: Paul was at the core of the Beatles' Apple symbolism. Their logo is an apple cut in half, as Paul's role was cut in half, divided between the two players. It honored the first half, the first to play "a Paul" role in the Beatles.

Steven Paul Jobs, however, had something different in mind for Apple Computers. His would be the third Apple to change the world, launching a new era of accessible light and knowledge.

The first world-changing "apple" was Eden's forbidden fruit. Taking the serpent's advice to exercise their freewill, Adam and Eve partook to be as the gods who possessed the forbidden secret knowledge and wisdom.

The second world-changing apple was Newton's. His epiphany about gravity while sitting under an apple tree in 1666 led to him enlightening the world with scientific and mathematical reasoning.

The world's third great Apple (originally selling for $666.66) launched personal computing that could potentially bring the whole human family into the powerful global intelligence network. The personal computer ushered in the Aquarian age of freedom. It gives mankind the ability to overcome world tyranny that has been maintained all along by suppressing information.

Secret societies (having gnosis forbidden to others) naturally see the "fall of Adam" as the rise of mankind. According to the Sumerians, Ea (whose title, Enki, meant "Lord of Earth") liberated humans by giving them gnosis forbidden by Enki's half-brother, Enlil ("Lord of the Command"). To control humans (the slave-race), Enlil forbade empowering them with light and knowledge. Enki provided that forbidden gnosis, and formed Earth's first secret society, "The Brotherhood of the Snake."

In the Sumerian stories, we see Enlil and Enki's rivalry as they curse and bless humans: Enlil forbids enlightenment. Enki provides it. Enlil casts the humans out of Eden. Enki makes them clothes. When the humans grow out of control, making too much noise and bother for Enlil, he tries to drown them in a great flood. However, Enke warns Atrahasis (or Utnapishtim)—renamed Noah in the Bible—to build a big boat and to fill it with animals. Those who prefer Enke over Enlil, say Enlil's Bible is biased.

38[(52)]

"All Together Now"

"All Together Now" was one of those songs that we recorded well before deciding to release it. I quite liked the song, and recorded it not long after I wrote it; but the up-beat mood did not fit our albums until later. We recorded this skiffle song on 12 May 1967, back when we were still recording material to release on our *Magical Mystery Tour* album. It was intended to be a sing-along song that was not only easy enough for children to sing along, but also one which provided an easy concept for the adults gathered all together now to sing with me. In not so many words, I was saying that the reality of me entering **the** Beatles as the substitute for our **departed Paul can be known as easily as** counting to ten, or as reciting **the alphabet.** It's as easy as tea. As easily as you may look and see a ship out in the harbor, or learn how to chop a tree, or skip a rope, you should see me. As easily, learn to open your eyes and "Look at me!" Do you see anything at all that is different, such as the changed eye color?

Billy's Back!

Remember learning your colors? It is entirely elementary. Children learn to distinguish "black, white, green, red . . . pink, brown, yellow, orange, and blue" by willingly looking at them to tell each color apart. Still, to see the difference between each color, you have to look at them. No one ever saw me. If our fans ever really looked at us, why couldn't they see me? They did not look closely enough. When Brian and I first discussed me impersonating Paul, I said I **did not think** we looked enough alike. He replied that **our fans** believe what we tell them. Had they **looked**, like distinguishing yellow from orange or blue, they would have recognized some stark differences. For example, the one who is inches taller also has a longer shaped head. People only see whatever they expect to see. Until told otherwise, they go on seeing only what they had always seen.

The point is for **everyone** to join in the song of seeing me. I sing, "**Look at me.**" I can imagine hearing them answer, "**We** see you!" It gets even better, and is a hearty **laugh in light of** what we really have you sing. **Paul** lost his head in a car crash. No longer **together**, it knocked his head off. Here **I am standing** in for him, as if I were Paul **with you again**, happily singing this underlying message, "Look at me all together now!"

Following the idea that the best place to hide a gag is in plain sight, I had everyone repeating the secret clue again and again for emphasis, and even had "All Together Now" as the title. The musical climax is on the first half of the sentence, "Look at me all together now!" **This message is** the good news **that the celebrating crowd**, singing along, evidently **does at last see me.**

The joke goes on. Even though they see that Paul's head had been lost, there **I am** as him leading the song. It is as though he were **resurrected**. They all sing of me being **back together again** as though I were he. Although Paul had been dead, now he, unbelievably, sings again. **He is as Humpty Dumpty** except that this time, all the King's men **restored** his life, putting his broken pieces **back together again**. I am saying, **"Look at me all together now!"**

I recorded the master track, and then played it all backward. Hearing sounds compatible with John's "Strawberry Field Forever" message, "I buried Paul," I added in the same message. I sang along with the backward track, creating a backward harmony. I sang, "I buried Paul" (metaphorically). Where it is "all together now, all together now, all together now, all together now" going forward, we have the fab corpse in focus going backward as "I buried Paul. I buried Paul. I buried Paul. I buried **Paul**." He is kaput, dead, and buried. "Poor boy has **lost his head**" ("Flies and Bees to Emily"). **But then he's back** together again! It is a miracle! He is all together now! When has anyone ever had one's head knocked off, and yet live? It is a marvelous deception.

If the song has not been playing in your head, go get it now and play it while this key is fresh in your mind. **You will** laugh your head off; but that's okay. **Endure it well. You know** that you too will be all together again soon enough.

This song, with its **blatant** simplicity, is one of my favorite musical **jokes about Paul** that I have made. My favorite by John was "You Know My Name (Look Up the Number)," which also ended up on the shelf for a couple of years. We began recording it in 1967, and finished it in 1969. Recording these songs turned Paul-stress to hilarity. They say, "Laughing and crying is the same release."

39⁽⁵³⁾

You Know My Joke.

"You Know My Name (Look Up the Number)" was one of my favorite songs to sing, and the best joke of a song that John ever wrote. When John came by to pick me up one day, he saw a phone book up against some lyrics on the piano. I had left it there **just** as I had found it a few days before. "You **know my name.** (Look up the number!)" had been written across the cover by a certain visitor. Now, **I already** found it amusing; but enjoyed it even more when John **suggested** I sing it in light of the fact **that no one really** did know my name. I added, "Even if they **did look** up the number, they would have it wrong." **We are not the same** number. Paul was nines, I was sixes.

Making the joke complete, John later turned up at the studio and said, "Billy, I've got a new song, 'You Know My Name (Look Up the Number).'" I asked the words. He repeated, "You Know My

NOTE: Coming from William, it is high praise to say that the song was "the best joke of a song that John ever wrote." William's true personality more closely resembles Vivian Stanshall than the rock icon. Although he loves to work hard in production mode, he is otherwise jovial, humorous, and clever. While others see a serious Ra or Horus in him, he would sooner see himself as Loki incarnate: a fun, playfully mischievous, shape-shifting trickster.

Name (Look Up the Number)." He laughed, knowing that I was about to.

Already I was laughing along with him. I asked, "What's the rest of it?"

"Make that your mantra," he said. As I repeated my question, he said, "No, no! That's it! That's enough! There are no other words! Those are the words! It's your new mantra!"

When we recorded it, I invited Brian Jones (of the Rolling Stones) to join in on the fun. We all had a crazy good time at it. I first asked Brian just to cheer him up; but his saxophone also added to the song's hilarity. It had been about a month since his arrest for possession of hemp. His trial was another three months ahead of him then. John explained the humor of the phonebook lines. This joke was of the stock the Stones knew well. It gave Brian a laugh too—which was refreshing in light of the stress he was feeling. **This was** not the first time that we explained **Paul** lyrics to each other. Keeping the world **in the dark** over Paul's death was hard to do. **Both bands were anxious** to share enough with each other **to keep us all sane.** We had to tell somebody. Confiding in them helped.

We recorded "All You Need Is Love" the following week. Then, later in June, or maybe even July, John and I went to Brian's flat and played the song with him for the first time. The thing that led up to playing it was his talk about being in jail. He was arrested on 11 May. Although jail time was over, the impending court date haunted him. He said being in seclusion is not bad at all when it is voluntary, but that forced loneliness was one of the cruelest punishments ever executed on this small earth. Having become the sergeant of loneliness after leaving behind some aspects of my William life, I pretty well understood something about what he was feeling. John suffered loneliness his whole life also. It drove his work. We all experience it. Some get hit harder than others. It hit Brian when locked up. He said, "When the prison door slammed, I could hear it lock. That's when I was alone."

"Last thing George heard from Paul was a slamming door," John said. "George didn't know what it meant, or how alone it would leave us." John told Brian again about Paul's big argument with Epstein before Paul and Donna's fatal ride. Paul had been angry. He slammed the door and left, leaving them all lost without their old friend. Paul had seen it all before in dreams, but could not overturn his fate when it came down to it. If only he could have recognized what was happening. It is very clear that **if he had not gone** on that fateful ride, **I could not have taken his** place. This role engulfed my **whole life.** It is the gig of a lifetime. It gave me all **I would have**. I am grateful for it. Yet, some qualities of **my own life** were better when I could return home to my role **as myself.** Now, I am outwardly successful; but I have lost a part of myself. When Paul's door slammed, sealing his "untimely" death, much of my own life was slammed shut with his.

When John listened to Brian talking about the slamming door, it triggered old memories and emotions, provoking him to write a song. That is how we had all trained ourselves. Experiences lead us to creative outlets, usually songs. We were much freer to collaborate with others than most outsiders would have supposed. We did not worry about giving away ideas. Slamming doors vibrantly animated John this time. He suggested that we all write a song that began, or maybe ended, with Paul's and Brian's slamming doors. **It would be the** same song, "one door with **dual meaning**," but without my "Paul polish," which was the basis of "All You Need Is Love."

My perfectionism always bothered John. He would knock out a song, track it, and then let the engineers do whatever they thought best. Sometimes he would complain about something they would do to it, but usually did not care. John and Paul were both glad to move on to something else, or on to nothing at all for that matter. They bored of work easily. I was the opposite. **I would** tweak it one way, then another. I would **add new tracks**, then take some back off. For me, **they were** never done a moment before I felt they could not be **much better.** That is just my way. For the change, I would do the opposite now and then too. My *Driving Rain* CD was totally opposite that way. I went for some spontaneity, freshness, like the rain, more than my usual well-worked pieces. It almost sounded too unrehearsed for me; but I fancied doing one that fast. **We recorded it** in mere weeks and then pulled it **all together as fast as** I am told the early **Beatles did it before I came** along.

Everything slowed down for my endless vision and detail work. **I made them all crazy** spending over 700 hours **on my first Beatles album**; but I wanted it to be perfect. I got faster, but not as fast as Paul and John had done it. Not, that is, until recent years. Lately **I have pushed myself** to be more like Paul. Funny that. ***Driving Rain*** was my thirtieth album since **the Beatles**; but I still cannot escape Paul's shadow. **Decades later, I** still have to prove myself to him. It is **still** for him that I do it as much as for myself. I **must work** day and night for Paul McCartney if I am **to** be him.

Owing to how I would **drive John crazy** with all the polish I wanted for each song, John often lashed out at me in frustration. He respected **my** skill, but was accustomed to having his **work** over and done with for more immediate **rewards**. My focus on detail causes delays. **The Beatles** virtually faded away from fans while we worked on *Sgt. Pepper's*. Many people thought the band had ended. In a way, they were right. Some critics called the Beatles a has-been band. Finally, all of that yelling turned to awe and wonder with the unveiling of *Sgt. Pepper's*.

Overtime proved worthwhile. **John** could see that it was far beyond any album that they **had** made until then. Yet, better was not his priority. It **frustrated** him that it took so long with me at it. All of **them** were upset with how I called all the shots. Although they humored their new leader, it seemed like an eternity to them before we finally released *Sgt. Pepper's* 1 June 1967.

Later that month, we taped "All You Need Is Love." Though positive sounding, it was of John's own frustrations with my laboring perfectionism, and about how he missed Paul. In spite of the song's very upbeat mood, the message was that I could not accomplish anything exceptionally beyond what everyone or anyone else could do. I should stop pushing him to do what could not be done.

"You can learn how to play the game. It's easy. All you need is love." The game we play alludes to our *Sgt. Pepper's* cover where "LOVE" represents the knight, queen, bishop, and rook. It's easy, unless you need a king. He's dead. For Brian, John quoted *Through the Looking Glass*, "It's a great huge game of chess that's being played—all over the world," and said that I, the new one as Alice now, "wouldn't mind being a Pawn, if . . . I might join—though . . . I should *like* to be a Queen." Doing the queen roll, **I was set up** for jokes. Still, it is a good line or two **from Lewis Carroll.**

Brian listened attentively to "All You Need Is Love," which John stopped half way in to explain its real meaning. When he started again, Brian watched the chords, and then picked up an acoustic guitar. He instantly had the whole thing. The first three times we reached the end, Brian shouted, "Play it again!" And so we did. Each time, he sang and played with more gusto than the time before.

"No more!" I sang, preventing another "Play it again" round of "All You Need Is Love."

"Too bad," Brian said, "I was just starting to get into it!" Fortunately, we did not sing that whole ordeal again, but **Brian and John kept** on with the "We loved you" line, **modifying as they** went. Over the evening, we all **contributed little bits and** pieces until Brian eventually **completed it** as his "We Love You." The Rolling Stones recorded it soon after. When they did, John and I sang backup.

Even though John and I wrote most of it, we did it to give Brian a good time. I did not ever object to letting him have the credit. John, however, seemed a little more bothered by it, probably because it originated with his own song in the first place. Opening with the slamming prison door made it virtually John's from the start anyway.

Musically, Brian's "We Love You" was not ever something I coveted. I did not fret about wanting Paul's name on it. It was mostly for amusement. "All You Need Is Love," which led to it, was a far better song. Even though John wrote his out of frustration over how long it took to do *Sgt. Pepper's,* I value it for its double meanings and call for love. I can better understand his frustrations now. Fading toward obscurity as I tinkered perfectionisticly had its price.

In "You Know My Name," I, the man of a thousand voices, showcase my most publicly accessible non-Paul vocal sound as I use my Vivian Stanshall voice. **John and I had** lots of fun with it. Mal Evans had **a good time too.** He contributed some of the backing vocals. It was the kind of ridiculousness that, had I written it, I would have given to the Bonzos. If I had, it would be too unknown for me to mention it now. For that reason, I am glad John wrote it rather than Vivian Stanshall, my Bonzos persona. Nevertheless, it was a comedy act, which is what the Bonzo Dog Band did best.

Pressing the question about my name, I am as Rumpelstiltskin, the old fairy tale character. In England, based on Joseph Jacobs' translation of

NOTE: After using the song, "Live and Let Die," in *Shrek the Third* (2007), there was discussion about Sir Paul possibly providing the voice talent of Rumpelstiltskin in *Shrek Forever After* (2010). With that lingering possibility, but without an agreement for it, William included his symbolic connection with the character. That way, if he were to play that part, fans could have already understood that association before seeing the movie.

the tale collected by the Brothers Grimm, we know that little villain as Tom Tit Tot. In the traditional version of that amusing old story, some commoner sought to look important by boasting that he had a daughter who could spin straw into gold.

The king called the man's bluff. He locked the girl in a tower with straw and a spinning wheel. He insisted that she spin the straw into gold by morning, for the next three nights. If she succeeded, he would let her go. Otherwise, she would be executed. When she could not do it, a gifted substitute showed up to do it for her. See me there. **I am the substitute**.

This magical mystery guy **who made the gold** secretly, let her take the credit, **but was paid for it.** He got her necklace for the first night's work. The king was amazed. The next night, the substitute willingly worked for her ring. The king was again impressed. The third night, the substitute (who had been producing the gold [hits] without his own name ever receiving the credit) agreed to do his magic for the girl one more time if she would pledge to him her first-born child. To keep her [or Paul] alive, she agreed. Without the substitute ever revealing his name, he continued his magical work. He made more gold than ever.

Overcome with awe, as well as greed, the king married the girl. When their first child was born, payment came due. The girl, now the queen, **offer**ed all her wealth to keep the child. **The substitute** at last agreed to give up his claim to **the big payment** if the queen could guess his name. **Then all his fortune** ended when she learned his name. Since **I have** that same risk, "you know my name" only in fiction.

40[(57)]

From "Ob-La-Di, Ob-La-Da" to Boogaloo

"Ob-la-di, ob-la-da. Life goes on," was a catch phrase that was always said with a Jamaican accent by a guy named Jimmy Scott. I use to see him often at the clubs. The idea was that whatever happens, life still goes on. "**Ob-la-di, ob-la-da**" means about the same thing as "**bada bing bada boom**." It is a phrase showing that **things happen** as intended without requiring much effort. Until the day you die, "Ob-la-di, ob-la-da, **life goes on**." It's a done deal. It's as easy as pie. **Voila!** Whatever is to be is whatever happens. The expression tells us that everything runs its course. Ob-la-di, ob-la-da. One thing always leads to the next until you die; and even then, life goes on.

"Bro" (short for brother) in Scott's dialect was "bra" (usually spelt, "brah"). Brother Paul tells me, "Life goes on, Bra." I also enjoyed thoughts of bras.

On one level, a boy and girl fall in love, marry, and bring children into this world. Everything flows freely. Voila. Life happens.

Death concepts, particularly the death of Paul, take the song to a higher level. The lower level is a metaphor for the higher. On a lower, Desmond meets a girl named Molly, gives her a ring, and they live their lives together singing, working, and raising the children.

In the UK, a barrow is a pushcart. "**Desmond** has a barrow in the market place" means he **sells goods** from his cart, next to all the other carts that are pushed to that same greenmarket or farmers' market.

Every line works on that level, but also perfectly on one suggesting that Paul is entombed under the ground—since the word "barrow" also signifies an ancient burial mound. From a metaphorical way of understanding the song, the biological Paul is Desmond; I am Molly. **Desmond is** in his tomb, even while still **active in commerce.** Molly is a singer in the Bonzo Dog Doo-Dah Band (and also sings as a session musician).

Desmond says to Molly, "Girl, I like your face." **Obviously**, my face was very important to Paul. He clearly **likes my face**. And what do I say to Paul now **as** I take him by the hand? "Ob-la-di, ob-la-da, life goes on!" The life of Paul goes on through me. **I am "how the life goes on."**

As this love story goes on with the more apparent meaning, Desmond goes to a jewelry store, buys a twenty-carat golden ring, and gives it to Molly. Or, in real life, the buried Paul gives me his gold. The obvious implication is that **Desmond and** Molly marry, or that Paul and **I merge, become one.** As has been said of marriage, "They twain shall be one flesh." What does Molly do once she receives Desmond's treasure? She does exactly as I do for the late Paul: "As he gives it to her [Billy], she begins to sing." What does she sing? "Ob-la-di, ob-la-da, life goes on." That is what I am singing to everyone. Besides in this song, it is the message I have sung for years. Starting when I received Paul's wealth, I began to sing that his life goes on through me.

Paul and I, as "Desmond and Molly Jones," had been joined together for exactly "a couple of years," averaging in when this song was written (22 months) and released (26 months). In those two years, up until "Ob-La-Di, Ob-La-Da," it was a good union. "In a couple of years they have built a home sweet home."

Letting them laugh, I sing, "with a couple of kids running in the yard" of Desmond and Molly Jones. It deserved the scripted backup laughter: "Ha! Ha! Ha! Ha! Ha!"

Since the merger had gone well from a monetary standpoint, referring to the musical commerce that I do as Paul or Desmond, I sing, "**Happy ever after** in the market place." I am happy **in the work**, but not ever after in our home **with the children** (that is, with the bandmates). **Business is good.** Keeping it successful, I, the parent who was always in charge, let the children (bandmates) lend a hand.

Making my debut as Billy Shears, through Ringo, **I asked for**, and got by with, help from my friends. **Our worst days** included having my face worked over with injections, surgeries, and exercises. **The** nights had me back singing in the studio. Molly, in **the** song, spends her days doing her pretty face. When **the** day is over, "in the evening she still sings it with **the** band." What am I, or Molly, still singing with **the** band? "Ob-la-di, ob-la-da, life goes on!" I'm how **the** life of Paul continues. I am "how **the life goes on!**"

Really, today, most people cannot appreciate how absurdly conservative the world was when we wrote all these songs. I repeatedly inserted the word, "Bra" to tie in Jimmy's Jamaican "Brah," and to break the bra taboo. It also tied to John's song, "Girl," in which Paul and George sing, "tit, tit, tit, tit, tit, tit, tit, tit, tit."

Having Desmond staying home to do his pretty **face** at the end was just a recording accident. I sang **everything** great in that take, after several imperfect attempts, but sang that one part wrong. I decided to let it stay because my many takes for perfection were driving all the rest of the group crazy.

I liked the song a lot and thought we should **release it** as another hit single. However, George felt it was trite; and John totally loathed it for several reasons, not the least of them being how it made **each** of my bandmates, John, George, and Ringo, the **metaphor**ical children of Paul and me. John said it **gives a story** about a meaningless relationship. He said, "What? These two get married and then go **on living happily** ever after just because he liked her face? Do these two ever fall in love? Do they ever get beyond their looks?" I replied rudely about Yoko's looks, but wished I had spoken from love.

Speed was another issue. Just as I had John speed up "Revolution 1," resulting in the hit, "Revolution," "Ob-La-Di, Ob-La-Da" had been much slower. One night, after days of takes that still weren't right, John nearly knocked me over as he burst into the studio. High as a kite, he stormed over to the piano, and shouted, "All right now, we're going to do 'Ob-la-di, ob-la-da!'" He pounded out **the entire song** as loudly and furiously as he could. It **sounded great**. I was glad to use it. It made me sing **much faster**, but that did not bother me at all. **It made the song better.**

Speaking of John being high, I altered that last line to make a drug reference, changing "sing" to "take." "If you want some fun, take Ob-La-di-la-da!" You can see that that line has nothing to do with my Paul merger, or with anything else in the song.

John's great disdain for the song carried over into **ridicule** that came later. When he was drunk or high, he **was often** verbally abusive to me. It was always **the drugs talking.** He would accuse me of hiding what I was doing from him, or of spending months to get my songs covered in "Billy Shine," not to do good work, but to make his look inferior. Sometimes he would accuse me of having stolen his band from him, or that I took advantage of him when he was most vulnerable with the shock and anguish of losing Paul. At other times, he would criticize me for being too much of a workaholic to have any feelings for my bandmates. I could go on, and on, and on, and on. He surely did. It was especially bad when the chemicals got him going.

Later, he would sense my pain, and know that he did it again. He would turn to me, slide his glasses down to the end of his nose to see over them, and tell me, "I love you, Billy." This pattern repeated itself numerous times.

Having that song in his arsenal to sling at me, he called me "Desmond" off and on for a few months. Each time I'd think to correct him, I'd stop myself after one time when he caught me in his snare. I said, "Desmond is Paul." We had already been over it many times; but he seemed confused.

"Oh," he said, acting is though he did not know. "I thought you were Paul,"

"No," I said, "in the song, I am Molly. Paul is Desmond."

"Good to get that straight now, Molly," he said, laughing at me. "All this time, I thought it was about you becoming Paul. So, this was when you became Molly? Is that right?"

Ordinarily, **John and I got along** well. We were rather close. However, **sometimes** resentments were unloaded, **particularly when** he was drunk or high. **He was capable** of cutting malicious humor with episodes interspersed wholly void of all humor whatsoever. **Sometimes he** was funny, but hurtful. Other times he **was just mean**. Then later, when he could see he had gotten **to me** again, he would usually apologize. John's Desmond jokes went from annoying to much worse.

Letting **John's stupid Desmond humor** get to me **was a mistake.** By resisting it instead of laughing Desmond off, I unwittingly encouraged it. After a time, they shortened it to "Desi." It was months before **Ringo let me** in on their joke. To this day, I don't **know for certain** who started it. One evening when **I was** not there, someone said that I sounded like **Ricky Ricardo** (on the American situation comedy, *I Love Lucy*). Ricky, played by Desi Arnaz, popularized his kind of boogaloo music.

Unless you happen to be a big fan of boogaloo music, you probably understand how they used it as ridicule, calling me "Desi" until I finally knew why, then calling me "Boogaloo." The term, boogaloo, was probably coined around the time Paul died in 1966. It is a fusion mostly of popular African American, R&B, soul, mambo, and son montuno music. When John, Mick, George, or Ringo used the word, however, it meant singing like Ricky Ricardo. Boogaloo, like Ricky, was more Cuban in the beginning.

Saying **I was Desi or Boogaloo** in private was annoying. **Nevertheless,** to maintain band image and earnings, they kept **their ridicule** from our fans until I **dissolved the band.** Then, the Boogaloo silence deal expired. **They jabbed me** whenever they could **in those** early post-Beatles years. They made **Boogaloo references** in hit songs that the general public could not understand. It was gibberish to them. Yet, the esoteric crowd knew; and that inner-circle included many of my close friends and associates. I cared about those connections. Only they fully understood the Boogaloo references because only they had the Desi background story. They made the Boogaloo songs to embarrass me. They succeeded.

"Back Off Boogaloo," written by Ringo, and produced by George, who also played guitar on it, attacked me and my music. Referring to "Ob-la-di, ob-la-da," in which **I took over Paul's** work cart, or his "barrow in the **market place**," and from which they called me Desi and Boogaloo, Ringo kicked out: "Wake up meat head. Don't pretend that you are dead. Get yourself up off the cart."

Billy's Back!

Out to stick it to me, he says I too seem dead, and ought to get off Mc*CART*hey, leaving his name, fame, fortune, and business, "the cart," or "barrow in the market place." Ringo was saying that my music failed to measure up to Paul's standard, and that if I were going to go on making music in his name, I had better shape up: "Get yourself together now and give me something tasty." John's "Come together over me" line, and my own "All Together Now" has an echo here. He tells me to get it together as Paul or to stop using his name. He sings, "Everything you try to do, you know it sure sounds wasted."

Going on with Ringo's "Back Off Boogaloo," repeated gallingly throughout the song, he is directly attacking me. He says I think I am a groove because of my personal choice in shoes and socks—as if my looks had anything to do with my music. Mostly, Ringo just goes on and on telling me to "BACK OFF!" I told him to "F*CK OFF," and resented not using stronger words.

On his "Back Off Boogaloo" single cover, **Ringo** had a big picture of Frankenstein. He **used that** character by Mary Shelley because it is a **monster** made of dead human remains. Ringo is **showing** that I, Boogaloo, am a monster made of **the dead Paul.**

NOTE: Ringo wrote "Back Off Boogaloo" in criticism of William's first two Paul McCartney albums (*McCartney* and *Ram*). George Harrison helped Ringo develop the song by adding some chords and finishing the melody. In September 1971, Harrison produced its recording in Apple Studio. The year before, he had also produced Ringo's "It Don't Come Easy." "Back Off Boogaloo" was released as a single on 17 March 1972, exactly ten months after the release of *Ram*.

His record cover was rather amateur compared to all the covers full of clues on our Beatles records. However, Ringo never was heavily involved in that end of our Beatles presentations. I highly doubt if any outsiders understood his use of Frankenstein.

Doing that song whet John's appetite for Ringo to sling another at me. Following Ringo's lead, John made another song for Ringo to sing ridicule of me Ringo had sung that **I think I'm** a groove. Now he adds that I think I'm "**the greatest** in this world, in the next world, and **in any world!**" John and Ringo revile me for thinking that I am better than Paul who is in the next world, the spirit world. Well, yes, it is true. I am greater. He was my forerunner. I am the most successful songwriter in history.

Singing the entire song in first-person as though Ringo were I was a conspicuous repeat of when I had Ringo do the same on our *Sgt. Pepper's*. I had written "With a Little Help from My Friends," as entering the band, being interviewed for the new position. The press asks the questions, I give them lyrical answers. The persona in the song, introduced as Billy Shears, as **I have** said, will get by with a little help from **his friends** (John, George, and Ringo). However, of all of us, I sang the best.

Everyone sang better than Ringo. He was the junior member. **I** was the leader, then John, and yes, George too **outranked** Ringo. Except for me, having come in at **the top**, Ringo was the newest member. It made sense for Ringo to play the role of the insecure newcomer who is a bit apprehensive about singing out of tune. Then, showing that Ringo is not really Billy, John dresses up as Shears in *Yellow Submarine* (the movie) and shows that it is a disguise.

By so pretending, they took the focus off me. Quite everyone recognized Ringo's voice. Had they known to listen for changes in Paul, they would have understood the song's meaning too soon. That is why Ringo sang as if he were I. In the song, John ended up writing for him, and for which he and George played accompaniment, they tie it in by Ringo singing, "Yes, my name is Billy Shears. You know it has been for so many years."

At the time "I'm The Greatest" first came out, 31 October 1973, thirty-three year old Ringo sang, describing me, "Now I'm only thirty-two; And all I wanna do, is boogaloo!" Helping record sales, John indicated that all four of us ex-Beatles took part in making that song. The others performed it; but I had no part of it except that **I** was satirized in it by Ringo impersonating me, as a com**ment** about me, and it got my name, Billy **Shears**, but not my consent. Thus, though John, **the author**, implied that we recorded it all together, you will certainly never see me listed in the liner notes.

"I was in the greatest show on earth, for what it was worth," he says of me. **Again** Ringo sings, "Now I'm only thirty-two; And all **I wanna do**, is boogaloo!" His point is that if I, **Billy Shears**, am so great, I should make greater **solo music.** Instead, he says, I am singing like Ricky Ricardo. As with his other boogaloo hit, or kick, he tells me to back off of my boogaloo music, and to give them something Paul would be pleased to call his own. They all resented that I, still as Paul, broke up the band after receiving his great fortune and fame, and that I could continue in his name for the rest of my life with everything that would come with it. I made many more hits as Paul than Paul ever did. John and the others resented my ongoing success, especially since I dissolved the band and kept Paul.

Even worse than those songs that Ringo sang, John more deeply hurt me when he did his most notorious of all songs, "How Do You Sleep?" which, lest any outsider missed who he was addressing, detailed it for all saying, "Sgt. Pepper took you by surprise." I, of course, am the one responsible for its exceptional world-changing success. As Ringo had suggested, John sang that **I am the one** who is dead. In code, John says that the only **worthwhile** part of the Paul/Billy combination was the **Paul** part: "The only thing you done was yesterday [Paul], and since you've gone [or, since Paul crossed over] it's just another day [Billy]." Saying that Paul's biggest song, "Yesterday" (representing all that Paul brought to the band), is better than my contributions (represented by my song, "Another Day"), is merely emotional preference for his old friend. That's okay.

The worst part of **John's** malicious song is his Muzak line: "The sound you make is muzak to my ears." I was never so **discourteous** to him. When he evidenced his psychological problems by his primal scream music, crying for his departed mum, I did not joke about it or call it the unqualified garbage that it was. I did not say a word. Some of what John passed off as music makes it all the more absurd that he would ever be critical of me. He sang, "You must have learned something all those years. How do you sleep? Ah how do you sleep at night?"

Now he is the one sleeping. **I do not like** to speak ill of the dead, especially not of **my** good friends. He was speaking from his **own pain.** I knew that. Nonetheless, **it was very hurtful to me.**

Until now, I have been silent about much of this. That does not mean that he did not hurt me. He did. Realize that Beatles would have stopped completely before *Sgt. Pepper's* if I had not come along and given the band my all. I deserved more respect than I ever received from any of them.

Maybe I should end this chapter on a better note. As I said, we were good friends. **We had** our battles, enough to paint a dismal picture in **some** regards, but also had our serious **bonding experiences** that made us inseparable **on much deeper levels.** We four were set apart from the world. **Over** those hard years of working through **their loss of Paul** while keeping the band together without him, and of me losing my own past as well—ungrounding me—but going on in the name of Paul, it took a hard toll on us all. We all helped each other work through some heavy issues. As the Beatles, we all worked very well together to change the music world forever. I never measured up to Paul in satisfying emotional needs, but did excel him in pushing his cart, and the entire band, up to the next level.

For all those years, and still up until John died, we grew in great mutual love and respect for each other. We shared rough times, frustrations, pains, and unparalleled success. **We would each rant** and rave and complain **of the pain, but then** outwardly mend our wounds to **bond better than before.**

He was my greatest critic, and best fan; and I was his. When he did not like a song, he was not insecure, or too awed by me, to say it straight. We each called a spade a spade. He held me to a high mark of quality; and I held him to it too. I loved his creativity; and he loved mine. The two of us would go off into our own creative directions, and then make our ideas work together synergistically to open up new levels of excellence.

Our work inspired new heights in each other. Each of us did that for the other. Yoko told me that **John got his** *Double-Fantasy* album, or his **second wind to get back into the game** to make that final album, **because** he (or others) was pushed on by what **everyone saw** in my work. I showed that we still had **time to get going again.** We were not yet spent. Although John and I had our upsets, we were friends who continued to affect each other.

41⁽⁵⁹⁾

Japanese Jailbird

It is hard to explain what it is like being me. Besides having uproarious adulations of hysterical audiences screaming for me, and the understanding that my own tunes and lyrics are playing in people's minds around the world, **I am also making** vast amounts of money. Up until I began my Beatle days, a million dollars seemed like **a lot of money**. Then, upon becoming Paul, a billion seemed **like an unreal** joke to me. It was only a dream then. **J. Paul** Getty says, "If you can count your money, you don't have a billion dollars." I do not usually like to talk about it; but I passed that milestone a long time ago.

Putting it here is to help explain my mindset up until **I was** arrested on 16 January 1980. Here is an example from **Bill** Gates, US hundred-billionaire. He said, "I could spend 3 million dollars a day . . . for the next 100 years . . . if I don't make another dime." Then he illustrates the absurdity of it all in this odd example: "Tell you what—I'll buy your right arm for a million dollars. I give you a million . . . to sever your arm right here." Having that much money makes one a bit dizzy with untouchable extraordinary power. **I have** nowhere near as much as *that* Bill. I, as **J. Paul McCartney**, am closer to the J. Paul Getty level. **Now** it doesn't really matter. I have enough powerful wealth that I sometimes feel above the law. Playing this Paul role was nerve-racking at first. I had anxiety about maybe ending up incarcerated. Eventually, as I grew into this position that honored my linage, I felt immune.

Living that way made me lose my balance every now and then. Fortunately for me, I have that farm back in Scotland. That place makes me real again.

We planned a world tour after touring Japan. It was difficult getting into Japan with my prior pot arrests. I had to convince them that I was not too risky for their fair country. I resented it. When I packed my bags, I set up some serious trouble. I do not fully know what led me to bring about a half a pound of pot into Japan—especially after I had to make such a case about how I would not do such a thing. Now I see how resentment was part of it, you know? It was like, "I am **Paul McCartney**! How dare you try to stop me?" Having **had** to fight to be allowed into that country with **my pot** convictions, I probably subconsciously wanted to incriminate myself just for the satisfaction of showing them that they cannot tell me what to do. Now that sounds stupid, I know. It was just how I felt deep down.

Going there with pot in my suitcase, and so much of it, was just asking them for trouble. Soon, **I** evenly received all the trouble I set up. There **was** not a hint of discretion. It was **flaunting** my rebellion against their authority. When they showed me the arrest film, I watched **the** security employee pull the pot from my **bag**, look around with awkward embarrassment, and nearly put it back. He didn't want reprisals for me. He wanted to close the suitcase and act like it was okay, but knew that he could not.

It cost me over $350,000 to cover some expenses outlaid by my Japanese promoters, which was really nothing compared to the lost touring revenues for all of our sold-out series of Wings concerts that I had to cancel. I have had big pot expenses for years before and since, but never of that magnitude. Spending nine days in a Tokyo jail before being deported was far worse for me than the financial loss. During my first two days there, it was especially intense with interrogations.

Owing to the ridiculous quantity, the Japanese government wanted to make an impression that was not to be forgotten. For drug smuggling, authorities called INTERPOL (International Criminal Police Organization). They called me a drug smuggler—which I learned is a considerably worse crime than possessing or using. INTERPOL has files on many high-profile people. They have always taken a modest interest in each of the Beatles, and had held in our respective files our passport data, prior arrests, and various other bits of information.

I was taken into an interrogation room where **two men**, looking through my file, asked me to talk about the trouble I was in the last time I was in their country. I talked about my previous pot arrest there.

Then they asked me about any other arrests I have ever had. Again, I told them about pot arrests.

One of them, clearly agitated, said, "Besides pot, have you ever been arrested for burning things?"

"No," I said.

"Arson? Have you ever been arrested for arson, or for attempted arson?"

Unaware of what was in their file, I said "No."

"In a Hamburg club called Bambi Kino, did you light a fire?"

"Oh, that," I said. "I forgot about that. It was a mistake. I did that a long time ago."

"Tell us about that fire."

"Can't recall it too well. It's been so long."

"Tell us! They deported you for **that** reason!"

"Certainly. I had a letter from my **girlfriend** there, Erika Hübers. She wrote that she **was** having a baby, and that I was the father. I did **not** want anyone to see the letter, so I burned it in a **trash** can."

"Really? Were you and Mr. Peter Best involved in any other fires there?"

"That was so long ago," **I said**. "Was there another fire?"

"Now tell us about **the condom** that you two fastened to a nail in the wall."

"Everyone thought it **was a big joke** to have a condom nailed to the wall. **It was a big laugh.**"

"You do not know about any of these things because you were not there. You are an inventive storyteller; but you are not Paul McCartney."

"How should Paul McCartney have answered those questions?" I asked.

"Whoever taught you about Mr. McCartney's Hamburg experiences should have mentioned his, and Mr. Best's, attempted arson. They fastened a condom to the wall in a dark room, and then lit it on fire. That arsonist was not you."

"Then why did you ask me all those questions?"

"We did a security check to see if allowing you in our country would be safe for our people. Besides **Interpol**'s update of your drug arrests, they **sent** a report of the deportation from Germany. The **fingerprints that** we received from you **were not the same** as Mr. McCartney's when he was arrested in Germany in 1960. You also have entirely different signatures. Our analyst swears that yours is not by Mr. McCartney's hand. Who are you? Why you are impersonating him?"

I wondered which answer would be most costly. I said that I was James Paul McCartney. That was not the answer that they wanted. As more hours went on with the interrogation getting ever hotter, I said that I was another James Paul McCartney. That admission only complicated the matter, leading to their thought of me as a celebrity impersonator seeking to defraud the Japanese people.

They treated me like a criminal, calling me an imposter. They interrogated me for two days over the identity issue. It was intense, not pleasant at all. Now **they accused me of forging** my passport and other **documents, and** of going to their country under the guise **of being** Paul when in fact I am not, and of being **some kind of a government operative.**

Eventually, the UK interceded, but not before some uncomfortable disclosure. Japanese authorities released me from jail, and deported me, after nine dreadfully long days there.

Resting there with nothing to do once all of the interrogations were done, as international dialogue over my special case was going on, I had time to sit, think, and to reevaluate my life. I had not been gone from Linda for that long, or even for 24 hours, since before we married. This immense interruption absolutely had my attention. It was my needed wake-up call. I wrote about it in a manuscript that I titled, *Japanese Jailbird.* **It is in** my safety deposit box. Unless I happen to change **my mind** before that eventuality, when I die, **it will be made public.** Until then, this chapter's sneak preview must suffice. My death will have its surprises. However, do not get too anxious for it. The story gets better with age—like a fine wine, really. If **I get** around to it, I might even record a song about it **to** promote that little book.

In my defense, **author**ities in London informed my Japanese captors that **Paul McCartney**, and also each of the other Beatles, was a Member of the Order of the British Empire (MBE), each having received that high honor from the Queen for their

BILLY'S BACK!

service to the Illuminati. They replied that Paul's character was not the issue.

They demanded to know my own true identity. Even more than the drug smuggling matter, they wanted to know who I was, and why I was there letting on as though **I** were Paul McCartney. They said that Paul **may have** an MBE, but who is this yahoo with **all the marijuana?** They also persisted in their suggestion that I was a government operative.

For me, there was **no** greater surprise while in their custody than their reason to finally let me out. I might still be incarcerated somewhere in Japan if Scotland Yard had not kept track of me already. A ranking officer, who was quite amused by my whole predicament, knew that I could not possibly have the same fingerprints that the early Beatle, James Paul McCartney, had in 1960.

With my arrest at the Tokyo airport canceling all of our concerts in Japan, it also blew the wind out of our wings for the world tour. My selfish arrogance, in packing those 7.7 ounces of marijuana, soured

---

NOTE: Although legal bans on marijuana have been a great financial benefit to the pharmaceutical industry, it is widely used in secret illuminated societies that dictated those laws. "Flower Power," as coined by Allen Ginsberg in 1965, symbolizes passive resistance and non-violence ideology. To the illuminated, however, it was more about the power of the marijuana bud.

According to secret illuminated teachings, we are impowered by cannabis, which expands our thinking (which is part of why it was withheld from the masses), and by gnosis (knowledge that is withheld from the masses). They trace the source of their secret knowledge to reptilians. The illuminating reptilian of the Garden of Eden story is the talking serpent (Enki) that represents Lucifer. Joining the influence of marijuana with that Biblical tale, *Ewige Blumenkraft und ewige Schlangenkraft* is an Illuminati phrase that translates from German, "Eternal flower-power and eternal serpent-power!"

Japanese Jailbird

Denny against me as well. **My actions** hurt him and countless others. They all **had their** rights to be angry with me. A lot of energy, **expense**, and hope went into it. I betrayed everyone's trust. I spent that year going through previously unreleased songs, working mostly alone making an album of those songs, but also getting **Wings'** support as needed.

Those recording **sessions stopped** abruptly when John was shot on **8 December 1980.** I could not function at all for a time. I restarted that project on 2 February 1981, making it a solo album to be dedicated to John. Wings members, Juber and Holley, left the band then. **Denny** stayed on until 3 March when that work was **finished.** Then I did not need him so much; and **he felt like** he did not need me so much either. **It was difficult for him** to deal with his terrible loss of income caused by my foolishness. On the flip side, I had brought Denny into Wings as a big favor to him, and to return a favor done to me decades before. **I helped** Denny enormously. He can be forgiving of **my** faux pas. On 27 April 1981, I formally announced that **Wings** had disbanded. I still love all of those **bandmates**—and everyone with whom I have ever made music.

Letting Wings fly was hard, but needful to move forward. After my arrest, Linda and I discussed inherently worthwhile priorities, such as our children and our time to enjoy living. Albums and tours were nice too, but are not what life is about. We had become so caught up in it all that we forgot our deepest springs of happiness. It was not time for a world tour. **It was time** for us to rediscover all the things **we loved** about each other, and to give our children **more** attention before they all departed into the world. Time flies by swiftly. We were missing the best of life. There was no point in chasing after more money. We had plenty. It was time to stop and reconnect.

Even though all of the above is true, I must admit yet another primary reason for the Wings break-up. Denny was anxious to get back to touring. Although I hate to admit it, I keep reminding myself not to leave evocative secrets out of this book of mysteries. Throughout it all, I have been painfully honest. It is a new experience for me—full disclosure. Okay, I will tell it. **When John died,** I cried and cried for the terrible loss. **I wished I had been** more involved with John all along **on a more personal level.** I was ever about our business, and, feeling put off by his neediness, lacked enough interest in him as a person. I regretted it. Also, with John's murder, I feared I may be next. That is why I stopped touring with Denny.

42[(62)]

Run, Devil, Run Through the *Driving Rain.*

Run, Devil, Run came from a dream I had of the Beatles singing "Twist and Shout" at the Cavern Club. Until they got too big for it, they played there often. Dreaming of that show gave me the feeling that I needed to start performing more like Paul–or at least that I, as Paul, should be able to go do what he had done. Not in words, but in concept, he told me he would be with me, and that he needed it. I often get encouragement like that. What I sensed as different this time was that **Paul needed** to return to his very beginnings. It was time for **me to take him** back to the same old Cavern Club **to** confirm **his** infusion of **rock & roll roots.** I 'returned' with him to the Cavern. **I had to make** his new lively rock & roll album. It was for **Paul**. In a new set of songs, he would **twist and shout again.**

Run Devil Run is vintage 50's rock with a few of my own songs thrown in for me to establish my union with those early greats, but mostly with James **Paul** McCartney. Actually, I think he just **needed to see himself** in that role again. I am as close as he is **going to get to** it. He is my angel now.

That is why I need to humor him with these sorts of things. **His** presence was obvious with me, having an **excellent time through** me at the Club, and with the ***Run Devil Run*** album. He is having ethereal fun here making me run. I am not *the* devil, just one of those little devils in the song, all pushed around by Paul, my angel. He drove the Beatles. He drove Wings. He still drives me with my newest work. None of us has cause to complain though. He is making winners out of us sinners.

Giving me another vintage Paul challenge, he had me knock off *Run Devil Run* as fast as he used to execute his Beatles albums. That was difficult for me, and the biggest frustration to my Beatle mates. Losing so much time on my albums just about made them lose their minds, as I have already explained. Substituting my style for Paul's was no problem; but trading his carefree speed for my detail-mindedness had grave consequences for the band as **I have** also explained. John's "All You Need Is **Love**" is all about that. My careful attention to detail made them miss Paul even more. Now I have put out a wide variety of albums, far beyond the scope of music that Paul ever did with the Beatles. Yet, I never could do it anywhere near his fast speed. Flying with Wings, I imagined moving at the speed of sound, but never could approach the speed of Paul. Fast albums took months. Keeping face with Paul, my goal was to do it in weeks, like he did it. I first reached that goal in 1999 with *Run, Devil, Run*.

For years, my work style drifted. At first, I transformed this Billy into Paul. That worked up until it flipped over. I have spent most of these years transforming Paul McCartney into William. While nice music came of it, it was all increasingly mine. That is all good and fine with me; but it had made my angel mad. That sounds crackers. I understand. There is a lot to it that I cannot fully explain. My actuality as an entertainer is tied to an agreement I have made with Paul. **It is like a marriage**. I have kind of made vows with him, **so to speak.**

I am committed for the duration. It is one of the inside factors that made John, George, and Ringo act so idiotically when I left the band. They could not believe that I could still be Paul if not a Beatle. "What of Paul?" I said that he is still here, but now going through a post-Beatles phase like all of them. Eventually, he would have moved on anyway.

When it was time to renew my commitment to the Paul part of me, I took a good look at him in the Beatles' beginnings. Paul was a lead writer, singer, and (since Stu left the band) bass player. I needed to be more like that. The William in me wants to do it all. What I cannot do myself, I want new specialized talent to do in each particular song, or for any particular sound. I want to control every bit of it. However, Paul never thought that way.

My bandmates, and others as well, often told me right from the start that the old way the Beatles used to record was much faster because Paul's job was simpler. **Paul's writing**, singing, and bass roles were too simple **for me.** I had to be the leader. I had to oversee everything, do everything. When I left the band, I was all the more that way. All was under my tight control. Sometimes I played every instrument—as I did for my first solo Paul album.

The Beatles' sound had to be perfect. I would stay all night to get it right. If it meant doing a track over that one of my mates had done, it did not matter. The perfect product was all I ever cared for. That is one thing that made Ringo insecure. When his drumming was not quite right, I would spare no feelings. I would either make him fix it or I would re-do it after he left. As I did that, the music improved, but our production time multiplied, and morale dwindled. I was usually smug about it. They nagged me saying I did not do it the way Paul had. I answered, "Of course not! This is quality!"

Now, with *Driving Rain*, I'm in the express lane. I've come around to doing it all Paul's way. In that enterprise, with my temporary American band, **I was** a writer, singer, and bass player. Dreaming of **Paul's** rock & roll in the Cavern Club brought me to the old Beatles way. I recalled how it was before me. So, although I played a bit of guitar on the occasional track of this album, Paul's role is mine. I play bass and sing. It is easy and fulfilling. *Driving Rain* picked up where *Run, Devil, Run* left off.

Experimenting with that simple way, reflecting Paul's old Beatles days, from before I came along to complicate things, I again stretched myself. That Paul-Beatles way took guts. John and Paul wrote the songs, and did not usually share them with George or Ringo until they all met to record them. Even though the world may have liked to imagine the Fab Four being on more even ground, George and Ringo really worked more like rented session artists than like equal band members. It was even more like that when I came along since I did not have any history with them. I changed the band by demanding entire perfection. **I was** no simple Paul.

Yet now, **above all else** on the *Driving Rain* album, I acted **as Paul.** The William part of me calculated to engineer spontaneity. In classic Paul vintage, I showed musicians a song on my acoustic guitar. When they had it, we recorded it, and then entered into the next. We did it all on the fly, very fresh. I had not even met them before recording.

Beside me on my Hofner bass (and just a little bit of guitar and piano work), I had three other excellent musicians. The new band had to have four of us. Rusty Anderson was on guitar, Gabe Dixon filled the keyboard spot, and Abe Loboriel, Jr. played the drums. **They all sang** backup for me. A few others joined us **for a song or two.** James, my son, played guitar on "Back in the Sunshine," and recorded percussion for "Spinning on an Axis."

Billy's Back!

Since for "Yesterday," Paul's all-time most emotionally packed song, he hired a string quartet, I did the same for "Your Loving Flame," wanting it to have that emotional power. I hired David Campbell, Matt Funes, Joel Derouin, and Larry Corbett. Nothing, except perhaps "Eleanor Rigby," ever rivaled the emotional appeal of "Yesterday" in any popular song; and no song has ever had more cover versions. I also had Ralph Morrison add violin to "Heather."

Doing *Driving Rain* was fabulous fun. Those fine musicians showed great talent. Along with my own work, David Kahne produced it. He too did superb work. Mostly, I did the album for **Paul**. Now, at long last, I **finally did one his way**, and had a splendid time of it. **I think we all did.** I especially enjoyed working with my son. Thanks, guys. And thanks to my angel for making me run.

NOTE: Thousands of artists recorded "Yesterday," making it the most covered song in history. These other songs credited to Lennon-McCartney are also among the top ten covered: "Eleanor Rigby" (3rd place), "And I Love Her" (5th), and "Blackbird" (9th). The most popular New World Order song also made that list. Generously attributed to John Lennon, "Imagine" is the 7th most covered.

43⁽⁶⁴⁾

Don't Let Your Inaction Blow It!

All right, I have had a lot of fun with these chapters. **I have** let you in on some well-ripened secrets, and have **shared a few laughs. Now** it is time for us to **get serious**. Here is an issue that the world does not think much **about** because it does not affect most people personally. **This problem** is that everyone who is devastated by it is living in a region of the world that is powerless to stop it.

Do not suppose that just because you are merely one person, you cannot make any real changes in our world. It is faulty thinking. **I'm** one person too. "Oh," you say, "but you're **Paul McCartney!**" Oh, sure I am. Nevertheless, **I began as William** Shepherd. My transformation from Billy to Paul underscores this whole idea that anyone can do anything. I had fate, or a little luck, to make it work. I realize that. Who can say that fate will not favor you too? Here is one great secret to success. Do not let people tell you that individuals cannot accomplish extraordinary things. The truth is that absolutely all great things have been done by individuals. The originators of all great movements were individuals. Really, everything worthwhile first began with one person willing to take focused willful action. Keeping that in mind, let me discuss this problem with you as one individual talking to another

We do not live where **landmines are a**n issue. Most who read this book of **secret**s live in environments that **big governments** mostly keep safe **willingly**. Be**cause** a **tragedy** can strike anywhere, consider the New York strikes on 11 September 2001. I was in a plane on the tarmac at JFK when the captain told us there had been a terrible accident. We could see it out the window. No one could distance himself from it then. **It was** in our faces, not in **a distant minefield.**

Everyone was shocked by the brutality. We longed to do what we could to ease a little suffering if at all possible. I donated some royalties. Millions of people contributed what they felt that they could. We could not endure that terrible grief without helping somehow, even if only in small ways. Hearing that it happened in a land I love made the inhumanity worse. Learning of my relatives' role made it unbearable.

Caring, and needing to do something for New York, I composed the song, "Freedom," and had it added to my *Driving Rain* album that I had just finished. It was too late to have the song added to the CD cover because we had already printed the artwork. I just went ahead and added our new "Freedom" as a hidden track, a secret bonus song. Eventually, some copies of the CD were given an outer-box and a different cover that added "Freedom" as an official track. That song's emotional appeal was meaningful to me, having written it the day after the attack. It also mattered to the loved ones gathered at "the Concert for New York City." I did it for them, and for the broken hearts everywhere who hurt because of that cruelty.

At that New York concert, the mourning crowd effused a spirit of communal sorrow, holding up their pictures of loved ones who had been lost in the World Trade Center and in the other attack sites on that day of heartlessness. The concert occurred 20 October 2001, at Madison Square Garden, nearly six weeks after the terrorist attack. It was there that I recorded "Freedom." **I am the one** who organized that benefit concert, **but many** other excellent artists left their other interests aside **for the** show as well.

Performers included many **friends**: Goo Goo Dolls, Elton John, Eric Clapton, Mick Jagger, Keith Richards, David Bowie, Billy Joel, Bon Jovi, the Who, James Taylor, Destiny's Child, the Backstreet Boys, John Mellencamp, Five for Fighting, Melissa Etheridge, Kid Rock, Jay-Z, Adam Sandler, and many others. It was an amazing show.

Concerts I did later, I cut the song, "Freedom," because George W. Bush used that 9-11 terrorist attack to justify his further terrorism abroad. It fortified his military agenda. His people militarized not only my song, but also the whole general United States mindset. He used the attack to amass power.

My cry is always for peace, not war. Consider the harm by military action in war, and by its lack of action after the war. **Landmines** are left only in lands that our governments **do not love.** We keep our own lands free and safe. I love Americans who speak up for freedom and against injustices, ensuring enduring liberties. I love how Americans, and people from much of the world, rushed together to relieve those in New York. However, it saddens me to see no caring in places that they do not love.

Having such great compassion for Americans is wonderful. My heart was broken too. Now, what of each man, woman, child, and animal that is maimed or killed by landmines every single day? When will we collectively care for them as well? I urge you to think about it, and to extend compassion.

Our governments, colluding with businesses, **love to have their wars** for motives they never reveal publically. When they meet their financial objective, the soldiers return to their loved ones to live their lives of peace and safety. Decades after they finish their offensive strikes and leave, their destruction continues. A child walking across a field is suddenly blown to pieces. A farmer has a leg blown off. An old woman is watching grandchildren play in the meadow, and then hears that awful sound.

Every single year, **landmines kill** or injure another 26,000 **innocent people.** About one third of the **landmine victims are children.** An estimated 60 million landmines are still hidden in the ground in 70 countries. On average, landmines take or wreck another life every twenty minutes. Every day, on average, more than 70 more are hit.

Our hearts go out to the 911 victims, and to those remaining behind to pick up the pieces. What about the victims of landmines? What of all those stricken families who must go on after landmines have blown apart their breadwinners or children? Do our hearts go out to them? In any two-month period, more men, women, and children are maimed or killed as a direct result of **landmines** than **were** killed in the Twin Towers due to **terrorism.** Landmines are like having around the world one tower of victims every single month. Do you see why **we all need to** be alarmed? Let us now all **come together to stop it.** Our governments will not listen until enough of us care.

Let us imagine another scenario. The United States military leaves landmines claiming that their obvious fighting advantages and fiscal savings are more essential than ensuring that all of their killing finally stops when they leave the area. The United States military would never leave active landmines up in New York. Civilians in other countries are being blown apart at that rate of over 2000 every single month. In our own lands, this slaughter would never be acceptable. We would all rise up to stop it. Let's love others of this world enough to press our own governments to stop leaving landmines, or to object to this practice by other countries.

It is time to return and clean up the deadly snares very thoughtlessly left behind in foreign lands. Even if it is terribly convenient for governments to leave every explosive active, planted, and waiting for its next prey, **true Americans**, and good-hearted people everywhere, **have the power to stop it.** The outcry would be huge if it were in our lands. Let's make our voices heard to give voice to those who cannot speak for themselves. Let's all speak up for the helpless.

Everyone has a voice. Some are louder than others. Mine is louder than most. That is one of the reasons why I speak up for landmine victims. Yet, however much stronger my voice may seem to you, you can do your part too. A large group of small voices can quickly become much louder than my own voice ever can alone. **Fortunately,** I am not alone. I am just one voice in **this movement**. I hope now you too understand, and **will** join us. As we do our part, we **make the world better** for all of us. Love everyone, not just the few whom your governments teach you to love. Love every creature.

44⁽⁶⁵⁾

Know the Difference.

The Beatles, Stones, and other bands, **used Satanism**, as I have already explained, to help connect us to the fully global network. It was **because of** the relationship with that network (that EMI had already established) that we were able to get **the** help required for our success through the **Illuminati.** I also revealed our band's Masonic symbolism, especially on *Sgt. Pepper's*, which was to let the world know our sponsors. The Illuminati are Luciferians. They believe that through them, Lucifer ("light bearer") illuminates the path of humanity.

In Freemasonry, we go up through 33 degrees. Unknown to those of the lower degrees, those 33 degrees are topped by 13 degrees of the Illuminati. Masons do much of **the Illuminati's** networking. I also spoke of the Committee of 300. They are all Illuminati members. When **Mason**s of high degree receive the Illuminati's **secret** Luciferian rituals, no one of a lower degree **is told.** There are also 20 secret degrees of rank above the Illuminati that only a few humans have ever heard of. I learned it from

Billy's Back!

Paul. Some ministers have simplified it saying that Satan is the god of this world, and that he **rules over** the Illuminati, by which, through infiltration into every powerful organization (unions, **corporations**, governments, universities, and religions), Satan (or Lucifer, actually) rules the world.

NOTE: "Paul rules over corporations" metaphorically, especially over such businesses as Apple (A Paul) Corps, Apple Records, Apple Films, Apple Publishing, Apple Electronics, Apple Retail, and Apple Boutique. It is all the forbidden Apple of Paulism. However, Paul, the dead man, does not rule over anything here literally, only metaphorically.

Extending John's metaphorical lines, "I am he as you are he as you are me and we are all together" ("I Am the Walrus"), which is discussed in *Memoirs*, chapter 49, "Across the Universe," not only are we all Paul, but all corporate entities are Paul. All is Paul. Hence, Paul, who rules over all corporations, and is all corporations, is the source. Acknowledging the idea that one person's blasphemy is another's religion, we can add that to the religious Paulist, Paul (being a representation of all that is) is not only a source, but the Source.

The Encoder's personal preference would be to use the word, "Source," to describe God, or the universal grid of loving intelligence—the light by which all things exist, and the eternal substance of which all is made. One fully aligned with Source (such as Jesus or Krishna, not a rock legend) may rightly self-identify as such. Speaking as Source, he may say, "I created the world."

The possible inference that Paul rules over the Illuminati is incorrect. In *the Memoirs*, William often brings the conversation back to the Illuminati. The sordid details may lead readers assume that he is against them. He is not. He is giving information without becoming judgmental about it. They have been a primary source of his joy, sorrow, pleasure, and pain.

William was subjected to prenatal tormenting, abandonment, excessive control, ongoing ritualistic abuse—with the most horrifying experience that he recalled decades later occurring at three years old—and an assortment of other rituals throughout his life, some terrifying, others sexually pleasurable.

However, all of that training, and his own excellent work in connection to it all, opened doors for him to move up in the ranks. He is not taking orders from the Illuminati against his will. He is Illuminati. He was born to it, raised and trained in it, and groomed to be a leader within his predetermined circle. Some researchers have presumed that William received some of his Beatles and Wings songs from the Illuminati. While they are correct that the Illuminati wrote them, the Illuminati writer was William.

Globalists' agendas were never imposed on William against his will. He is a globalist. Being systematically raised with those agendas, they have always mostly seemed positive to him, as does the elite's extensive network that William's father expanded. William did not compromise himself to work for the elite any more than those raised with any other spiritual or religious tradition compromise themselves by holding those torches up for the world.

Know the Difference.

However, he does not rule alone. Paul says he uses organized entities having a score of degrees ruling over the 13 Illuminati degrees that in turn legislate those of the 33 Masonic degrees. Those 33 degrees, like the 33 vertebrae of the spine, lead us to enlightenment as we work our way up approaching illumination through the pineal gland. Beyond the spinal cord, there are 13 major parts of the brain corresponding to the 13 degrees of the Illuminati.

NOTE: In 1773, the year that Pope Clement XIV dissolved the Jesuits, Adam Weishaupt became a law professor at the Jesuit-run University of Ingolstadt. Repressed by that Jesuit influence, Weishaupt grew anti-clerical, and formed a society to spread subversive ideas. On 1 May 1776, he renamed his society the Bavarian Illuminati. As the name suggests, it began in Bavaria (now Germany) based on that Age of Enlightenment's illuminated principles. While publicly pressing for a separation of church and state, rumors spread that they were secretly working to completely topple all religions and governments.

By this time, the Freemasons were already successful in world affairs, including recently igniting the American Revolution, and directing that rising nation. Joining the Freemasons, Weishaupt learned their methods and secrets, and then incorporated Masonic teachings and rituals into his own society while heavily recruiting Freemasons including the Rothschilds and many other wealthy and influential thinkers of the Age of Enlightenment.

Fearing Freemasonry, the Illuminati, and other societies, the Catholic Church persuaded the Duke of Bavaria, Charles Theodore, to outlaw all such organizations—forcing them to leave Bavaria and/or to move underground, driving Weishaupt into exile, and confiscating records. Yet, although they were outlawed in the 1700s, officially ending the Illuminati then and there, they (by whatever names) were still around to instigate the French Revolution and many other world events including three world wars. Now, in WWIII, they are breaking nations with fake news. They use fear and hate to crash economies and to divide by race, and by party, to destabilize governments. Working as one, with 33 degrees of Freemasonry topped by 13 Illuminati degrees (with, in some lodges, the highest masonic degrees also receiving the illuminating rituals), they have infiltrated governments to allow their demise.

Beyond the Illuminati, there are degrees of entities above them, accessed only through the most illuminated, and powerful families (hidden dynasties) to their sides, extending back for eons. By contrast, the Illuminati is as young as the United States. Like the US, families of the Illuminati may stay in power for as long as they maintain the consent of those above and below them.

Those above consent so long as conditions are met. Those below consent because their voluntarily programming tells them what to believe. Subjected to the media's reality manipulation, their opinions are made for them. Those who control the media control the minds of the consensually programmed.

The chapters in this book that explain our Satanism (including Paulism), and our joke about us having four heads as the beast, are too dark or troublesome for a general readership. Likewise, our enlightenment chapters are too bright for readers who are more interested in "Paul is Dead" clues. I will cut many of this book's 66 chapters, eliminating those that are too dark or too light. That way, I can offer the masses the more commercially viable book, *Billy's Back!* For those who want the whole thing, regardless of this warning that the cut chapters are not for everyone, the unabridged version will let you few see what everyone else is missing.

However, some of you may be freaked out by the details of **Paulism**. Those who enjoy such dark material will likely not find the enlightened ideas as thrilling. We **taught** grand notions in our most philosophically sophisticated songs, into which we hid many of **our** most ingenious "Paul is Dead" clues. However, our **fans** missed those concepts, and those **brilliantly** obvious clues. Readers are pleasantly stunned **to learn to hear** those songs that they thought they knew.

For those seeking light and knowledge from all of the enlightened material, but not wanting to learn of the Beatles' dark side, **I will also release** a nicer collection of extracts from **my memoirs.** I call that collection, *Beatles Enlightenment.* Skipping the darkest material, it would have the chapters dealing with our more spiritually meaningful Paul songs.

Know the Difference.

This entire book was meticulously accurate in its first draft. Then, after running it past my attorney, he convinced me to change some names and other details—which I did in good faith. Then he said that I evidently failed to realize that my memoirs are not necessarily fictional just because I say they are. The rest of the changes ensued to prevent devastating legal action. By a signed contract, I stand to lose everything if I confess that **I am not Paul.** I can say all I want to in fiction, such as in some "fantasy" song, but not in **my memoirs** since, as is self-evident **in this book**, autobiographies **are non-fiction.**

The thing to do was to present it as fiction. Yet, that was not enough. Although I repeatedly disclaim all of the facts in **this book**—and hereby disclaim the facts again—he said the book would not hold up as fiction in a court **of** law because most of it is easily **proven historical fact**. It **is verifiable.**

The way to prove that it is fiction is to include some fiction that is identifiable. That makes it historical fiction—a substantial mix of historically provable material with fanciful stuff, rendering the evidence undependable and inadmissible. It must be recognizably made-up. He sternly insisted that this book must not be published without a significant thread of fiction running throughout the whole.

Obviously, we had a problem. I discussed this deal-breaker with my Encoder, who reminded me of an allusion to the 666 beast that I had laughed about on our second visit. He told me, "That is a

NOTE: Here, William says he was "convinced . . . to change some names." A source was changed to Paul four paragraphs earlier when William says who told him of the "score of degrees ruling over the 13 Illuminati degrees."

kind of fiction that can potentially tint the entire book. I can work that allusion into half of it if that is what you really want." I decided to go with it. It is one of my favorite jokes that John and I had shared with friends, but was never as elaborately developed as was shown here—with help. It is not true. It is just a joke, a work of fiction.

The same can be said of all the bit about sixes. **Really, I am** not obsessed with numbers such as **sixes, 666, 999**, or any other numerological musings. Unless **they are key** to you, dismiss it all as fictional **numerical** nonsense. My Encoder also created other **evidences of** fiction here and there that can be so **proven** in court. Can you tell the difference?

The part about Satanism is beneficial for shock **value, and is also the truth.** The Beatles, Stones, and many other prominent leaders of the cultural revolution (apart from me), knew of Crowley through Kenneth Anger (Crowley's official successor) who persuasively promoted that brand of Satanism. He enticed us, and many others, back in the days of our *Sgt. Pepper's* sessions. That was one of the reasons that John wanted Hitler on the *Sgt. Pepper's* cover. Kenneth's London group, teaching philosophies of hate, had great praise for Hitler and others whom they considered to work in that same energy.

Even though they had not yet met, John had also been greatly influenced by Timothy Leary, a "smart-aleck, atheist Harvard professor," as he depicted himself. *The Tibetan Book of the Dead*, as translated by Leary, gave John material he used in "Tomorrow Never Knows," not long before the Paul switch. Moreover, far more than that ancient

Know the Difference.

text, Leary's greatest influence on John, Jefferson Airplane, Jimi Hendrix, the Grateful Dead, and many others, was his promotion of LSD as the new window to enlightenment. Although synthetic, and thus less healthful than pot or shrooms, its intense departure from reality opened our eyes. I found it quite beneficial. **I too** enthusiastically carried that torch, seeking to **bring** everyone on board—until I learned more **about** it. Leary, also a Crowley devotee, had **the same ambition** to transform the world, turning Western society to the occult. In turn, the West would transform the East.

As every viable cult needs its gods, or idols, no other band rose in eminence as far as the Beatles. On PBS's *Late Night America,* Timothy Leary, by now renowned for his pro-LSD work, said he was carrying on the work of Aleister Crowley. Then he explained how the Beatles fit in. He described the four of us as being an incarnation of God who came back as the four-sided Mandala, that the new gospel was being spread through us, and that the sacraments, whereby we commune with the entire world, are the drugs that we promote.

I am explaining these connections to show how we became so **big**. We were, as I said, the good boys of **rock and roll**, and the Stones were the bad boys of rock. These **positions**, different, but the same, needed to be filled **for the Tavistock project.** We, the good boys, showed our Crowley affiliation with his picture on *Pepper's*, but did not explain his Illuminati connection. The Stones had the opposite image to sell. They were more blatantly Satanic.

Each band image carried out the same agenda of the Committee of 300, which, consisting exclusively of Illuminati members, are all Luciferian Satanists. Helping to spread paganism motivates them partly as unifying vehicle to break down formal religious structures. Luciferianism also breaks down political and institutional loyalties, to unite the world in a New World Order. Promoting Luciferianism is less often for intrinsic empowerment than for affiliation. Let disintegrating allegiances to nations, religions, and traditions create **a revolution** as a portal for the world to receive what **is coming**. The new structure is here. **We are well under way.**

All of this explanation of Satanism is included to show that it was not some satanic power from the netherworld that gave us world dominance. I connected through Crowley and Paul, not through the devil. Our work with Satanism was not to infuse Crowley doctrines of hate, but to use the Illuminati's professional networks. By helping them succeed, they empowered us globally. **Their interests were** entirely political. Mine were **entirely commercial.** We each helped the others get what they wanted. The perfectly coordinated agendas of several Illuminati

---

NOTE: Through the opium trade, the East India Company (EIC) stripped the Far East of its wealth (requiring unfathomable restitution from the Rothschilds four centuries later in order to be permitted to pursue their global agenda). From the EIC's Council of 300, the aristocracy formed the Committee of 300 (also known as the Olympians) in 1727. That supranational council presides over politics, banking, commerce, media, and the military. The Council on Foreign Relations, and every nation (directly or indirectly), works under their direction—as permitted by those in yet greater circles.

organizations (such as the Committee of 300) were put into play **by deliberately aligning us** to tear down existing institutional, societal, and political barriers effectively enough **for their NWO** agenda.

For example, when they brought us to the USSR, Russians got a taste of **our Western society** as never before, which **snowballed into** them and many others seeking further **globalization**, leading, as planned, to the removal of the Bamboo and Iron curtains.

Our Crowley connection was not as tied to his philosophies as to his global network that was readily available to us. Under the guise of Satanism, many bands jumped on board the Illuminati's networks. A bit humorously, it appeared that Satan

---

NOTE: John internalized how the global elite had successfully used him, manufacturing Beatlemania as a calculated step toward breaking down order everywhere to create a new global society under their own leadership. He saw how his own rigged success contributed to the plan to control society through music and hero-worship as a step toward generating enough anarchy and chaos to eventually culminate in mankind demanding a New World Order. John said, "Our society is run by insane people for insane objectives. I think we're being run by maniacs for maniacal ends and I think I'm liable to be put away as insane for expressing that. That's what's insane about it."

Typical of how the illuminated carry out their work, John was told how the Beatles would be used. All was by consent. Nevertheless, typical of why such societies succeed even after giving advance notice, the weight and far-reaching implications of each operation cannot be comprehended by those who cannot fathom the bigger picture. Also typical, the most information is given to those with the most to gain from it, making them co-conspirators, not opponents.

John and Paul were told that they would be given music and other support to usher in the New Age. Placing them at the top of the musical pyramid, and with them the world's most famous writing team, the Beatles would endure forever. John later acknowledged, "Changing the lifestyle and appearance of youth throughout the world didn't just happen. We set out to do it. We knew what we were doing." They understood why they were so generously supported, and gladly received what they could without any possibility of fully comprehending it. The weight of it all did not begin to hit him until Paul died. John then became unstable. He lost interest in quality work, and would have quit altogether had he not been controlled by William, Yoko, and heroin.

orchestrated their success; but it was the Committee of 300. **Those who played along**, promoting sex, drugs, and Satanism, **were empowered**—not for their work in the devil's evil playground, but rather **to further the disintegration of** values that held all **societies in**tact. Imagine the intended impact of **the world** seeing us "good boys of rock" with LSD.

The media, also controlled by the Illuminati, promotes all those who promote that disintegration. As for the Beatles and Stones, assistance was direct. For others, it is indirect. **For** us, George Martin had leads (through **EMI's** military intelligence) to those making **societal transformations**. They would not lose the band when **Paul crosses over**. They would send me **to provide new directives.**

Aleister Crowley comes up rather frequently in these Memoirs. Doing a quick search, I see Crowley listed 33 times to be exact. On average, that is a reference to Crowley by name in every other chapter. Each chapter that refers to him also tells you a bit about my connection to him. In earlier editions, I used this space to warn my fans not to follow him. I do not want you to use my book to rally support for Satanism, Thelema, or even Paulism in any radical way. Extreme religiosity makes people spiritually sick. In my chapter that discusses the tension in Ireland, I show you what **excessive** rigidity can do to people. If you think one **religion makes** people good, and another makes **people bad**, how do you explain Christians killing each other for not

---

NOTE: William is less set on concealing Aleister Crowley in current editions of *the Memoirs of Billy Shears*. In addition to his last name occurring 33 times in the text, there are another nine occurrences in the *Memoirs* footnotes. "Crowley" occurs six times in a total of only three *Billy's Back* footnotes.

following Jesus the right way? In the Bible, it is the religious fanatics, the Scribes and Pharisees, that Jesus condemns, not prostitutes, gays, or anyone else.

Crowley, as the father of modern Satanism, was as original in that role as I am in my Paul McCartney role. He did not invent it. He simply improved on what was already there. He excelled in it by bringing order to existing ideas, and by focusing energy and action on his intentions. I did the same as Paul.

What most folks fail to grasp about Crowley is his extensive network. He built connections in the highest levels of government and prominence, not merely in the UK, but in Western Europe, the US, and through enough people in those places to reach the rest of the world. If you knew Crowley's lovers and children, you would re-think all you know of world affairs.

Okay, back to the dark side of Crowley and Anger. Anger, born Kenneth Wilbur Anglemyer, had changed his name to suit the essence of the Satanic nature. He became angry. **I prefer happiness**, as most sane people do. Although **I appreciate the** work he did to present Crowley's **ideas**, I only agree with

---

NOTE: Intentionally acquiring a Satanic nature is absurd since it opposes peace and happiness. "Satan" (from the Hebrew שׂטן) means adversary or accuser. In this upside-down world, some who express the greatest hatred for Satan may be the most Satanic—the most inclined to adversarial positions of judging and accusing others. Hence, they are angry, refusing the peace of understanding.

To Luciferians, it is blasphemous to say Satan to mean Lucifer. However, rather than being offended by that error, most recognize it as coming from a Christian perspective. Satan and Lucifer are opposites like black and white. The same being has both attributes just as we all do. By accepting the totality of ourselves and of others, our wholeness allows our opposite aspects to work as one like a black and white chessboard (a Masonic symbol).

Resisting our darkness strengthens it by trapping energy there. Accepting ourselves, without judging our darkness, frees us to choose either light or darkness. The global elite seek both, having the contradictory belief that they can be adversarial (Satanic) to opponents, but illuminated (Luciferian) personally. It is as inconsistent as accusers (Satanic) seeking the Holy Spirit.

what serves me. **What best serves me about** Kenneth Anger and **Aleister Crowley is** not their teachings, but **the influential network.** That web, enlisted by the Committee of 300, was the long road on which to drive the Beatle vehicle carrying the new world message. Networking in Father Crowley's camp gave us power in this world. As for teachings, notice that I also quote from Jesus, Confucius, and many others. Since I believe that we can learn from everyone, I do not mind quoting anyone. Whether the messenger is a devil or an angel, it is mostly the message that interests me. Since the sacred books from around the world talk about the devil, I have the feeling that it is also okay for me to tell you what **Lucifer and his servants** have been doing.

All **of Crowley's Thelema philosophy**, he built upon a collection of ideas **taught** for millennia by nearly all religions. It stems from **the principle** of submitting to God's will. That idea **of** submission grew to include deferring **our own will** to God's for our own special divinely appointed missions in this earth school. I buy into that idea. **I believe** that the Divine not only foreknew **Paul's coming** replacement, but also prepared both of us **for it.**

For better or worse, I see that my role changed the world. The evidence is staggering. I am not religious, but am spiritual enough to see how it all played out. Eventually, it became clear to me that no one could hijack this planet away from God's control. Most religions would agree with that. Whether you think of God as the grid of universal intelligence, or as an exalted Father of our souls, or as anything else that is omniscient and omnipotent; if such a Divinity made this world, to be consistent, we may rationally guess that He, She, They, We, or It also runs this show.

I realized that God, or the universe, of whatever **you may personally** call this loving creative force, **sets everything in place** for whatever mission or work **that we are sent here to fulfill.** If God rules earth, then nothing monumental can happen down here that God did not either direct or allow. For reasons that we cannot comprehend, whatever God allows must be for our own ultimate good. Having a particular mission to accomplish in this world, I came and did what the universe made possible, and basically willed me to do. How else could I have accomplished all of that?

Lingering traditions say that God could not have worked with me that way because I am not righteous enough. Although none of us seem purely holy, the Divine expresses though all of us anyway.

With each Beatles phase, the primary message was to give or receive love. We sang, "All you need is love." It began with silly romantic love songs, but suddenly matured into being more concerned about the brotherly love that was lost with Paul, and about the infinite love that connects all people for global humanity. To "Let It Be," requires a loving acceptance of people and circumstances as they presently are. Our primary message has always been to love. Have romantic love, but also extend liberating divine love unto the oppressed Irish, to those who suffer from acts of terrorism, or from leftover landmines. Love the poor and rich alike. Love the weak as the powerful. **Love everyone.** Then I would ask you to **love every creature.** Respect all life enough to **give up eating meat.** Start with all mammals.

On the other hand, the source of Aleister Crowley's suffering, more than any other, was his veneration for placing pursuits above love. He advocated will over love rather than willing love. For each of us, our greatest potential for happiness is in doing what we love with whom we love.

In this book, I have explained—and given you background information for—ways that Paul and I are conspicuously dissimilar. I will recap some of the highlights. To those who knew Paul and me, the most obvious differences are in our personalities.

Paul was first John's friend, then a bandmate. They watched their time go by, being perfectly content to sit around and talk about nothing. Finally, when it did come down to work, **John and Paul enjoyed** knocking their lyrics back and forth, **"co-writing"** a lot of their material. Then they would go to the studio with the others, work a song to completion, and leave it to go on to the next song, and on to the next. When done, they resumed talking about nothing interesting, just enjoying being friends. John would lead. Paul would follow.

NOTE: The official romanticized narrative that John and Paul sat for hours at a time knocking around lyrics and talking about girls is part of the fiction that made the Lennon-McCartney writing team—and the Beatles—much bigger than real life. In the early days, the only lyrics that they figured out together were the ones that they heard on the radio and wanted to play in clubs. Once they signed on with EMI, lyrics, music, and instrumentation were generally provided for them. When William took control of the band, they were challenged to write more of the songs themselves.

Know the Difference.

All of that changed when I took his place. I became impatient talking about nothing just to be making connections. I was more into making money, and into getting things going. In collaborations that I did with John, it was later on in the creative stage. For example, we would each individually write our tunes and lyrics, and I might suggest putting them together, blending them into one developed song. I would have ideas about tracks that we could add to his songs to give them a richer sound. Or, he would sing a funny backup line in one of my songs, or tell me to speed it up. That is how it was.

After we wrote our own songs, we would both play with them to make them better. He would sing a song too quickly, and I would say, "Slow it down!" I would play one too slowly, and he would shout, "Play it faster!" It was not co-writing in the way that he and Paul had usually done. As kids, they would lay around looking up at clouds and say lines back and forth to each other. Sometimes as one started a tune, the other might improve upon it. Their song writing was an ongoing celebration of their long immoveable musical friendship.

That is why they shared their writing credits. **Nothing** was officially Paul's or John's. Everything either **wrote**, much to my own great frustration, was **"Lennon-McCartney."** Lennon was the leader. When I came along, I was the leader, and so you would think he would agree to listing the writers as "McCartney/Lennon." When John shot down that idea, I suggested that whoever actually wrote each particular song should have his name first. That idea did not fly either. John clung to branding every song, "Lennon-McCartney."

Our work habits were entirely different. I would regularly make track after track until the rest of them were ready to revolt. Then I would spend days, weeks, or longer, tinkering with them all, redoing nearly all of it sometimes. My personality was about as opposite from Paul's as it could be.

Another major difference was that the Beatles was my band. I made that condition before I would sign on with them. With me at the helm instead of John, we did things differently by design. **My focus** included a higher quality standard than they **had held** to before. I, as I said, invested more time. **It** was **up** to me to select each album theme. I would come up with it, write some songs, and then tell each of the crew what I expected from them.

For all who knew us, the personality differences always spoke the loudest. However, I thought the physical differences were also rather obvious.

Nothing seemed more blatantly conspicuous to me than our height difference. I am inches taller. Baldness was another factor; but most fans were unaware of his premature balding because their early mop-top style had it combed forward. My hair color was like my kids'. James looks just like me.

Where Paul's hair did not fully cover his ears, that too is something to notice. On the Internet, our ears are easily compared. Paul's round ears are attached at the bottom. My ears, which you can see have a completely different shape, are not attached at the bottom. My earlobes hang down. Our images also show our head shapes. His is round, like his ears. Mine is longer—like my ears. Injections added voluminous walrus cheeks for my added facial width, making it seem rounder; but no surgery changes the entire shape of the skull. If they had done so, my head would not match the rest of my body. Each differing skeletal frame matches its own head shape. Watch my cheeks change from album to album.

I told you about the trouble I got into in Japan because **my fingerprints did not match** those on file from **Paul's** 1960 attempted arson arrest. Likewise, **just as** my accusers in Germany, my Japanese captors found that **my signature did not match Paul's.**

Genetics is the most positive way to distinguish each person. Since my DNA did not match Paul's, I have successfully overturned his paternity suits. His relationship in Germany, for example, produced a child, one for which we paid support, and required evidence that I was not the father. What better evidence than my DNA? I proved that mine was not a match for Paul's German daughter.

Voice biometrics, also as unique as fingerprints, tell the same story. I told you about the University of Miami professor who showed that our voiceprints do not match, proving that we are not the same Paul.

I taught you how to hear our voice distinctions now so that you can **easily recognize** the differences. **Paul's voice** is throaty and scratchy; and he has an accent from Liverpool. My voice is fuller and lower.

I told you about how we sped up the recording of my voice when I sang, "When I'm Sixty-Four" in order to raise the pitch, making it a bit closer to the sound of Paul. I also explained the numerous ways we had tried to convince the world of his death since 1966.

I do not know what else to say. **I have explained** in this historical book exactly **why we could never** come out in any non-fiction setting and **talk about it.** I can only say it in a song, or in a novel such as this.

Everything exposed in this book to prove my identity is true and historically verifiable. I have added some fictionalization in order for me to show that this is a work of fiction in the event that I ever need to prove in court that it is a novel. However, the facts about me not being Paul are all easily documented. Neither the fingerprint mismatch in Japan, nor the DNA discrepancy in German courts, lacked hard evidence, but generally went unnoticed. Likewise, the voice signature mismatch shown in an old reliable magazine (*Life*), was not taken seriously enough to change public opinion. **I am** pointing it out in hopes of **helping you understand** it. I have tried to show **that this switch is** genuine. Karma made Paul's dread **a reality.** Now, with this revealing book, I say it as plainly as possible. Since novels are fiction, this book does not break the nondisclosure agreement.

I have only scratched the surface of the hundreds of clues that we all most meticulously embedded all throughout our songs, record art, and films. I could

Know the Difference.

fill volumes. However, **I** covered it all well enough so that I can **make the point.** We spent hundreds of hours making **all of those clues** to convince all of you. **Behind closed doors**, we laughed at your gullibility for blindly believing that Paul lived on. Publicly, we **said** it was bloody stupid for people to read any **"Paul is Dead"** clues into any of our material. Publicly, we could not believe that people would think that we had any part of it. Until I say I am dead, I am still alive! We would swear that we had no idea that those elements could give such an impression. We made fans feel stupid for believing that Paul had died, and wanted you to have the sensation of being too wise to fall for such a hoax, when in fact, the opposite is true.

Since we had to add some fictionalization to make this book qualify as a novel, I decided to add this chapter so that you could know the difference between what is fact and what is fiction in this book. Beyond the point of vulnerability, I have opened my heart and soul to you, and revealed loads of secrets. Some of them, most of you will never believe. That's okay. I wouldn't either.

Letting this material sink in may create a struggle between wanting the truth and an ego not wanting to be proven wrong. The absurd ego willfully rejects all that is outside of its narrow vantage point. It chooses to be limited. I do not. **You** are free to re-think any position, and **are free to know** that this book exposes **the truth that "Paul is dead! ... Really dead!"** (I am quoting my *Sgt. Peppers* album, as explained on page 228.)

Based on my life expectancy, I shared these facts soon enough to give me some satisfaction in this lifetime, but too late for them to be used against me in earthly courts. A trial involving this material would last years longer than Paul tells me I have left.

Going to all the trouble of writing this book, and of having it all encoded for an entirely new literary experience, was for this one purpose: **I** want the world to know me before I am gone. I **want** you to know the real me, not merely the role **you** have come to know. I want you **to know** who I am. The world does not really know **me** except for my role as Paul.

Owing to my well-established over-identification with **Paul McCartney**, for you to know that he **is not who I am**, I went to some length to show you our distinct differences. Now you can distinguish between **Paul** and me, and can now be certain that he **died** out on that lonely road so long ago, back **in 1966.** We can put that matter to rest in order to move on to who I really am. **I am** still playing as Paul; but now you can see **William** as Paul, and not merely as Paul himself. **Now you** know. With that knowledge, you **can call me** by either name. Visit www.**BillyShears**.com for more on *the Memoirs of Billy Shears*.

**Most importantly,
love everyone.**

*All the best to those
who love my Memoirs,
and to those who don't,
with love from your scarab,
the Gold-Winged Beatle.*

Come see us at

www.BillyShears.com

Printed in Great Britain
by Amazon

82571342R00231